About the author

Born 1st May 1948 in Kent, the author was educated in Kent and Surrey. She was then employed in the computer industry before moving to Cornwall, and then on to Mauritius for five years. Returning to the UK, it was back to Surrey and Kent. She now lives on the Isle of Wight with her second husband. She has two grown up sons, and four grandchildren.

First published by Beachy Books in 2017

www.beachybooks.com

1 2 3 4 5 6 7 8 9 10

British Library Cataloguing in Publication Data.

A catalogue record for this book is available from the British Library.

ISBN: 978-0-9562980-8-9

Design by Philip Bell (Beachy Books)

Typeset in Libre Baskerville and Lucida Handwriting

LIZZIE

Rosey Messing

Rosey Messing.

18.VI.17

Limited edition 20 of 50.

Beachy Books

www.beachybooks.com

For Lois, Pam, Lyle, Rochelle, Ernie and Barry in Canada
and my dear Mum, Cis

Contents

Introduction and thanks

My mother was born into the Monson family in Harrow in 1923. Inspired by her eldest sister, Joan, and extensive family research by James William Monson of Alberta, Canada, I set out to find out more about my mother's ancestors from Boyle in County Roscommon, Ireland. My aunt had whetted my appetite when she returned from a visit to Derrymaquirk, one of the family dwellings still farmed by Ernest Monson. She had touched on the surface of things and made a few notes.

This gave me a thirst to look deeper, and it became a captivating obsession for a while which led me to visit other family members, as well as farms, libraries and graveyards. I've also pored for hours through computer archives.

As well as confirming many truths, I have also laid doubt on the long held beliefs that the family land was meted out by Oliver Cromwell for services rendered, and also that our family was connected to Sir Francis Drake. Every family has its own fantasies of past fame and fortune. I believe these are ours.

There is proof that the Monsons, Barons and Baronets of Carlton in Lincolnshire, have been significant in history, but no proof of any clear link with our Monsons. Sir John Monson (1599-1683) supported the Royalist side in the Civil War, while his brother, William (1607-1698), was a Parliamentarian. Admiral Sir William Monson (1569-1643) served under Elizabeth I with Sir Francis Drake and was the author of 'Tracts', naval histories about the Spanish Armada.

My contact with Nicholas Monson, 12th Baron of Carlton, Lincs, and direct descendant of the Royalist, Sir John Monson, hasn't brought to light any direct link between the two families, though Nicholas, himself an author, has cheekily suggested that there's nothing to disprove that a link could have been forged on the wrong side of the blankets!

How I came to find a fascination with the life of Lizzie Monson, my grandfather Hasluck's cousin, was through my family research. She and her sister, Minnie, set out from Ireland to a brave new life in Saskatchewan and I was intrigued by Minnie's short pencil-written account found behind a family picture by Minnie's grand-daughter, Helen Brown Rogers. It is a record of part of the journey to the new homestead in Saskatchewan:

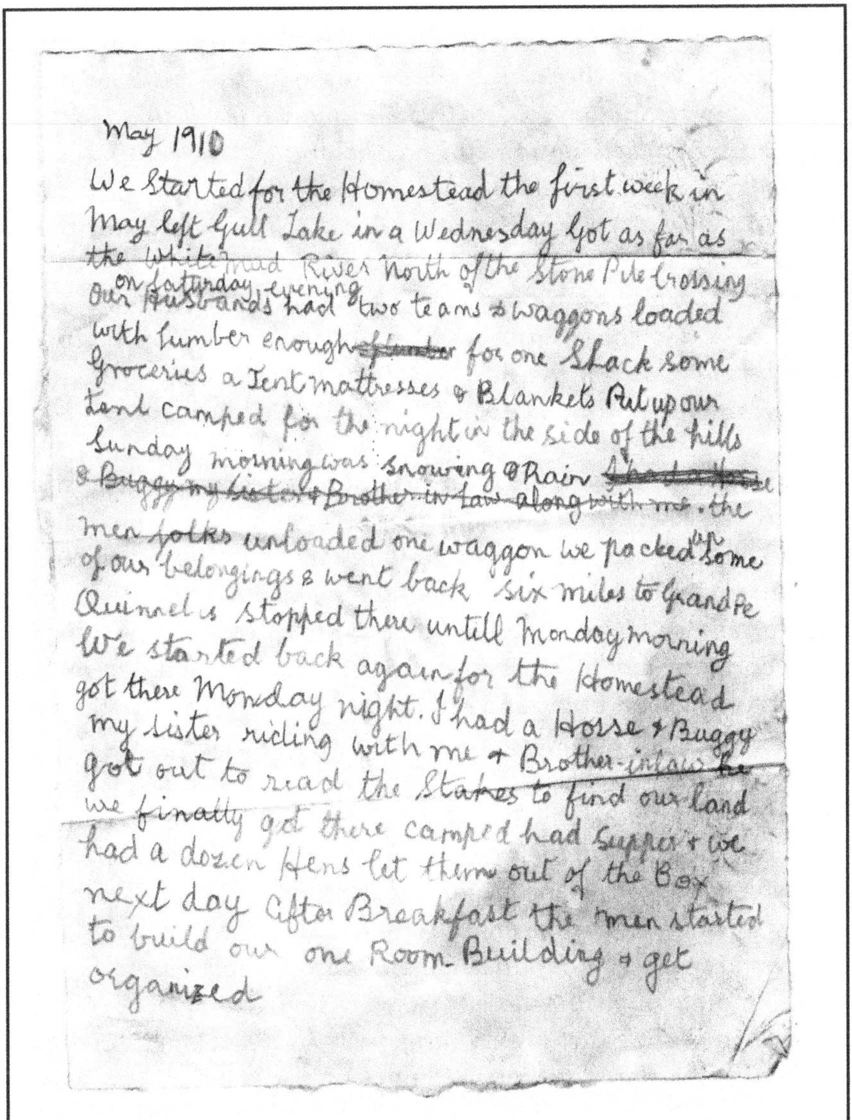

May 1910

We Started for the Homestead the first week in May left Gull Lake in a Wednesday Got as far as the White Mud River North of the Stone Pile Crossing on Saturday evening Our Husbands had two teams & waggons loaded with lumber enough ~~of lumber~~ for one Shack some Groceries a Tent mattresses & Blankets Put up our tent camped for the night in the side of the hills Sunday morning was snowing & Rain ~~I had a Horse & Buggy my sister & Brother in law along with me~~. the men folks unloaded one waggon we packed up some of our belongings & went back six miles to Grandpa Quinnel's stopped there untill Monday morning We started back again for the Homestead got there Monday night. I had a Horse & Buggy my sister riding with me & Brother-in-law ~~he~~ got out to read the Stakes to find our land we finally got there camped had supper & we had a dozen Hens let them out of the Box next day after Breakfast the men started to build our one Room Building & get organized

Minnie's diary page from 1910.

"May 1910
We started for the Homestead the first week in May left Gull Lake in a Wednesday Got as far as the White Mud River North of the Stone Pile Crossing on Saturday evening Our Husbands had two team & waggons loaded with lumber enough for one Shack some Groceries a Tent mattresses & Blankets Put up our tent camped for the night in the side of the hills. Sunday morning was Snowing & Rain The men folks unloaded one waggon we packed up some of our belongings & went back six miles to Grand Pa Quennells stopped there until Monday morning We started back again for the Homestead got there Monday night. I had a Horse & Buggy my sister riding with me & Brother-in-law he got out to read the Stakes to find our land we finally got there camped had Supper & we had a dozen Hens let them out of the Box Next day after Breakfast the men started to build our one Room Building & get organised"

It got me thinking about the great adventure that Lizzie and her sister Minnie, and later two more of their sisters, embarked upon, leaving behind all they had ever known to look for a new life which led to them marrying and homesteading on the wild plains of Canada. It was a daring and brave step into the unknown for each and every one of them borne mainly of necessity as Ireland and the family farm had little to offer them. Lizzie and Minnie were the first to leave the nest in 1908, with Tillie and Martha following two years later.

I have visited Coolnagranchy, their childhood home near Boyle in County Roscommon, still standing but now used as a cattle barn. I have seen the graves of their mother, Mary, nee McMaster, and one of their younger sisters, Blanche Florence, at Croghan Church, where the family worshipped over a century ago, and the graves of many other relatives in Boyle Churchyard, another Monson family church.

The more I found, the more I wanted to find. Having done my best to research Lizzie's first twenty three years in Ireland, and briefly in London where she stayed at the house of my grandfather, and his parents and siblings, I then felt compelled to discover more about the seventy years she spent in Canada. To this end, in May 2015, I took a trip to Saskatchewan, discovering five of my third cousins. Four of them, Pam and brother Lyle, Rochelle and Ernie, are Lizzie's grandchildren; Barry is Minnie's grandson. I spent a wonderful time with Pam, Rochelle and Barry, walking the land once farmed by Lizzie, Minnie and their husbands. They took me to Climax Cemetery and I came across, albeit too late for them all to tell their own tales personally, many of the family characters that I had been hearing about and had come across in my research. The most significant memorial stone of all was for Lizzie, or Gram Fallis as she was known by her Saskatchewan family. I wallowed in the reminiscences of Lizzie and Minnie and their families, so generously shared by all the cousins I met. While visiting Pam in Regina, Saskatchewan, she took me to visit her mother. It was one of my greatest pleasures to meet Lois, Lizzie's oldest living daughter. I marvelled that Lois, at ninety one, and just three months younger than my own mother, was still as sharp as a pin; but sadly she was struggling with her sight and hearing. With Pam's help, Lois had so much to tell me about her mother and the family and was happy to share it all with me.

My thanks go to all who provided information and evidence.

This is the story of a very brave and strong woman. It is very much based on fact and truth. As I was not present, I have used details discovered from my research, and dipped into my imagination to fill in the areas where information is not available or complete, and to tie the tale together. I have fashioned a mix of fact and fantasy, with a clear ear for the truth. It is a history worth telling but cannot be completed without the inclusion of some inventions. I trust that all will forgive me for any inaccuracies.

1

Early days in Ireland

1884-1908

The year is 1979, and I sit in my armchair in my little duplex bungalow in Climax, gazing out beyond the boundary hedge of caragana bushes at the prairie land that occupied so many years of my life. I can see it taunting me still from beyond the hedgerow, dusted by the wan autumn sun, the wind as relentless as ever at this time of year. This is the prairie that consumed my every waking moment for over twenty years, and has stayed with me in my dreams for seventy years or more.

It has its own special beauty. The sky and the prairie spread out to meet in infinity, each reaching forever in any direction you choose to look. The seasons bring such changes, some of great beauty, and some of unendurable destruction. Days can be warm and hazy, the blue skies studded with feathery clouds, and ending in stunning sunsets. Or they can bring storm clouds, with anything from a squall to a full blown thunderstorm. The worst times are when the land is hit by a tornado, or there are floods, or when there is an endless drought and the winds blow the dusty land into every nook and cranny. We homesteaders suffer a constant fight with the elements: the sun, the rain, the wind, the snow. Even the grasshoppers can conspire against us and destroy the harvests of our efforts. And yet I feel a part of it, despite the confrontations it has brought over the years.

My life here in Climax in the Canadian province of Saskatchewan has been full of a mix of hardship and happiness, but then my life has always been like that, even during my first twenty one years back in Ireland, and the two I spent in England with my Aunt and Uncle.

I was born Elizabeth Monson at Knockadoo in the south west of County Roscommon. I was sometimes called Eliza but most often known as Lizzie. My sister, Minnie, and I left home in 1908 in the hope of finding a better life here in Canada. Two more of our sisters,

Tillie and Martha, followed two years later. Though quite different from those years growing up in a family of twelve children, it's had its own challenges and sadnesses, its own joys and fulfilments. Despite everything, though, it is with great pride that I feel we four sisters played a small part in the cultivation of the lands that I now look out upon.

I came into the world on 12th November, 1884, at Knockadoo Estate. It was here that my father, Thomas Monson, lived and worked. He married my mother, Mary McMaster, the year before, when he was twenty nine and she was eighteen. Both came from Church of Ireland families. Mother's older sister, Kathleen, also married into the family to my father's cousin, John Duke Monson.

Although we were friendly enough with local Catholic families, it was completely unheard of that any of us should marry outside the Church of Ireland. Even though there was a shortage of marriage partners for many young people, it was frowned upon to wed a Catholic – God forbid we marry a Papist! This sometimes resulted in close relatives marrying, as was the case with my father's sister, my Aunt Mary Ann, and her first cousin George Thomas. As for my sisters and I, some of us sought a new life further afield and found our eligible bachelors far from our land of birth.

The other thing with the Catholics was their wish to have Ireland as a republic and released from British rule. It was all founded in history and came to a head in the time of Oliver Cromwell, over two hundred years before, when Catholics were oppressed and lost their lands to Protestants, and often their lives, at the hands of the English. I sometimes wondered if our family land was originally Catholic owned but, when I asked my Uncle Edward, he told me that it had always been ours.

We were ever aware of a discontent bubbling beneath the surface and from time to time there was news of small troubles, but really it never had any great effect on our lives in Roscommon except for a gentle underlying mistrust that Protestants and Catholics had towards each other.

In Ireland at that time, life was never easy, and there were many mouths to feed. My father's father, also named John Duke, was the fifth son of John Monson, my great-grandfather, who had farmed at

Grange and Derrymaquirk, both near Boyle in County Roscommon. John and his wife had lived to a ripe old age; I was told it was a hundred and three and a hundred and four. It was generally the way in the countryside at that time that, once parents chose to pass on the farm and land to a son, only then could he marry and bring his wife to the farm. Other sons would either leave home or stay on the farm but not marry, and work as unpaid help for their brother.

My great-grandfather continued with the farm late into his life, so, with no chance of establishing themselves in the locality, two of his sons, William and Thomas, left home to seek their fortunes in Ohio, North America. Those who stayed behind, George and Edward, worked unpaid for their father for many years and eventually took over Grange and Derrymaquirk, leaving the smaller farm at Coolnagranchy to my grandfather. Throughout our family's history, when the land could not support all the Monsons, some found it necessary to leave home to go north to Ulster or Scotland, or to England, or even overseas to North America and New Zealand.

The great potato famine in the 1840's had also taken its toll, though our family was lucky to live on the land and able to grow other crops. My father was born at the end of the famine when, for ten years running, the potato crop just rotted in the fields and many starved. Father told me that over one million people died and another one and a half million left Ireland as they would have surely perished otherwise. That was more than a quarter of the population either dead or emigrated.

With nowhere to establish himself, my father took work as a steward on the Knockadoo Estate to support his new family. But we were not to stay there for long. When my grandfather died, eight years before his own father, my father inherited Coolnagranchy and we moved to the farm. I don't remember anything about life at Knockadoo as it was shortly after my first birthday when we moved from there. Some time later, I remember Father telling us as children that his employer was an English aristocrat. Father would keep us in fits of laughter, trying to copy his employer's posh English accent. However, I suspect that working on the Estate was generally not so much fun.

The family grew quickly – a new baby every year or second year – there was no birth control in those days. Mother was eighteen when she wed, and then spent the next eighteen years of her life either pregnant or breast feeding. How hard it must have been - we were always hungry, and there were clothes to be made and washed and mended. As well as the general housekeeping and doing her best to make ends meet, Mother also had to help out with jobs on the farm.

So I was the only one of the twelve not born at Coolnagranchy, and I was christened Elizabeth, after my father's mother. My brother, John Duke, named for our grandfather, was the second-born, then followed eight sisters, Mary Anne, Ellen Matilda, Martha, Sarah Jane, Eva Lena, Lillian Rebecca, Blanche Florence, Kathleen. At last came another son, Thomas, named after our father, and finally, Victoria Queenie, whose name honoured Queen Victoria who died in the year of her birth. Our father affectionately shortened his daughters' names, so we ten girls were known as Lizzie, Minnie, Tillie, Martha, Sarah Jane (not shortened for some reason), Eva, Lillie, Blanche, Kate and Queenie. Our Victoria Queenie was born shortly after the death of Queen Victoria, greatly mourned by the nation even though there was discord between Ireland and the British government.

I have always considered myself fortunate that I was born into such a family; I knew of other farming families where the girls were the lowest ranking in the family, less cared for by their parents than their brothers were. They were unpaid slaves. I always knew we were lucky. We were all loved and cared for equally. It's true that there was little to go round and we all had to help with the chores, but we never felt we were treated unfairly. And there was always lots of laughter.

Sitting here in my chair, my thoughts wander back to my childhood – almost a century ago. Life was hard, but we were all happy, and all such good friends. How did our mother manage to get us all fed and clothed, nursed through illness, off to school each morning, ready for church at Croghan each Sunday some thirteen miles away? How could it be that I, the oldest of us all, have lived longer than almost everyone? In fact, the only other of my brothers and sisters still alive is Eva, who was only five when I left school, and was just leaving school herself when Minnie and I set off for Canada.

Coolnagranchy near Boyle, County Roscommon – the farm where we all grew up.

The Coolnagranchy Monsons circa 1902
Back: Sarah Jane, Martha, Lizzie (me), John Duke, Minnie, Tillie, Eva
Seated: Father with Thomas, Mother with Queenie
Front: Lillie, Blanche, Kate.

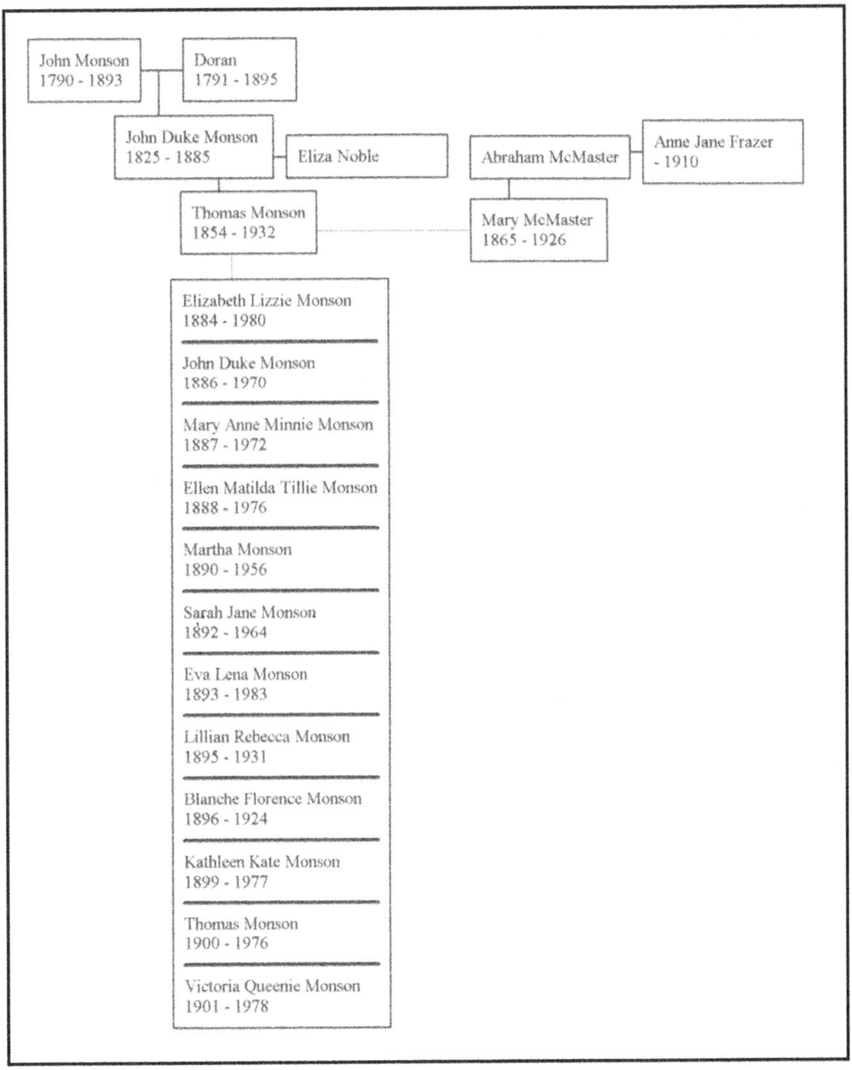

Ancestors and siblings.

Many of my brothers and sisters lived to a good age, into their seventies or eighties, but not two of my sisters, Lillie and Blanche, who had never left home or married, and died at thirty six and twenty eight respectively in the saddest of circumstances.

As the oldest, Mother relied on my help with the younger children, especially after I left school, aged fourteen. We all knew how to read and write. This was probably my greatest blessing. How else could I have kept in touch with my family over the miles and the years if I had not had the gift of literacy. So too the ability to understand numbers has been a godsend to me. I'd enjoyed my time at school, and had many friends. I worked hard and hoped that I would get a good job, perhaps as a book keeper. That was not to be, but I was able to help Mother keep our farm books, and I carried those skills on with me into my married life. Prospects were poor for our family – so many daughters – and jobs and eligible husbands so few and far between.

Although life was quite hard when I was a child, there was always some fun to be had, always something going on. The farm itself provided us with many pastimes as well as our daily chores. One of my jobs was to make up the mash for the chickens each morning. They always seemed to know well in advance when I would be coming out of the kitchen door to see to them, and there would be much scrabbling and scratching in the hen house when I slid open the door and they all rushed to get out and compete for the steaming mash. Then I would check their water tray and top it up from the rain barrel which stood in the yard next to the barn, then do my rounds, looking for eggs in the hen-house and around in the hedgerows. We always kept at least a dozen hens, maybe two dozen if we could get them; eggs were an important part of our diet, sometimes the only protein food available. And we always had a cockerel too, strutting and bossing and full of his own importance, not forgetting his early morning wake-up call. I can't forget one cockerel that didn't know when to stop; he crowed from morn till night. One day, he went suddenly silent – and there was chicken in the pot that night!

Once I'd seen to the chickens each morning, I then went to help Mother with the younger children. For so many years, she was either pregnant or breast feeding, so her time was greatly taken up with the babies. As we grew bigger, Minnie and I were the ones to get everyone's breakfast, usually porridge, and make sure that all the children who were old enough were ready for school. My brother, John, was always out with Father at the crack of dawn, or well before daylight in the long winter months, and the two of them would appear as if by magic when we put the bowls of hot, steaming porridge on the table. I think John would have preferred to stay all day helping Father, and he made a big fuss most mornings I can remember before he set off with us in the direction of the schoolhouse.

We all went to the same school at Ardsallagh, about half a mile away. In all the time I was there I only had two teachers, Miss McGahern and Miss O'Reilly, except for a student teacher called Mary Leonard, when I was eight, who didn't seem much older than the girls in the top class at school. She stayed for about a year before going on to another school. She told us that she was born and spent several years in Sligo Workhouse. When her mother died, she was lucky enough to be taken in by her aunt who encouraged her to think about becoming a teacher. Her tales of the workhouse made us all very sad and we grew to realise how lucky we were, even though times were so challenging.

Miss McGahern was the main teacher and lived in the cottage next to the school, while Miss O'Reilly lodged with an old couple in a small cottage close to our farm at Coolnagranchy. We would see her most days when we were making our way to school. It wasn't so far to school, a little shorter if we could cut across the fields in dry weather, so it would take us about fifteen minutes at the most, much less if we were running late! Often we would walk with Miss O'Reilly and she'd ask us about the farm and what we were up to and all sorts of other things. I think her name was Colleen, but of course we never addressed her as anything other than Miss or Miss O'Reilly. She came from near Dublin and moved to County Roscommon when her parents had died so she could be closer to her brother, who worked in Boyle as a mechanic and was her only relative. She was always very friendly when we were walking, but much stricter once we arrived in school, as she had to be.

Our school was a single-story stone building, with a big wooden door which led into the main hallway, and that in turn led off to two classrooms. Out the back was the playground, split in two by a stone wall to make the two playgrounds – the larger one for the bigger boys and the smaller one for the girls and younger lads. The single toilet, we called it the privy, for the whole school was a small stone building at the end of the playground dividing wall. It had a wooden door with a metal latch, and one window up high in the wall. It was a dry toilet with a wide wooden seat, and there was a bucket and scoop with ashes and soil to sprinkle into the toilet. There was no handyman or odd-job man at school and the bigger boys had to see to digging out the toilet from time to time, and loading the soil on to the handcart to take to the field next door. When he was older, my brother John always complained bitterly when it was his turn to help with this, but then I guess it wasn't the best of jobs.

When we went in the main door of the school, there were hooks on the wall for us to hang our coats and hats. Turf was stored in a pile in the hallway, so when the weather was wet outside, the hallway was a damp, miserable and smelly place, what with the wet coats and muddy floor and the pile of turf. In the cold months, we were all asked to bring dried turf to school for burning in the open fireplaces in the two classrooms. It was the only heating and everyone always clamoured to sit as near the fireplace as possible as only those nearest the fire got any warmth. The fire was another bone of contention with John as the older boys had to look after the fire, lay it and light it, keep it going, and clean the hearth and take the ashes out to put in the toilet bucket, and put the extra on the pile. Not long before I left school, in the year that I reached my 14th birthday, a new metal stove arrived in Miss McGahern's room, the bigger classroom for the 4th, 5th and 6th classes. The stove also took some looking after but was more efficient at providing heat to the room. It was positioned in the centre of the classroom, so the heat got to more people. It was also much less smoky.

Each classroom had four heavy dark wood tables and benches, each about ten feet long, all facing the teacher's desk, which was raised on a rostrum by the fireplace. We had to get up to ten pupils on each bench; it depended how many children were registered in school that year, and how many were attending. Some would stay away because of influenza or other illness, or would have to stay home to help their families, and often one or two of the lads were missing, unable to make it due to a beating from their father. Most of the time the classrooms were full to bursting. Miss O'Reilly took the younger children outside quite often, while Miss McGahern was the principal teacher and had the hard task of teaching us all The Three R's - reading, writing and arithmetic. It's always amused me that they were so called. How strange that the misrepresentation of them all starting with the letter R should be encouraged in an environment where spelling is taught and held to be important. Spelling was also part of the curriculum, along with grammar. We also learnt geography, which fascinated me, and, in 6th class, the girls were introduced to book-keeping and the boys went out and about to learn about animal husbandry.

I loved learning and did very well. My brother John was not quite so keen and often threw a paddy in frustration, much to the amusement of his classmates. His name often appeared in the punishment book and notes would arrive home, much to Mother's dismay. But there was no corporal punishment in our house, and, after a few words of admonishment, Father would set John a task out on the farm. Invariably it was something that John was happy to do, so it wasn't much of a punishment and certainly didn't stop him re-offending. When Mother asked him about the problem, he'd tell her that he knew all the letters, but he just couldn't make out the words.

I often think now that John was born at the wrong time. In those days, no-one understood why some people had such difficulties, particularly with reading. Nowadays, there seems to be a better understanding of these things, and John would probably have been identified as being word blind or something and given help, rather than him flying into a frustrated tantrum. He was often ordered to the storage area at the side of the classroom to get the slipper. Those punishments never did him any good – he just found reading almost impossible and no end of reprimand and punishment could change that. Little wonder that he disliked school so. He seemed to fall foul of the slipper more often than most. If he'd been a girl, it would have only been a slap, or maybe a whack with a ruler on the back of the legs. Of course, my name never appeared in the punishment book!

I think back to my first day at school. I was probably aged seven, and Mother delivered me at the school gate with a quick wave, then rushed off home, doubtless to get back to John, Minnie, Tillie and Martha. Mother was heavily pregnant with Sarah Jane at that time, so the trek to and from school must have been very arduous for her, and twice a day at that. Miss O'Reilly had some other new students that day, as well as about twenty five other children in the 1st, 2nd and 3rd classes. Two of the girls from the 6th class were given the task of supervising me and the four other new students. They took us out and showed us around, and then we sat on an old rug in the corner of the classroom while they told us stories. At break-time, they stayed with us in the playground and warned us not to go into the big boys' playground or we would get knocked flying or get hurt. The big boys' playground was certainly a bit of a battleground, and the lads were very boisterous. Up to the age of eight or nine, the boys stayed with the girls. After that they were thrown to the lions – it was a dog eat dog environment which I am happy I never had to enter, but it was possible to witness the goings-on from a distance when visiting the privy.

When John had been at school some time and graduated to the big boys' playground, he often came home with a black eye, grazed knees or torn trousers. Mother was always upset, and fed up that there was more mending to be done. Father, I think, rather encouraged young John, and he seemed proud of him, his one and only son, pleased that he could stand up for himself and that he was a manly boy, certainly no softy, and not frightened of using his fists. At that time, Thomas had not yet been born; he didn't arrive until two years after I'd left school.

I remember the school day as starting at nine o'clock, with a half hour morning playtime, and an hour's break at lunchtime when we would have soup brought in by Mrs Cubby. It alternated between barley and pea, and we each had to supply a small bowl from home which we brought to school at the start of each term. If you forgot your bowl, it was a crime worthy of an entry in the punishment book, and you went without soup until you rectified the situation. Most people's bowls were wooden, but I was very proud to have a pottery dish – terracotta with a white and blue glaze which I think once belonged to my Grandmother Eliza who I'd never met, but I think I was named after her. Regardless of whether it was summer or winter, the soup was always piping hot, though often a bit watery. In the cold, damp winter months it was more than welcome as it not only warned your tummy, it also warmed your hands.

Afternoon lessons were interrupted by another half hour break, then the hand bell sounded at 4 o'clock and it was time for home. Mother brought and collected me from school for the first days, sometimes bringing John and Minnie with her, though it did slow down the journey as they were only five and four. One afternoon, not long after I'd started school, no-one came to get me. I guessed that the new baby was on its way, so I made my way home alone. Sure enough, Sarah Jane had entered the world, so now there were six children in our family. I made my own way to and from school after that, sometimes walking with Miss O'Reilly but often on my own, until John started school a year and a half later.

The two classrooms in school were quite plain, just square rooms with a single window, and with the storage area for books and paper which the boys so dreaded if they were for the slipper. We also kept our lunchtime soup bowls in a wooden box at the side. As well as the tables and benches, there were blackboards. Each room had a blackboard on the wall, and Miss McGahern also used a moveable blackboard on wheels, so she could set different work for the different age and ability groups. When I was in Miss O'Reilly's class, we each used a slate and chalks to practise our letters and numbers, then progressed to dip pen and ink in Miss McGahern's. It took some time to learn how to hold the pen properly and form the letters on the rough paper. Writing was a messy job and my middle finger on my right hand soon formed a small lump which was almost always black with ink. Filling your ink pot was a hazardous task – the large bottle of black ink stood on the rostrum just below the teacher's desk and we were at risk of reprimand if we spilt a drop of the precious liquid while transferring it into our ink wells. Some poor children were not very steady of hand, especially when Miss McGahern stood over them or glared from her desk; she was a person who had eyes everywhere – she missed nothing it seemed. We were fortunate that, although she was firm, she was never unkind or unfair. I imagine that a stricter teacher could have filled a punishment book just with entries relating to ink spillage! We were each allowed a small piece of blotting paper which had to last for a term, invariably long past the time that every inch of it was darkened by spills and blots and unable to soak up even the smallest drop of ink.

I was lucky that I was right-handed. Some of the children showed a natural tendency to do things with their left hand, and this carried over into trying to learn to write. The constant admonitions and raps on the hand towards those who were obviously left-handed were sad to see, and there were many tears and tantrums. Of course, my poor brother John was included in this group, and his frustrations often led to yet another entry in the punishment book.

The first task in cold weather was to clear the grates and get the fires going. The older boys were in charge and they met with varying success. Sometimes the fires were already lit if one of the boys had got to school early enough, and this saved a lot of time and often saved us all from a smoky classroom while the turfs took. At the times of the year when the fires were needed, the classrooms, in fact the whole school, invariably had an earthy, smoky smell which was transferred to the pupils and their clothing. This was often a blessing as personal hygiene was not always the top priority with some of the families. Some children also had head lice and the teachers would work away with the nit combs and rub in a little ash on their heads in an attempt to fend off the eggs and tiny creatures that nestled in the unfortunate child's hair. Sometimes we Monsons were included in this torture. I was never sure which was worse – the itching or the treatment.

The winter snow provided another task for the older boys and it was their job to clear the snow from the pathway between the gate and the main door, and to make sure that the step was cleared and scattered with ashes to stop ice forming there, with the inevitable slips and accidents.

Before the start of lessons each morning and afternoon, the teacher would take the register and record the details in the roll-book. Sometimes, the older girls were asked to call the names and mark the book. It wasn't unusual for the morning and afternoon rolls to differ – someone may have turned up late in the morning, and sometimes a pupil would go missing who had been in school for the morning roll.

This was more usually boys than girls and meant a note home to their parents when they returned to school the next day or even later. Who knows if those notes ever made it home, and whether parents were actually literate and able to read what was written. In summer, there were always less boys in school than girls; they would be off helping their fathers on the farms and smallholdings.

In the older classes, there was not much variety in each day's lessons. We always started with reading – altogether and out loud to start with, then we were expected to take it in turns to read a paragraph or two while everyone else followed in their books. There were never enough books for us to have one each, so sharing was usual and books would be passed along the table for the next boy or girl to take their turn. John always got in a real panic when it came to his turn to read. Our reading matter varied from formal school text books to prayer books and geography books and sometimes, in the top classes, we got to read real storybooks. My all time favourite was "The Secret Garden" by Frances Hodgson Burnett, and I also loved the poems and rhymes in "A Child's Garden of Verses" by Robert Louis Stevenson. But all books and reading were a joy to me.

Before morning break, we also did grammar, often based on something that was read earlier. Miss McGahern wrote the rules on the blackboard for us to copy in our copybooks, then we were charged to find examples in our reading books and text books.

Morning break soon came and we were all packed off outside, whatever the weather, which often meant dressing up in coats and scarves and hats, and gloves or mittens if you were lucky enough to own them. If needed, the boys would stoke up the fires, and they often lingered around the hearth if the weather outside was particularly bad. Who could blame them. But mainly, we all loved the time spent in the playground. The girls had their skipping, with all the old rhymes such as "Bluebells, cockleshells". I still know all the words I think:

Bluebells, cockle shells, ee-vy, i-vy, over.
My mother said that I never should
Play with the gypsies in the wood.
If I did, she would say
'Naughty little girl to disobey, disobey ...'

The younger boys in the girls' playground also joined in with "Red Rover" – where we stood in two teams facing, and a child was called from the opposite line to break your line. If they couldn't, you kept them in your team. It sometimes got a bit rough but it was all great fun. And "Queenie, Queenie who has the ball?" and "Pussy four corners" were other great favourites with boys and girls alike. John told me that the big boys also played "Red Rover" in their playground, but it was altogether much rougher, along with another game they called "Lift Off" which involved catching people, lifting them then throwing them to the ground. The games in the boys' playground led to many bruises and grazed knees and bloody noses, and occasionally broken bones.

The period between morning break and lunch break was taken up with arithmetic. Once more, we copied from the teacher's work on the blackboard. Some days we were learning something new, and on others we were tested and had to take down sums and equations from the board to work out in our copybooks. We learnt our times tables, and how to work out pounds, shillings and pence, and that there are twelve inches in a foot, three feet in a yard. I test myself now to see what else I can remember. Now what was it? Oh yes, five and a half yards in a perch, forty perches in a furlong, and eight furlongs in a mile. Some of those rules learnt so long ago have not been particularly useful to me in my adult life. But learning how many yards there are in a mile has probably been more helpful to me when we were working out how many fence posts were needed to set the boundaries to our land here in Saskatchewan.

From time to time in the arithmetic class, we were invited to solve a sum on the board. I found arithmetic quite easy, so enjoyed the class, and never minded being called up in front of my peers. I know that some of the other pupils, including John of course, found the whole subject a nightmare. I guess that I was one of the lucky ones.

We also learnt Roman numerals and I've retained that knowledge to this day. I can still work out that I was born in MDCCCLXXXIV and the year now is MCMLXXIX. So I am now ninety five years old – XCV in Roman numerals. These days, I always enjoy working out what year a programme or movie has been made when it's displayed at the bottom of the TV screen.

At lunch time, we all collected our bowls from the store area and queued up in our classroom for Mrs Cobby, the dinner lady, to ladle out the soup. We were allowed to sit at the tables to sup it, then rinsed our bowls at the tap outside the main door and returned them to the storage box. Then we were shooed outside until the bell was rung for afternoon school and registration. Of course, soup took much longer to drink in bad weather!

My memory of afternoon school was that it included spelling tests, and sometimes geography – with tales of far away places that always fascinated me. Spelling tests could be quite fun. We all stood in a line around the wall and Miss gave the first person a word to spell. If they failed, then the next person tried the same word, and so on until someone got it right. They would then move up the line past those who had faltered. Then there was a new word for the next person to try, and so on, until everyone had been given a chance to spell a word, and moved up if successful. Then it would start at the top of the line again. The aim was to get to the top of the line – and to stay there if you could – which I often did as spelling came easily to me. Not everyone had the same success, and I'm sure that not everyone enjoyed it as much as I did, especially not my brother, John.

Afternoon break was followed by writing – another opportunity for blackened fingers. When we were learning to write, we laboriously copied words from the blackboard, then practiced and repeated them as neatly as we could along a ruled line. As we progressed, we still had to draw lines to guide us and we were set the task of copying words from the board, or sentences from a reading or geography book. Later, we were set the task of writing a story on a topic set by Miss McGahern or by one of the class if they were invited.

At the end of the school day, all had to be tidied and put away, with the floor swept and the blackboards wiped clean. This was a task for the older girls, and they worked on in the school building while younger brothers and sisters played outside, waiting to be escorted home. I didn't have to do these chores during my last year at school as Miss McGahern had chosen me as her special helper, and it was my duty to ring the bell for start and end of lessons, and to help get out books and paper and so on for each lesson. I also helped to supervise the break time activities in the girls' playground and saw to any grazed knees or bumped heads. I imagine that my teacher saw me following in her footsteps, but I had other ideas of being a writer or a bookkeeper. Neither of those aspirations came to pass, though my bookkeeping skills became an important and practical part of my life.

In my early days at school, the walk home was a lonely one, but by the time I was in Class Five, there were five of our family in school. Even after I'd left school at fourteen, I was still tasked with the school trips and, for seven or eight years, I went to and fro each day with four or five of my siblings, and this went on until I left home in my early twenties to live for a time with my Aunt and Uncle in England.

Children came to Ardsallagh School from other farms and holdings from the area near Coolnagranchy, all of them from south of the Boyle River. There was no crossing from the north until you got into Boyle itself, which would have made far too long a journey for getting to and from school each day. Children came from Ardmore, Ballymartin, Carrowroe, Cloonshee, Knockarush, Lisserdrea and Derrymaquirk, among others.

At times, there were a lot of Monson children in the local schools, up to ten or more at any one time. Not only were there my brothers and sisters and me at Ardsallagh School, also our Monson cousins (actually second cousins) from Grange were attending Grange School – Harold, three years older than me, George, just six months my senior, then the two girls, Ellie and Kate, who were good friends with Minnie and me. After the girls came Robert, Abraham, William and finally James, known as Archie, who was the same age as my brother Thomas, both born in 1900. Only our Queenie was younger, born the following year. In all there were nine Grange Monsons, only two of them girls. Our family from Coolnagranchy was sort of the opposite with twelve children and only two boys. Our Mother's older sister, Kathleen, was our Grange cousins' mother, and their father was our Father's cousin, John Duke, so it was very much a family affair.

Our Great Aunt and Uncle, Edward and Ellen, were still living at Derrymaquirk all the time I was at school. Their youngest son, our Uncle Edward, worked on the farm and never got married until his father released the farm to him in 1905 when Edward was thirty five and his father well into his eighties. I only ever remember our Great Uncle as being very old. Uncle Edward's first son, William, wasn't born until just before Minnie and I left for Canada, shortly after the death of Great Uncle Edward. So there were no cousins of our age at Derrymaquirk at this time, otherwise there might have been even more Monsons at school!

The farm at Derrymaquirk should have gone to one of Uncle Edward's older surviving brothers, but they had all chosen to leave Ireland to seek their fortunes, either in America or England. This included Uncle George, whose son, Hasluck, was born two years after me. I would have liked to go to school with Hasluck - he was my favourite cousin. We met each other a couple of times when we were growing up, when his parents came home on a visit from England. Then I got to know him better, also his brother, Duke, and sister, Edith, when I lived with their family in England before I set off for Canada. Hasluck and I became firm friends and this has continued through our letters to each other over the years. Who knows – if his parents had stayed in Ireland, he and I might have wed, just like his father and mother who were also first cousins.

We had yet more cousins at Carrick-on-Shannon. They were the children of Aunt Kate, one of Father's sisters married into the Haire family, who farmed locally. Her husband was called Johnston and they had six children. We didn't get to see them very often as it was some distance, and the older children were a few years older than us. If we got the opportunity, I loved to visit their home, called Killukin, and struck up a great friendship with my cousin, Molly Haire, three years my junior, who I have kept in touch with over the years.

Near the end of our time at school, at the age of fourteen, we were set a test based on all the subjects we had learnt and we were each given a grade which was recorded on a certificate. We were assured that this would be helpful to us when applying for a job. In fact, some children took the test earlier, even at ten and a half I think and, if they did well enough, they might leave school early. I suppose we could have left early too, but Mother was always insistent that we get as much education as we could, so we all stayed until fourteen.

So I did the test at fourteen and got an excellent grade. Despite that, I never found that the certificate did me any good as there were so few jobs available. I never achieved my ambition of being an author or a book-keeper. In our final couple of months at school, the girls had the opportunity to do book-keeping with a lady who came in on a couple of afternoons a week, while the lads went out with a local farmer to learn about farming and care of stock. Not everyone stayed on at school once we'd been given our certificates, but those who did persevere also got a mention on their certificates of these extra studies.

I never know how my parents managed it, but our birthdays were spread quite well across the year, though it was obviously more by luck than judgement. January was John, February Kate, Sarah Jane was in May, and Lillie in June. Minnie's birthday was in August, with Martha and Eva in September, Thomas in October, and then Blanche and me in November. Queenie and Tillie were both born in December. So, whatever the month, there was almost always a celebration to be had. Presents were always of a practical kind – usually something knitted or sewn by mother, and we children would try and make something from straw or wood – a little doll or a gewgaw of some sort.

Shortly after I had left school, around the time of my fourteenth birthday, Miss O'Reilly called at the farm, the only time she ever did. She brought me a gift to congratulate me on my glowing results and to celebrate my birthday. It was "A Little Princess", a book by Frances Hodgson Burnett, the author of my favourite book. I believe it was her personal copy. How I treasured that book – in fact, I still have it to this day in my bookshelf of children's literature that I have kept over the years for my own children and their children and children's children. I love to hold that book and feel the joy that I felt some eighty or so years ago when Miss O'Reilly gave it to me. It wasn't new at the time, and it has been used again so many times, but it will never lose its wonder to me.

I have always had a special fondness for Miss O'Reilly. I visited her in her home on a few occasions after I left school. It was a quiet, calm haven – so unlike the noise and constant clamour of activity in our home farm at Coolnagranchy. Once I heard that Miss O'Reilly was sick. My younger sisters said that she was not in school. Mother let me take her some soup and soda bread. On one of the occasions when I went to her home, I met her brother there. He seemed very nice. They looked a lot alike, though he was much taller; Miss O'Reilly was not much more than five feet tall and quite a bit shorter than the members of our family.

Our farmhouse was always busy, especially as more and more young Monsons arrived on the scene. There were three rooms upstairs, all used as bedrooms. Mother and Father slept in one in a big bed and there always seemed to be two or three cots in there, usually a new baby and then other children up to the age of three or so. After that, they came into the bedrooms with the bigger children. In the early days, John and I were lucky to have a room and a bed each to ourselves, but once Martha was born, my room filled up quickly. John was luckier, being the only boy for about fourteen years, and had a room of his own for some time. Finally, once the girls' room got full to overflowing, he was given a bed in the alcove just by the top of the stairway, and then Minnie, Tillie, Martha and I had one room and the smaller girls had the other. John's bed was quite small, but he wasn't. He had grown tall, like Father, so John was never satisfied with the situation.

The girls' rooms had one large bed in each, shared by all. We knew no different and we all snuggled in, pleased to keep each other warm, especially during the cold, damp winter months. As we grew up, we four older girls formed a special bond which lasted for the rest of our lives; we were the ones who left Coolnagranchy to spend our adult lives here in Canada.

By the time Minnie and I left home, the little ones had long outgrown the cots, and Mother and Father had their room to themselves. Once the youngest two, Thomas and Queenie, were big enough to sleep with the others, there were by then seven in one room, which included young Tom. He never had the benefit of a bed of his own until John left home, and we four oldest girls kept our places in the other bedroom. I imagine that Sarah Jane and Eva were greatly relieved when Minnie and I left home as they moved in with Tillie and Martha to replace us. When the time came Tillie told me that, although they were sad to see us go, they could hardly wait to move their few belongings into the room.

Each room had a chest for our clothes and some shelves for our few belongings. No-one ever really had clothes of their own; if it fitted, you wore it. For everyday wear, the girls all had dark woollen shifts with a white smock on top, and in the winter, we wore long, thick stockings. Underwear varied. Quite often, especially in summer, the younger girls wore none, and we older girls wore drawers. Our brothers had shirts made of rough cotton, a smaller version of what Father wore, breeches cut to just below the knee with long socks, and a belt or cord to keep their trousers held up. John invariably sported a cap, a hand-me-down from someone in the family, which he proudly wore all the time around the farm. Mother often had to reprimand him for wearing it indoors, and he was forbidden to wear it to church, even if it was raining or snowing.

Once clothes were no longer serviceable, they still had their uses. Cottons would be used as nappy cloths for the babies and toddlers and as period cloths for us girls once we reached an age where we needed such protection. Anything else was turned into dusters and rags for wiping and mopping up and cleaning, or ripped up and made into rugs for the floor. And once things had reached the end of their usefulness, there was always need in the spring for a warm, cosy corner for an orphaned lamb, brought to the kitchen for warmth and milk in an attempt to save its little life. Nothing went to waste.

We all had our Sunday best, for going to Croghan Church. Mother and we older girls wore a woollen dress with a white bib or collar, or a woollen skirt with a white high-collared blouse. The younger girls had white pinafore dresses over long-sleeved dark tops. Father's Sunday best consisted of a suit and waistcoat, with a white shirt and scarf tied around his neck, and he would curl his whiskers and part his hair neatly, as was the fashion. John had an old suit of Father's which I remember Mother altering as needed – it grew as he grew – until he was as big as Father and she had let it out to its fullest extent. Mother was very skilful with a needle and thread – thank heavens, as we surely wouldn't have managed otherwise. She often sat up far into the night, mending and altering so we could all be dressed well. As I got older, I often found myself helping her with this never-ending chore. On the odd occasion when something was no longer needed but still wearable, it would be passed to our cousins at Grange or Killukin, and equally, they would return the favour.

We each had a topcoat from the shop in town, or at least something serviceable handed on from our cousins. Our younger brothers and sisters had to make do with our cast-offs, and I recall seeing all my topcoats and other clothes being passed down the line as the years went by.

Footwear was always in short supply. We had a few pairs of boots and it was a matter of vying for what you could get. Some years there seemed to be several pairs, even of the right sizes. Often some of the family went bare-footed. Father did his best to keep the boots going, and there was always great excitement if he came back from Boyle having visited the cobbler bringing the old boots with new soles, or with some new but second-hand boots.

The lower part of our home was made up of two rooms. The sitting room was out of bounds to all but our parents and visitors, except on the most special of occasions. Looking back, it was something of a waste of space, given that there were so many of us and so little room for everyone. The only time we children were allowed in the sitting room was at Christmastide and we were duty bound to sit quietly, most of us on the floor or at the edge of the hearth, where a fire was lit. We each took it in turns to do a small entertainment such as a rhyme or a little story. At Christmas, we went out and picked holly and wound ivy into wreaths which we used to decorate the hearth surround, and we would sing Christmas songs learnt from school and church. It was a very special and happy time.

The kitchen was the heart of the house, and the only place which was usually warm, mainly because of the cooking fire, set back in the wall opposite the main door into the room. On chains and bars within the fireplace hung the big pot and the kettle and the big spoons, and suspended from other hooks on the ceiling there were sacks of potatoes and other vegetables, and perhaps some joints of dried or salted meats, keeping them dry and out of the way of rats and mice. Next to the fireplace was the bread oven where Mother baked the weekly batch of wholemeal loaves that helped fill our ever hungry bellies.

Also in the kitchen was a large wooden table which we could all sit around. Father had his big carver chair at the end nearest the fire, and Mother's chair was next to his at the side, but she never seemed to sit down for two minutes – she was either tending the fire and the pots, or fetching and carrying, or seeing to one of the smaller children. Over time, more chairs were acquired or made until Father got a man in from town to build a high-backed bench along the wall and around the corner. The table was moved across next to it and the younger members of the family sat there. Father sold two of the spare chairs the next time he went to town and bought Mother a pretty mother-of-pearl hairbrush and comb set. How she smiled and even cried a bit at the joy of it, but also told Father that he should have spent the money on something more practical. But she didn't make him take the gift back!

The only other furniture in the kitchen was the dresser. Displayed on its shelves was the Sunday-best crockery – and Mother was very proud of this. It was blue and white and each plate was decorated with a Chinese temple and strange looking trees and also with a bridge and a boat. Around the edge of each plate was a blue pattern with some unfamiliar symbols that looked like letters but, as hard as we children tried, we couldn't read them. Mother told us that the decoration was called Willow Pattern and it told the story of two Chinese lovers. The crockery had been handed down from Father's Mother, our Grandmother Eliza. We children never met her as she died before any of us were born. Of course, it was only used on Sundays and very special occasions. Our everyday crockery and cutlery was kept in the drawers and presses at the base of the dresser and was a complete muddle of patterns and shapes and sizes.

Washing up and washing were done in the small wash-house outside the kitchen door. There were two big stone sinks, and a large wooden bucket for collecting water from the well, just nearby. Propped against the wall was the tin bath that we all used for bathing. Once a week, usually Saturday evening, it was carried to the kitchen and filled with hot water which was heated in the kettle and pots over the fire. The eldest went first, so I was very lucky. Then it followed in age order. The water was never changed, just topped up. By the end of the evening, all the young Monsons were scrubbed clean and with dripping wet hair – all ready for Church the next day. Mother took the saying 'cleanliness is next to godliness' very seriously! She reminded us of that often, when we complained about soapy water stinging our eyes – especially the girls as this was unavoidable when washing and rinsing our long dark tresses. The whole family had dark hair.

Once the bathing was finished, the older ones, usually John and I, used the wooden bucket to empty water from the bath tub outside the door, or out into the vegetable garden if it was a time of no rain. Then we all went to bed. That's when our parents refilled the tub and saw to their own cleanliness; we children were forbidden to leave our bedrooms.

I remember that, for a long time, Mother was constantly asking Father for a dairy. We had a couple of milk cows and she did her best preparing milk and cream in the wash-house, but it wasn't very practical or easy. Father finally found the time and he and a labourer from the next farm, assisted by John, built an extension to the wash-house, along the wall of the shaded side of the farm building, where it was always cool. From somewhere, Father also came across some big dishes for setting the cream, and a plunge churn to help with butter making. That made Mother very happy. Not only did we have milk and butter and cream for ourselves, Mother was also able to sell or trade some of the produce, along with some of the vegetables that she grew in the walled garden at the back of the farmhouse. When there was time, Mother also made cheese, separating milk into curds and whey, then tying the curds in a cloth and hanging it over a pot. This was not the cheese that we have today and went sour after a week or so, but it was jolly good on freshly baked bread.

Mother taught Minnie and me how to make the butter and it became one of our tasks. We milked the cows and filled the setting dishes with milk, then left it all standing in the dairy. Once the cream rose to the top, we took it off with a big skimming spoon full of holes and put it ready in the churn. Over the next couple of days, we added more cream to the churn. Then the hard work began – moving the plunger up and down in the churn until the butter had set. I quite enjoyed this task.

I'll never know how Mother managed as she did. Despite so many years of almost always being pregnant, or breast-feeding, or weaning one of the little ones; despite all her household chores and the washing and mending; despite the constant challenge of keeping the fire and later the range in, cleaning it, lighting it, taking out the ash, blacking the range from time to time; despite being at father's beck and call; somehow she also tirelessly managed her dairy, and her vegetables. Father was in charge of growing potatoes, the staple diet of all Irish people, but mother grew carrots, turnips, onions, peas and greens, sometimes parsnips, and also took joy in tending some flowers when she could. She loved her flowers, and sold some too, and our home always had sweet smelling buds and blooms in a vase on the kitchen table.

Because vegetables and fruit were seasonal, Mother worked to preserve and bottle everything she could. She was so proud of her Kilner jars, another inheritance from her mother-in-law, our Grandma Eliza. We older girls were all set to work, picking and washing and chopping up, and we quickly learnt how to preserve and conserve and pickle, skills that have been of great benefit to us throughout our lives. Even John got involved and was tasked to take the younger children out to collect wild plums and apples and hips – anything that could contribute to the family's store press for the winter months. Best of all, I loved making jams and jellies and chutneys from the fruits we grew or we found growing wild – greengage, plum, marrow, blackberry, quince, wild raspberry, crab apples, and sometimes Father brought some oranges from town. He once came home with two dozen oranges which he said cost him eight pence. At first, Mother was cross that he had spent so much, but he told her that he'd got a good price for a pig he'd sold and had a fancy for some marmalade. Mother cheered up once we'd made several jars of marmalade and, when father came back into the house later that day, she gave him a big hug, and there were smiles all round! We all enjoyed eating the sweet orange preserve and our other jams on the wholemeal bread that Mother made on the big table on baking day each week.

Bread making took most of a whole day each week, and by the end, the kitchen smelt of floury deliciousness. Later in the week, when the loaves were all eaten, we'd savour our home-made jams on soda bread or soda farls, which were quicker to make than the wholemeal loaves. I still love the smell of freshly baked bread; there's nothing more homely or comforting.

Bread and jam were our usual supper time foods, or maybe bread and curd cheese or soup. For breakfast, there was usually porridge, though a rare treat was bacon and eggs when Father had slaughtered a pig and it had been salted and hung near the fireplace to get smoked. Those of us at home, Father and Mother and those not at school, made a meal in the middle of the day of meat and potatoes and vegetables, and then Mother kept some by for her 'young scholars' as she called us, and we had our main meal when we got home from school. On non-school days, we all ate together in the middle of the day. Sometimes, if there were enough ingredients, Mother would make some cakes or biscuits on baking day, but those never lasted long with so many young mouths to feed and an increasing enjoyment of all things sweet.

Father was the one who did most of the purchases in town on market day each week, and John went with him in the holidays and then regularly once he had finished with school. Mother prepared a list of what was needed, usually locally grown oatmeal, flour, salt, sugar, and sometimes tea, and then there was also corn meal to be bought for the animals. It all depended on how well Father had done selling his wares at the market, maybe a bullock or piglet, or some chickens and eggs, maybe Mother sent him with some vegetables or flowers. Sometimes we had a surplus of milk, or Mother sent some of her homemade butter or cheese, or some jams or chutneys.

Mother only went to town if she needed something from the haberdashers, perhaps some thread or needles, or a piece of cloth to make a new garment or mend some others, or some cotton material for underwear or smocks. From time to time, she also bought wool for knitting or darning our socks and stockings, that is if she hadn't had the time to spin her own yarn from the wool from our own sheep. She always insisted that she should buy these things herself; she said that Father couldn't be trusted to get it right! Secretly, I think that Father was relieved as life was never easy when he got things wrong!

Sometimes in the school holidays, and later when we finished school, Minnie and I might go to town to give Mother a hand. If the weather was bad, it was not much fun, and we wrapped up against the cold or the wet, and knowing that the street in town would be muddy and boots and skirts and trousers would all have to be cleaned when we returned home. But on a warm summer's day, it was a very pleasant outing, jogging along in the cart behind Bessie, our dear old horse, looking out at the countryside, the hills and fields, the forever green-ness that is Ireland. The road went along beside the Boyle River, in some places babbling forever in a hurry over the pebbles, in others gliding deeply, silently, smoothly; bright in parts where the sun shone through, and moody elsewhere in the shadows of hanging willows. The route took us through the valley and up the slope past Boyle Abbey, with its arches and little tower, once a monastery I was told. I often tried to imagine the hooded figures of the monks and friars going about their daily services, drifting between the arches and genuflecting as the bell in the tower called them to prayer. Bessie plodded up the hill and on and into town and Father usually tied her up at the end of the main street so that he could easily carry his wares into the market square.

Town was always busy on market day, with everyone greeting his or her neighbour and stopping to pass the time of day. A trip to town was the time to learn what was happening in the area, or to hear who had died or what illnesses were doing the rounds. People in town lived in poorer conditions than we farm families, and didn't benefit from the fresh country air and the opportunity to grow and produce their own food. Large families lived in very close proximity to each other generally in small and squalid houses, with no water or toilets, and these poor conditions led to diseases such as tuberculosis, typhoid and cholera being prevalent. If we heard that there was disease in town, we put scarves around our mouths and avoided anyone we thought might be ill.

Father used to purchase the newspaper during his weekly trip to market. The Connaught Telegraph brought the local news to our household, and Father would sit by the fire of an evening, reading the news and throwing out comments about the price of this, or the scandal of that, or whatever tit-bits he thought would be of interest to his family. In fact, we generally didn't pay much attention, only if there was a report about someone we knew, and then there would be laughter or tears depending on the nature of the event.

Another way of getting things was to trade for them. Father might go to market wanting a young sheep, for instance, and do trade with another farmer for a piglet from our farm. No money would change hands, and he would come home that evening very pleased with his success, especially if he felt that he had the better deal. Mother traded her jams for vegetable and flower seeds. The new bench in the kitchen also came about through some of Father's trade. I recall him going off with John one morning to Lisserdrea with several of the chairs that would no longer be needed, and trading them for all the timber and nails that were needed to make the new bench in the kitchen. That evening at supper, Father laughed to tell us how pleased he was with the trade he'd made, especially as some of the chairs were quite well worn. He might have laughed, but most of the children had to stand for supper that day as there was a shortage of chairs to sit on, and for some days after that. After much encouragement from Mother, he got a man in from town to give him a hand and the new bench was constructed down the side wall and around the end of the table. And, of course, two chairs went to town and were traded for Mother's hairbrush set.

As well as the chickens on the farm, we also had a few sheep, kept mainly for the cooking pot, and Father always had a sheepdog. When I was little it was Jess, and later when she died, Jingo, took her place. At night, the dog was locked in the outhouse in the yard. Father never took a dog to town with him in case there was a problem with some of the stock at market, but at all other times while he was working on the farm, Father had a sheepdog at his heels, and the dog would wait patiently on the doorstep when Father came inside. Usually, there were about twelve pigs kept in the field we called Barn Meadow, though many more when it was piglet time of year. The sheep were in Dairy Maids, down by the river, and the two milk cows, Darkie and Jane, were kept in the big paddock along with our horse, Bessie, who pulled the wagon to take Father to and from town, and also took the family to Church in Croghan on Sundays, or to visit family at Grange and Derrymaquirk, and sometimes Carrick-on-Shannon. Mother also had her share of animals to tend; sometimes we had a pair of geese for their lovely big eggs and for the pot, and Mother might rear a few goslings and chicks for selling at market. Of course, we had a cat or two, to keep the mice and rats at bay. Each year, Father bought half a dozen, sometimes more, young bullocks and they were grazed in the field with the sheep and fattened up for market.

Whenever the cows produced calves, they were taken away from their mothers when they were big enough so that Mother could milk the cows to get the milk for the family. Some of the milk went back to the calves and when we were big enough, we all got involved with feeding them. Generally, it was quite fun, but got harder and more hazardous as the calves grew bigger – and stronger. Feeding a calf from a bucket was quite a skill. Sitting astride the calf, we pushed its head downwards into the bucket of milk, water and cornmeal. Our other hand we put into the calf's mouth to give it something to suck on. Calves' tongues are all rough and have always fascinated me, and I quite enjoyed this task. But sometimes it all came to grief when a boisterous calf arched its back and moved forwards or backwards, and we might find ourselves on the ground – and the bucket of milk all over the place!

An annual event was the arrival of a bull from Derrymaquirk, led in on a rope which was tied to the ring through the animal's nose. He was brought into the big paddock to be introduced to Darkie and Jane and stayed for a few days before being led back to Derrymaquirk again. We girls kept our distance from this bad-tempered, snorting beast, but we always watched on, fascinated at the high jinx; we certainly learnt much about the birds and the bees – though it was years before I realised that animal and human procreation were similar! I'm sure it's the same for all children – not imagining that your parents could be getting up to such things and then linking it to the arrival of babies. For farm children, we were very naïve. This continued for me, at least, until the mechanics of things were explained to the older girls shortly before we left school. The only other exposure we girls had regarding what to look out for was from the minister at Church on Sundays. From time to time, he would include a warning to all young girls of the wages of sin and fornication, but I was never really sure what he was trying to put across. When I asked Mother, she just said that we should be wary of what some young lads might be up to, using an example of this girl or that girl who had been put in the family way by letting her guard down. Really, it wasn't until I married William that I became aware of the bigger picture, and that, at the age of twenty five, was a big shock to me, even though Minnie had given me some advice after her wedding the month before mine. I laugh to think of it now. I have given birth to six children of my own. I have thirteen grandchildren, twenty three great-grandchildren and even five great-great-grandchildren. They all call me Gram Fallis.

Father, and John when he was old enough, brought home rabbits and pigeons and rooks for the larder. Mother was very able at making stews and pies from anything that Father and John brought home. Shooting was one of John's favourite pastimes and he was always off missing somewhere and coming home with something for the pot.

Coolnagranchy was quite close to the Boyle River and Lough Gara, and there were other loughs not so far away. Father and John went off fishing when they could, and a good catch of fish meant that Mother would prepare us a meal of fish and potatoes. From time to time, Father and John were invited to go fishing with our Aunt Kate Monson's husband, Johnston Haire, and his son, Jim. That was the same Jim Haire who later married our Sarah Jane. The Haires had a row boat on Lough Gara. Father and John usually came home with plenty of fish, and tales of the adventure of going off in the boat across the lake – there always seemed to be stories of the one that got away, and who fell in, and so on. Father would roar with laughter, and often Mother laughed till she cried and couldn't help herself as she rocked to and fro. I'm sure Father exaggerated a lot of the antics, just to get Mother looking so happy and relaxed.

If we had too many fish, Mother salted them then packed them in a tub for using later when we were short. She also salted other meats, so we were lucky that we rarely went hungry. We were fairly self sufficient really, what with meat and eggs and dairy produce from the farm, and a good supply of fish nearby, and we had vegetables and fruit, both fresh and preserved. Other wild foods that we took advantage of were mushrooms and puff balls which we children would go foraging for across the fields, and we also got to recognise other plants like stinging nettles and ransoms and sorrel, all of which got added to the menu if other greens or legumes were in short supply. It was always fun to come across puff balls that were getting old; we loved to kick them and make them explode in a puff of grey powder. I guess that is how they got their name.

August time was harvest time, and all the local farmers helped each other to cut the grass and build the stooks to dry the hay, ready for taking in and storing for the long winter months. This was always a carefree time for us young ones, though I now know how hard it was to get the hay cut at the right time to make sure it would not be spoiled. The younger children, particularly, were often in trouble for playing in the hay and spreading it about, but it was all smiles when the hay was all stacked and mother brought the harvest tea of scones and rich cream and homemade jam. Once the hay was turned and dry enough, it was brought in to the barn which stood at the edge of Barn Meadow. Here too the seed potatoes were stored, ready for planting when the ground was right. It couldn't be too wet, and we all learnt to be mindful of the terrible years of the Great Famine when the potato crop failed again and again, and people died in their tens of thousands. If our crop looked as if it was taking the blight, all of us who were big enough were engaged in scything or cutting off the browning tops of the plants and making sure that all was burned. That way, at least some potatoes would be salvaged, even though they might be small. In the early days, our potatoes were dug and picked by hand, which was very hard work. Later, Father got a potato lifter which took some of the toil out of the task, then things got easier still when he traded that and some cows for a potato digger which was towed behind the horse. We loved watching the digger as it threw the potatoes to left and right. There was still work for us children though, as the crop had to be collected up by hand, preferably when the ground was dry. We were instructed that we must pick up every single potato, even the smallest, otherwise there could be blight the following year.

Father always impressed on us that one and a half million people had died of starvation as a result of the potato blight only a few years earlier, and about two million more left Ireland in search of a means of surviving. They migrated to America and Australia and Canada, or went north to Scotland. In fact, two of my Grandfather's brothers, William and Thomas had both emigrated to Cleveland, Ohio, and my Father's cousin, William, left for Minnesota when he was twenty one. This was partly because of the hard times, but also due to the fact that, in each case, they were part of a large family where their father lived to a great age, and they saw no chance of inheriting the family farm. Their expectation was that they would remain unmarried and working for their father with no chance to make a living of their own. This seems to be a trait that runs through the Monson clan – a long life and many children.

So, Minnie and I were not going to be the first Monsons to cross the Atlantic in search of an escape from the shortage and hardships of life in Ireland; others had gone before and in much harder times.

At our farm, there was always a task to be done, and everyone in our family who was big enough was assigned to wood gathering duty, and that was a job that was not seasonal like the harvest. We could never have too much firewood, and we would go out with the wooden handcart to gather what we could from the nearby woodland. If a large tree had fallen, we would report back to Father and John, and, when there was time, we all returned with the cart to pile up the logs which John and Father cut. If we found a branch that we could manage, we dragged it back to the house. We had a timber pile next to the outhouse where logs were stacked. Smaller sticks for lighting the fire were kept in the end of the barn nearby in an untidy heap where they could dry. Father also brought in turfs for the fire, and later the stove, and we also took some of these to school for the fires in the classrooms.

Next to the outhouse was the privy. We had a double privy, two-seated so that Mother could take one of the children with her when she went to use it. The task of providing the bucket of ash was Father's, and John helped when he was older. As at school, John usually complained, and even more so when Father got him to help dig out the privy and dispose of the muck on the pig heap in Barn Meadow.

When I was young, lighting was by candle, and the job of making the candles was a messy one. Mother saved up pieces of animal fat and then boiled them together in a large iron kettle. We often added some herbs that we collected from the hedgerows, wild thyme or marjoram, to mask the smell of the fat which was usually quite rancid. This was then boiled in water and strained, and we dipped the lengths of cord into the hot fat and tied them on a rod to cool. We dipped them again and again, until the candles were thick enough, and then stored them in a wooden box, away from the risk of them being nibbled at by mice. We also made soap from animal fats and herbs, with the addition of lye which was made in a barrel using ash and water. The soap was also stored carefully away; it was too precious to be gnawed by mice and rats and spoilt.

I never realised at the time, but so many of the methods and skills that were part of my childhood would hold me in good stead in the early years of my life on the prairies of Canada, and some, my family and I still use to this day.

Sundays were traditionally observed as a day of rest, though in fact it just meant that Father and Mother had to get up that much earlier to see to the farm, and Mother had the extra task of seeing that we were all looking smart and ready for going to Church in Croghan. At the time, I never questioned why our family went to Croghan while the Derrymaquirk Monsons went to Boyle Parish Church where so many of our ancestors and relatives were buried. It was particularly strange as we were only a couple of fields away from Derrymaquirk. I believe that it was something to do with Mother's family, the McMasters; it was surely because Croghan was the family church of the McMasters, and it was an opportunity for Mother to meet up with her sister, Kathleen.

Once when we went to Boyle Church for the family funeral of my Uncle Edward from Derrymaquirk, shortly before Minnie and I went to Canada, I took a walk around the cemetery and noticed several Monsons already buried there. I found George and Catherine who had died when I was three or four, and I later discovered that George was my Grandfather's brother. I recall other graves for a Robert, a John, a Thomas, all familiar family names. Some I may have met as they had died in my lifetime, but I couldn't remember many of them. The oldest grave I came across was of John and Elizabeth of Grange, who may have been my Great Grandparents, but no-one I asked seemed quite sure.

The only other special church occasion that comes to mind was the wedding of Ellen, one of our older cousins from Derrymaquirk. I was seventeen and it was only a couple of months after Queenie was born. Ellen was marrying George Lonney in Boyle Church. It was a very cold December day, just after Christmas, and Mother had not been very well since the birth. The road to Boyle made things worse for her as we jogged along in the cart. Twice we almost turned back, Father was so concerned for her, but she was determined that we should get to the church. After the wedding service, we were to have returned to Derrymaquirk for the wedding breakfast, but Father put his foot down and said that Mother should go straight back home. So we children all missed out on the festivities, much to our dismay.

The other family wedding that took place was in April or May 1905. Edward from Derrymaquirk was marrying Emily Parker from Manorhamilton, up in Leitrim. We were all excited at the idea of another wedding, especially Minnie, Tillie, Martha and I. It was to be at St Clare's Church in Manorhamilton. Father explained that it was about forty miles away and that the journey would be too long. So Edward got married without the Coolnagranchy Monsons to witness the day, and we were all very disappointed. It seemed that something always conspired to spoil our fun when it came to weddings.

It was usual on a Sunday after church that we went visiting Grange, the farm of Uncle Duke and Aunt Kathleen. There was always amusement to be had, with so many cousins to have fun with. I remember one occasion when I was probably about eleven, several of us from both families went up to the big cow shed at Grange and were there for several hours. We discovered that we could jump out of the hayloft and onto the ground, and we made the landing softer by throwing out a big pile of the hay. Michael, the herdsman, found us and we were in great trouble, first with him and later with our parents when we returned to the house. In fact, we were in double trouble as we had been wearing our Sunday clothes and much was spoilt or muddy. From that day, Grange cow shed was out of bounds and we were charged not to wander away for hours at a time.

No-one was stricter than Old Granny McMaster. She was our grandmother on Mother's side, and lived at Grange with her other daughter, our Aunt Kathleen. When her husband, James, had died back in the 1870's, she left the farm over at Kilmactranny and moved into Grange with Aunt Kathleen and Uncle Duke. She was always there when we visited Grange, and ruled the roost with her strict and proper nature. As she grew older, she became very short-sighted, and we children had great fun trying to fool her as to which of us was which. Our fun was kerbed when finally she got spectacles.

Our parents
Mary and Thomas Monson.

Old Granny McMaster (Mother's mother).

Croghan Church where we worshipped each Sunday.

My childhood seemed to come to an end when I left school at fourteen. I had always been the main one to help Mother with the chores and the other children, but once I'd finished my school education, more responsibilities fell to me. I so hoped that I would get that job I'd anticipated as a book-keeper, but nothing was forthcoming and I never got the opportunity to escape the farm and spread my wings with a job in town or nearby. With no work available locally for me or my sisters, and no available husbands, our parents must have been very concerned for the future. Our farm just about supported our family as we were growing up, but with no solution in sight for change, the prospect of supporting ten daughters indefinitely must have been daunting. The future was not clear for the whole family. When John left to seek his fortune in 1905, it meant that Thomas, as the only son left at home, would be the one to take over the farming of Coolnagranchy from Father when the time came. But there would be nothing for us girls unless we could find our futures elsewhere.

2

Two years in England

1906-1908

In the Spring of 1906, Mother and Father decided to send me to stay in England with my Aunt Mary and Uncle George, those first cousins who had overcome the shortage of life partners by marrying within the family. I could never have imagined the new sights and experiences that were in store for me, particularly during the journey and then on my arrival at my Uncle and Aunt's home.

My Aunt and Uncle had come on a visit to Derrymaquirk and stayed for a few days with Uncle George's parents, Edward and Ellen. It was a great family occasion for everyone, though probably quite overwhelming for our Great Uncle and Aunt who were both in their eighties by then. We all went to Boyle Church together on the Sunday and it took three wagons to get us all there. After church, we returned to Derrymaquirk for a family party. Derrymaquirk was the grandest of the family homes and I always liked visiting there.

Mother and her sister, Aunt Kathleen, laid on a magnificent spread of meats and poultry, pies and pasties, and the house was full to bursting with children of all ages, some more boisterous than others, and parents, doing their best to maintain a little of the peace and decorum that was the norm at Derrymaquirk. Uncle George and Aunt Mary had moved away about twenty years before when Uncle went for work in the Civil Service, first in Dublin and then later they moved to England where Uncle was employed in the Board of Trade, and where my cousins were born.

Before their visit to Derrymaquirk, my parents wrote to my Aunt and Uncle and discussed with them the possibility of me staying with them in England. It was agreed that I should return with them to England, so their visit was partly to see family and friends, and partly to escort me back to their home in Middlesex. Back at home that Sunday evening, Mother and I set about putting together my belongings and tying them together into a bundle, all ready for my departure the following day. What a mixture of emotions I had, and Mother and I shared some tears as we packed my few possessions. I was twenty two and the only life I had ever known was there at Coolnagranchy with my parents and brothers and sisters and with my relatives living nearby. Apart from the first few months of my life at Knockadoo, of which I have no recollection, I had always lived on the farm at Coolnagranchy, and had few experiences away from home, apart from going to school at Ardsallagh, the weekly family outings to church in Croghan, and trips into Boyle from time to time.

Boyle was the biggest town I knew and I was always taken aback at the number of people who congregated there on market days. The thought of going with my Aunt and Uncle on a journey to England filled me with trepidation, to a land unknown and a new home that was far from the countryside that I knew and loved, with no animals and crops, no fields and hedgerows. I would be leaving behind all those I loved, with whom I shared my life's happiness and sorrows, parted from all those who knew me as no-one else did. The one thing that brought any solace to me in that moment was the thought that I would at last get to know my English cousins better. I had met Hasluck, Duke and Edith a couple of times before when they visited.

I had little idea what it was going to be like living in a town for the first time. I was grateful that my Aunt and Uncle would be taking me there as I could hardly imagine how otherwise I could find my way.

That night I slept badly, with nightmares of losing my way, or getting swept along by a sea of people in a land of strange noises and unknown faces. Several times, I found myself sitting bolt upright in bed, sometimes hot, sometimes shivering, sometimes struggling to get my breath. Since we shared a bed, it was impossible for my sisters not to be disturbed by my terrors. Poor Minnie, Tillie and Martha could not console me, nor could I bring any comfort to them. It all seemed so unreal and so unexpected, a parting that would change everything for us all. Mother had relied on me for so much, and now my sisters would have to step in to take my place. Martha had finished school two years before, and she, Minnie and Tillie had many chores of their own, but Mother had always entrusted more to me, including the task of getting the younger children to and from school each day.

There were five children in school at this time, with Thomas and little Queenie still at home, and Queenie quite a handful. She was always a cheeky little thing and made us all laugh with her antics. It's quite likely that we all encouraged her as well which didn't make things any easier, and Mother was often at a point of total exasperation with her – and us!

At last the dawn came, grey across the fields and hedgerows, and it was time to go. My face and eyes were red and puffy from my night-time horrors, even though I did my best to splash them with water. I really didn't want everyone to see what a state I was in, but I don't think I succeeded. I didn't want them to think that I was a big baby, especially as I had always been Mother's number one support, and it was to me that the little ones came running with splinters and grazed knees and all their problems, large and small. I was their second mother, always there for them when Mother was busy on the farm, or in the dairy, or mending, or washing, or cooking, for her work was never done and she looked to me, Minnie, Tillie and Martha to fill in when she was otherwise engaged. What would the little ones think if they saw me like this? How would they cope with my leaving?

Aunt and Uncle came over from Derrymaquirk in a jaunting car, and got down to bid farewell to my parents, and cast a cursory parting word to my sisters and brothers. Everyone was there to see me go, except for John, probably off somewhere on the farm setting traps or hunting rabbits. Despite my best intentions, I did not cope well with the whole affair of parting. I felt that Father did not approve of my sobs and tears, and that only seemed to make matters worse. Mother showed great fortitude and somehow helped me to manage the situation, though I was sure that she was suffering as much as I was. Aunt and Uncle got up on the jaunting car and Martha and Tillie gave me a hand while Minnie passed my roll of luggage to the driver who lashed it firmly on top of the large leather valise that my Aunt and Uncle had brought with them. Then we were off, leaving behind a very tearful family, with the little ones sobbing and clinging to Mother's skirts. So my life set off in its new direction.

Aunt Mary was such a comfort to me. She seemed to know all the right things to say, but also when it was better to say nothing. As we made our way to the railway station in Boyle, she tucked a blanket over my knees and gave me a beautiful reassuring smile that seemed to say to me that everything would be alright and that she would protect me in the times ahead. On the train to Dublin, she and Uncle chatted about their visit and talked about Uncle's parents at Derrymaquirk, and about all the changes they had noticed since leaving their own childhood homes back here in Boyle roughly at the time that I was born. Uncle had been born at Grange, then moved later to Derrymaquirk with his parents. Auntie and her brothers and sisters were all born at Coolnagranchy, my own home, a fact that I hadn't known before. She and I had more in common than I realised and I warmed to her with every passing moment.

When we reached Dublin, Uncle had some business to see to and left Auntie and me to take a look around the town. The shops were full of the wonders of the world, as far as I was concerned – hats and dresses and trinkets, all very grand; the like of which they certainly didn't have in Boyle. For me, the high spot of my day in Dublin was our visit to the museum. We saw wondrous and strange animals which were caught in far off lands, then prepared and filled with stuffing and brought to the museum. They were displayed in large wooden cases, with glass windows on all sides so the creatures could be viewed from all around. I had never seen anything like them before; animals that I have since learned more about but which, on that day in Dublin, were a complete mystery and wonder to me: lions and tigers and whales, every sort of bird and fish and deer and wolf and crocodile. I think that I was most fascinated by the hippopotamus and rhinoceros, the camels and the tall giraffe, all so unlike anything I had ever seen before. I did recognise some of the birds and ducks and fishes, the mice and rats and bats, as these I knew from home. But mostly, everything was so wonderful and unexpected and strange. Auntie and I went upstairs to a balcony high up above the main floor of the museum. There we saw more animals, and also looked down over the ornate iron balustrade at the displays below. I got a feeling of light-headedness as I had never before been up so high. I felt like a bird flying high above the ground, though my feet were still planted firmly.

After some time, Uncle arrived at the museum and it was time to make our way to the ferry that would take us to England. Mother had sent us with something to eat, so we had some lunch while waiting for the departure. It was good to have something to eat from home: Mother's wholemeal bread and cheese tasted so good, and Uncle disappeared off and came back with steaming cups of tea which were most welcome as the day had turned quite cool, especially when we were sitting out of the sunshine in the shadows of the ferry terminal.

At last the time came for us to board the ferry. A cold wind was blowing off the sea and I felt chilled and lacking the new optimism that I had found while exploring in Dublin with Auntie. But she came to my rescue again and pulled the blanket that had brought me comfort earlier around my shoulders as we made our way up the gangplank. Just as we stepped on board, the ship's whistle gave out a mighty blast which shocked me to my senses as if to force me to take notice of what was new around me, to take on all the novel and different experiences that I was going through, screaming at me to pay attention and not miss out on a moment of my new life. I realised that this was my opportunity to share these events with my family back home. My brothers and sisters might never have these chances so it would be up to me to report back to them.

Despite my new found confidence, I didn't much enjoy the trip from Dublin to Liverpool. The nearest I had been to sea before was a short trip in my cousins rowing boat on Lough Gara, and the rough waves across the Irish Sea left me feeling very sick and discomfited, but it didn't last forever and then we were in Liverpool. It was noisy and dirty and crowded with people who spoke in a way that seemed very strange to me. The evening was now drawing in, and Uncle said that we would find somewhere to spend the night before taking the train southwards to London. The accommodation was fine, in a large hotel near the train station, and another new experience as I had never stayed in a hotel before. I shared a room with Auntie and I guess that Uncle must have taken another room, though I never saw it. We had a meal in the dining room, something else I'd never done before, and I was very nervous about eating in a room with so many other people, many of them very smart in their suits and hats. The meal was very good though I can't say what it was because it was quite different from our simple fare at home of stews or meat and vegetables, and the array of cutlery and plates set before me was overwhelming. But the food was tasty, and it filled my hungry tummy and made me feel good. The night spent sharing a bed with Auntie went much better than my last night at home. I must have been quite exhausted, what with the sleepless night before, the emotions of leaving home, the journey and the new sights and sounds. I didn't remember my head touching the pillow. I must have slept soundly all night and I was surprised to be awakened by Auntie telling me that we needed to have our breakfast and be off shortly or we would miss the train to London.

Breakfast I do remember, with generous slices of succulent bacon, fried eggs and mushrooms, and white bread, much softer than the wholemeal from home. This was not a feast that I was used to but Father certainly enjoyed a similar meal on Sundays before we went to church. I couldn't believe that it was intended for me, and looked nervously at Auntie. She must have been aware of my hesitation and gave me a nod of approval. I ate heartily, savouring every mouthful and wondering that I could be so lucky as to have such a wonderful banquet. Once we had breakfasted, we collected our luggage and made straight for the railway station which was just close by.

What a busy, noisy, rude place Liverpool Railway Station was. Nervously I kept close to my Aunt and Uncle, fearing I might get lost and reminded of my nightmare on my last night at home, my fears of getting lost in a sea of strangers.

Soon we were boarding the train and finding our seats. I couldn't believe that Uncle had been able to reserve some seats especially for us. We settled down and made ourselves comfortable, putting our luggage and coats up on the string racks above our heads. Auntie suggested that I might like to sit by the window and she sat next to me, with Uncle sitting opposite us.

The train journey took most of the day, and I was constantly reminded of a poem that I had always loved called "From a Railway Carriage". It was from "A Child's Garden of Verses" by Robert Louis Stevenson and it had been one of my favourite books at school. The first few lines went over and over in my mind, in time with the rhythm of the train along the tracks.

Faster than fairies, faster than witches,
Rivers and houses, hedges and ditches;
And charging along like troops in a battle,
All through the meadows and horses and cattle.

The rhyme only left me when the train stopped in a station, or when my Aunt and Uncle engaged me in conversation, or when I dozed off for a while. The journey to London took several hours and greatly lifted my spirits as we ran through countryside, past trees and fields, over hills and through river filled valleys.

All of the sights of the hill and the plain
Fly as thick as driving rain;
And ever again in a wink of an eye,
Painted stations whistle by ...

It seemed that the poem had been made for my journey, giving me comfort and putting me in tune with all around me. Everything I saw was reflected in the rhyme.

And here is a cart run away in the road
Lumping along with man and load;
And here is a mill and there is a river
Each a glimpse and gone forever.

At one stage Aunt Mary asked what I was dreaming of as I had such a faraway look about me. I smiled and just said that I had a poem in my head about a train and she seemed to understand and smiled back.

Late that afternoon, our train reached its destination – we had arrived in London. I expected to finish the journey in a jaunting car – the same way as we had started out from Coolnagranchy the morning before. To my amazement, we walked out to the front of the station and there, Uncle got into a hackney cab and beckoned us to follow. This to me was the most wondrous of all our experiences so far and something that far exceeded any of my expectations. I would have so much to write home about.

It was some time later that we arrived at the home of my Aunt and Uncle in Willesden in Middlesex. All along the way, I was marvelling at the sights and sounds of London and the suburbs, and I felt a disappointment when we finally arrived, though also an anticipation to see our destination. Uncle gave some money to the driver and I stepped out to see my new home. It was joined to the houses on either side, something quite alien to me as all the family farms I knew stood in their own land, far from other dwellings. As with all the other houses in the street, it was brick built, with large grey stone bay windows upstairs and down, and a grey stone porch around the main door. There was no land in front of the house and it only took a few paces to reach the front porch. My eyes were drawn to the beautiful tiled floor. Aunt Mary approached the threshold, raised the lion's head knocker and rapped on the door. A few moments passed then a tall and very handsome young man opened the door, followed by another a little younger and shorter and a tall girl in a very fancy dress. These were my cousins, and the younger two, Duke and Edith, clamoured to take our luggage and were obviously keen to take a look at me. They were not at all as I had remembered them. My elder cousin, Hasluck, looked on, quizzically amused.

Aunt Mary saw that I was completely bewildered and ordered them back in to the front parlour where she said that we would join them shortly to make introductions. They disappeared through a door at the side of the hallway, chattering and laughing as they went. Auntie told me to go with her and I picked up my bundle which my cousins had left in the hall and followed my Aunt up the stairs. I noticed that the tiled floor in the hallway was even more elaborate than in the porch and my eyes were opened wide at the splendour and neatness of everything - the colourful rugs, the runner on the stairs with the decorated clips to hold it in place, the smooth brown rail and shiny decorative posts, and large wooden balls atop the posts. I wanted to take in everything at once but there was far too much for me to manage in those first few moments. I marvelled at the decorations on the walls and ceilings, the lamps fitted to walls and ceiling. This was so different from our farmhouse in Coolnagranchy, so different.

I followed Auntie to a bedroom at the back of the house and again I was in awe. There was a bed with a neat flowered cover, with decorative iron work at top and bottom that reminded me of the balustrade in the museum. The floor had polished wooden boards and a rug. Also in the room was a chest of drawers, a table and mirror with a large decorated bowl and jug, and a chair before the table. My eyes rested on a neat little fireplace set in the wall, and a small fire burned there, warming the room and giving a strange perfume which I later learned to be coal. On the wall a warm light burned from the gaslight. I couldn't believe it! A warm bedroom with a fire, and a light on the wall! In the whole of my life I had been accustomed to a cold and often damp bedroom, a room where we could see our breath in winter time, where we all cuddled together to keep warm each night. If there was any light, it was from a single candle on the window sill. We would sneak under the bedcovers to change from our day clothes to our night wear, and repeat a similar routine each morning.

My Aunt told me that this was to be my room and I could hardly believe that it was to be mine alone, with no-one to share any of it. I was speechless. When I'd left Coolnagranchy so tearfully the day before, I had not dreamed that any of this would be possible.

She told me to get myself settled and she would return for me in a little while. Once she had left the room, I looked around and my eyes filled with tears. It had never occurred to me that this could be happening to me, that any of this was possible. In fact I could never have imagined it as I had no previous experience of anything like this. I tried to take it all in and I stepped towards the small window which overlooked the back of the house. In the dusk, I saw a tidy garden, with neat paths and flowers and vegetables. How Mother would have loved this. I would write to her as soon as possible and let her know how wonderful it was. There was so much to tell everyone that I resolved to ask my Aunt for some writing materials so that I could write home to my beloved family the next day. I would make it my first priority.

Aunt Mary tapped on the door and asked if I had unpacked. I apologised and told her that I would need a few more minutes if that was alright. Quickly, I untied my parcel and put my few items of clothing into the drawers, my spare woollen skirt and two new blouses that Mother had found for me, my spare underwear and leggings, and two pretty handkerchiefs that Minnie had embroidered for me the previous Christmas. I carefully folded my nightdress on the bed and looked up to see a bright brass hook on the back of the door to hang my coat. Then I took my hairbrush and comb from the table where I had laid them out, and set about tidying my hair. It needed some attention after the rigours of the past two days. Before leaving home,

I had carefully braided my hair and wound it at the back of my head, but my hair was so fine and it always had a mind of its own and had strayed from its pins, with wisps of hair escaping from my carefully stranded plait. My fingers moved through my hair in search of the pins I had placed there, but I found only two. I would have to ask my Aunt if she had any I could use, but not straight away as I was mindful that my Aunt, and the rest of the family, would be waiting. I quickly undid my plait, then tugged and tugged at my untidy mane with my hairbrush and comb. Back at home, Minnie and the others had shared these with me; I wondered what they would be using now that I had taken them. I quickly plaited my hair again and wound a small bun at the back using the two remaining pins. Then I caught sight of myself in the mirror, another novelty for me, and went to the door and called to my Aunt. She emerged from a room at the front of the house, presumably her bedroom, and I followed her downstairs. She said she would show me where the water closet was to be found. I had no idea what she meant and thought perhaps she was going to show me where the water pump was in the back yard. What a surprise it was when she took me through the kitchen and scullery, both with even more decorative tiles, and on to a small room which looked just like a privy, but it was indoors. I couldn't imagine who would dream of having their privy in their house, it would be odorous and completely impractical. Seeing my discomfort, my Aunt chuckled and explained that things were changing and that everyone in London now had a water closet. She showed me how to make it flush to take everything away. She then showed me the bath and the gas boiler in the next room to the water closet and said this was much better than the old tin bath that she and Uncle had been used to back in Ireland. There were so many new things for me to wonder at.

I was so excited at the idea of meeting the family, though also apprehensive at what they would make of their country cousin and whether they would understand my broad accent. Aunt and Uncle still spoke in the accent of their childhood, though softened during their time in London, so I hoped that my cousins wouldn't be too taken aback at the way I spoke.

I had nothing to worry about. We went into the parlour and my Uncle was in an armchair near the fire reading the newspaper, with a lamp blazing bright at either side of the mantle. My cousins were all three sitting on other chairs around the room reading books. It was clear that they were under the strictest instructions not to make a great fuss. They all looked up and, as the oldest, Hasluck took it upon himself to break the ice. He told me he was twenty, which was just two years younger than me, and the same age as my brother John. I would never have guessed. He was smartly dressed in a dark charcoal grey suit and waistcoat, with a white shirt and light coloured tie. His hair was neatly cut and parted to one side and it looked as if it was oiled in place. He was charm itself, and welcomed me to England and hoped that I would be happy living with him and his family here at 74 Strode Road, Willesden. I felt myself blush. I was not used to such attention from a handsome young man. In fact, my only dealings with any young men were with my brother, John, and his ways were far from charming!

Hasluck introduced me to his brother Duke, full name Robert Duke, who was fourteen, and his little sister, Edith, aged thirteen, who he said sometimes preferred to be called by her middle name, Lenore, when she was with some of her friends. He said that she was called Edie at home – whether she liked it or not! She made a face and stuck out her tongue at Hasluck and we all burst out laughing. I began to feel more comfortable, but very much the poor country mouse. Our clothes were so different. I was dressed in my Sunday best, but felt so untidy compared with these three smart young people. Duke had dark blue breeches and jacket, buttoned high, with a high collared white shirt. Edie was wearing a very fancy green pinafore dress, with a white blouse beneath and a belt slung low about her hips. Her leggings were green and matched her dress and she had brown boots, and a yellow bow around her head holding back her curly shoulder length hair.

I thought I should return the complement and introduce myself to the expectant group, and tell them about my family back in Ireland. First I told them all about our farm at Coolnagranchy, near Boyle and they joined in that they knew some things about me and Coolnagranchy. They had twice visited when they were much younger but didn't remember much. But their mother told them that she had lived there as a child with her sister and four brothers, and it was when her father died that my Father, Thomas, had taken on the farm. This made me feel closer to them straight away. I then told them about the twelve of us, and that I was the eldest, and how I helped look after the little ones. They asked how big the farmhouse was, having to accommodate such a large family, and I told them that it was neither large nor grand. I was a bit embarrassed to share all the details with them as it all seemed so quaint and mean compared with the magnificence of their home. Of course, as the months went by and we got to know each other better, I felt more relaxed in their company and felt able to tell them more.

My eyes were suddenly drawn to some framed pictures on the mantle over the fireplace, including one of my own family. I recalled that one Sunday, when I was about eighteen, a photographer arrived at the farm to take a family photograph. We were all in our best church clothes and Father brought two chairs from the house and he and Mother sat down, Thomas on Father's lap, and Queenie on Mother's. My younger sisters, Lillian, Blanche and Kate, were ordered to stand in front of our parents and we older ones stood behind at the instruction of the photographer, who had set up his camera on a stand in the middle of the yard. We were all told to face the camera, but it took some time to get the little girls to stand still at the front, and Queenie never really settled down and wriggled and squirmed on Mother's lap. When all was as ready as it was going to be, the photographer put his head under a black cloth on his camera and told us all to stand as still as we could until it was done. He held something up and there was a great flash. We all started, wondering what had gone wrong, but it seemed that all was well. I had never seen the results of that day and was shocked and delighted to find the picture of my family at my Aunt's house. A picture of my family was going to be of great comfort to me as I could gaze on their faces every day, even though it was a record of us all some four years before.

I expressed my pleasure at seeing the photograph, and Uncle looked up from reading his newspaper, then folded it and placed it on the small octagonal table beside him. He took out a fob watch, opened the cover and announced that it would soon be time to eat. I wondered what sort of food we would be having, recalling my surprise at the meal I had enjoyed with my Aunt and Uncle in the hotel in Liverpool.

Auntie came into the room and confirmed that it was time to eat and I waited for Uncle to lead the way. Hasluck offered to show me the way to the dining room and I followed him out into the hallway then into the dining room. At home, we all took our meals around the big table in the kitchen, so I was taken aback at the idea of a separate room for dining, yet another surprise on this unusual day. And the beautiful polished table, every bit as large as our rustic table at home, had six of the most elegant chairs around it that I had ever seen, with carved decorative backs and beautiful material on the seats. Our chairs at home were plain wood and nothing fancy about them at all, and several of us sat on the bench that had been fashioned around the big table. The other fine-looking furniture and furnishings made me stop short in my steps. My Aunt, ever sensitive to my astonishment and bewilderment, came to my aid and guided me to the table and suggested that I sit on the chair next to Hasluck. He smiled reassuringly at me as I sat next to him and Auntie sat on the other side of me at her place at the end of the table. Uncle sat at the top of the table, and Edie sat opposite me with Duke next to her. I noticed against the wall behind Edie and Duke, that there were four more chairs matching those at the table. Another fire burnt warmly in the grate; so many fires in one house were more than I could dream of.

The meal itself held no surprises for me and I think that Auntie had planned it carefully to put me at my ease, though I was not expecting the silvery cutlery and beautiful plates, which reminded me of Mother's crockery on the dresser that had belonged to her mother. A young woman, probably about my age, came into the room carrying a large china dish with a lid which she placed on the table in front of my Uncle. She then went out and brought back a second dish, piled high with steaming hot potatoes. Hasluck introduced me to Bethany, telling me that she helped his mother in the kitchen. Uncle served himself a portion of the meat stew, then the dishes were passed down the table to my Aunt. She took a small portion of potatoes and stew, then invited me to help myself. My hand shook, nervous that I might spill something, but I managed without mishap and passed the dishes to Hasluck, who gave me a wink. How I enjoyed the meal, so familiar to me and my family back in Ireland, with potatoes and a rich tasty stew. When we had all finished, Bethany was called in to collect the plates and dishes, and shortly after returned with a large bowl of rice pudding. I felt less nervous spooning myself the creamy white pudding, realising that I was going to have to get used to serving myself at meal times. The rice tasted sweet and delicious. It was yet another surprise but a nice one. I was later to discover that it was the custom to have a sweet dessert as part of the daily main meal, but so strange to me as it was something that was not part of the custom back at home.

Once the meal was finished, Bethany came into the room to collect the bowls and clear the table, and Hasluck turned to me and said that we would all return to the parlour. At Coolnagranchy, Minnie, Tillie, Martha and I were responsible for doing the dishes after a meal, so I enquired if I could help. Hasluck chuckled and said that Bethany would do that, and my Aunt said that I wouldn't need to help that day but that this would be part of my duties in future. I rose from my chair and followed my cousins out into the parlour where we sat down on the comfortable chairs there.

Hasluck proceeded to tell me a little more about himself. I learned that he was twenty, just two years younger than me and that he was training to be an accountant at a firm in the City of London. He started his career at the age of seventeen when he had become a boy clerk with the same firm. I wasn't really sure what an accountant was, and plucked up the courage to enquire. Once he'd explained, I found myself on safer ground and told him that I had always wanted to work with figures and become a book-keeper, and that arithmetic had been one of my best subjects at school. Secretly, I wondered that, had I grown up in England like Hasluck, I might have had a better chance of achieving my ambition.

Edie then took her turn at telling me about herself. She said that she was in her last year at school and that she wanted to be an actress and marry a rich man. Duke and Hasluck rolled their eyes, and Edie raised her voice and accused them of not taking her seriously. Uncle came into the room and suggested that his sons go gently on their sister. He had obviously heard it all before.

When I asked Duke what he was doing with himself, he just shrugged and said nothing. I commented that both my grandfather and my uncle were also called Duke, though John Duke rather than

Robert Duke. Hasluck contributed to the conversation and said that it was a traditional family name and he was aware of at least seven Dukes in the Monson family since about 1800. I pointed out that I knew of another Robert Duke, one of the cousins from Grange. I asked Duke if he knew the origin of the name, but he didn't know, neither did Hasluck. Uncle George said that he didn't know either but it was one of those traditions that had been in the family for many years. Both on that day and in the weeks and months that followed, I always found it hard to make conversation with Duke. He was often so morose, doubtless brought about by his lack of direction and his general moody frustration at everything.

We continued to chat but I found myself getting more and more drowsy. Aunt Mary came into the room and joined the conversation, but soon she noticed that I was flagging and asked if I would like to go to my bed. I was very grateful as she led me from the room and up the stairs to my bedroom. She enquired if I needed anything and told me that I could go to the scullery to get water for washing. She also pointed out to me the chamber pot under my bed and said that I should bring the pot down to the back door in the morning. Breakfast would be at eight o'clock and I would be expected to be in the dining room in good time.

I must admit that I was so tired that I went straight to bed and fell fast asleep, only awoken the next morning by a tapping on my bedroom door. My Aunt opened the door and announced that it was half past seven and a good time to get up. She brought me a jug of warm water, another shock to me. Back home we splashed the sleep from our faces in the water butt outside the farm door. The only time we knew warm water was in the weekly bathtub. I couldn't believe that I had slept so late; at home we were all up at dawn, with the crowing of the cockerel in the yard. If I had slept until half past seven at home, we would never have had time to get all the chores done and everyone ready for school. I apologised, but my Aunt just smiled and said that she knew that everything would be strange for a while but that they would gradually sort themselves out. Today, I would be finding out what's what, and then tomorrow I would start learning the ropes from Bethany. Auntie told me that Bethany would be leaving us at the end of the week as she was going to be needed at home. Her mother was due to have her sixth baby and, as the oldest, Bethany would need to be there for the family. This all sounded so familiar to me and I looked forward to getting to know Bethany better. Her situation sounded so similar to mine back at the farm; we could compare notes.

There was one weekly task that I didn't get involved with, and that was doing the washing. Early each Monday morning, Amy arrived at the scullery door and it was her job to do the family's laundry. She took advantage of the bath and the gas boiler in the bathroom off the scullery to do this and used a mangle to wring out the clothes, a luxury unknown to us at Coolnagranchy. If the weather was fine, she strung the clothes out in the garden to dry; if it was wet, she put them over a washing rack in the scullery which was then hoisted high. The mangle and drying rack were things of great wonder to me and I thought of how useful it would be for Mother to have these to help with the weekly wash.

It sounded as if I was going to be busy here at my Aunt's house and wondered when I would find time to write home. I hadn't really considered before what I would be doing there, but shouldn't have been surprised as it was quite normal in Ireland for nephews and nieces and cousins to stay at their relative's homes and become unpaid servants of the household. I had seen this happen within our Monson families back home, including my cousin John Duke from Grange who, I learned, was about to join our family at Coolnagranchy to help Father with the farm work. I chuckled to myself at the thought that he would be taking my chair at the table.

Quickly I rose, saw to my ablutions, then dressed myself, sorted out my hair ready for the day, and went down the stairs, still amazed how splendid everything was compared to the humble environment I was used to. I went through the kitchen and found Bethany in the scullery, stirring a large pot of porridge on the cooking range. I had seen one of these ranges once at Derrymaquirk, but at Coolnagranchy we had no such device; we cooked on an open fire in the hearth. But I knew how to make porridge and was comforted that breakfast wasn't going to hold any great surprises for me. Bethany asked me to fill the kettle and put it to boil and I took the kettle and went to go through the door to outside, assuming that I would easily find the pump. She asked me where I was off to and I explained. She quickly put me to rights, pointing out the tap and sink in the scullery. Of course, I had no idea about the tap and she had to stop what she was doing and show me how to make the water come out. This was the first tap I had ever seen, and I felt that Bethany was a bit cross with me – but there was nothing I could do about it.

Once the kettle was filled and put to heat on the range, I was then charged with getting down one of the big frying pans so that the bacon and eggs could be cooked. This again held no mysteries for me as I was usually the one to prepare Father's Sunday breakfast for him, but when Bethany asked me to get the toast started, I had no idea what was expected of me and told her so. When we made toast at home, we used toasting forks and cooked the bread on the open fire; there was no open fire here. At my admission of ignorance as to how to make toast on the range, Bethany said that I should take over stirring the porridge and she would show me how to cook the toast. She took a large loaf of bread out of the large metal bin that stood on the table by the dresser and cut generous slices of the bread on a wooden board. She took a round metal grid that was propped at the back of the range and opened it like a book. Then she trapped two slices between the two sides, and put the contraption flat beneath a lid on one part of the range, next to where I was stirring the porridge pot. I was told to keep an eye that it didn't burn, while Bethany took down a frying pan and proceeded to cook bacon. Soon a delicious smell came from the cooking bread, and Bethany lifted the lid to reveal that the bread had changed from its original whiteness to a golden brown colour. Here was this strange white bread that I had seen before in the hotel. Bethany took a thick cloth to save burning her hands and tipped the toast on to a metal platter, placed two more bread slices between the grids and thus set another two pieces of toast on their way, saying that I could look after the rest now that I knew how. The slices of toast soon piled up and I loved the squared patterns on them made by the grids.

Finally, we filled a tray with freshly made tea and a jug of milk, and Bethany left the kitchen briefly, taking first the tea tray and then the large dish of porridge that she loaded from the cooking pot. Between us, we soon prepared two platters, one with eggs and bacon and the other with several slices of toast which I had proudly helped to prepare. When all was ready, we together made our way with the platters, both with lids, to the dining room and set them on the table. My Aunt instructed me to join the family at the table and Bethany returned to the kitchen for her own breakfast.

I soon found my place in the family's daily routine. Having received full instructions from Bethany before she left the household, I became adept at using the new tools and utensils, and cooking the new foods. My life's changed pattern suited me well enough, and I was soon at ease with my new family who were so welcoming to me, even though I was little more than an unpaid servant. I wanted for nothing, except the chance to see my real family from time to time, especially my Mother, and I very much missed my dearest sister Minnie, my closest friend since we were both tiny. I did get to write home about the journey and the first wonders of my new home, but that was only after almost a week and with the help of Hasluck who provided me with pen and ink and paper. Before that, I was so busy, learning the ropes from Bethany, and accompanying my Aunt to the dressmaker to fit me up with some work dresses, though they were in fact better than the clothes I had brought with me from Coolnagranchy. We also went down the street to the milliner, and Auntie bought me a hat – the first I ever owned. It seemed that everyone wore hats and I was to be no different. Since that day, I have always worn a hat when I go out into town.

On a second visit to the dressmaker, Auntie helped me choose some material for a new best dress. What a luxury that was. This was a new and wonderful experience and I was overcome with the whole idea. I had no notion of what to choose; there were so many beautiful fabrics, added to which I had never actually had a dress before, only smocks and blouses and skirts. In fact, I found that I could not choose, so overcome was I at the whole affair. The dressmaker, a smart young woman with her hair piled high, came to my aid and suggested a beautiful dark blue cloth with a simple uncomplicated pattern that she said would suit my colouring and my neat figure. A week later, I went for a fitting, and a few days later the dress was ready for collection. It was delivered to the house in a brown paper parcel. I was overwhelmed by my new outfit and the kindness of my dear Aunt.

As the days went by, I got more accustomed to my new surroundings, though I still marvelled at the handsome furniture and fireplaces and the beautiful curtains and furnishing in all the rooms, and at the notion of having a scullery and a kitchen as well as the parlour and dining room. It was a far cry from our single room in Coolnagranchy that served us for everything.

I was thrilled by the nightly visit to our street of the lamplighter, who came by to light the street lamps. I had only known about such things from my poetry book; there were no lamps or lamplighters in our country lane back home.

... For every night at tea-time and before you take your seat,
With lantern and with ladder he comes posting up the street ...

I got to know Hasluck much better. He always took the time to chat and to explain those many things that were so new to me. I learned that he was very fond of poetry; one of his favourites was Gray's "Elegy in a Country Churchyard" which he said he had learned at school. Of that, I only remember the opening verse:

The curfew knells the toll of passing day,
The lowing herd wind slowly o'er the lea,
The ploughman homeward plods his weary way,
And leaves the world to darkness and to me.

Hasluck was particularly fond of the works of the Scot, Robbie Burns. He never laughed at me for my comparatively childish taste in poetry, but determined to educate me in something more grown-up. It was with the greatest delight that he launched into his favourite, "Tam o' Shanter", and got very animated in parts of it. It all sounded very strange to me, but my cousin explained the tale of Tam who wouldn't take his wife's good advice and got too drunk. He ended up lost in the dark and bedevilled by witches and all manner of ghastly sights. The rhyme was all in Scottish and Hasluck loved spilling out the words in a brave attempt to sound like a rugged, throaty Scotsman. From time to time I would stop him for a translation, but he invariably waved his hand at me and ploughed on. He was determined to teach me the whole thing and laughed at me trying to change my Irish accent to mimic the words. I did quite well, and can roughly remember the tale, but only a few phrases stay with me now and they are very disjointed.

As far as I can recall, this is how the story goes. Against his wife Kate's advice, Tam o' Shanter goes off to town on his horse, Meg, to go drinking and enjoying the women with his friend, Johnny:

O Tam had thou but been so wise as taken thy wife Kate's advice ...
... Souter Johnny - Tam loved him like a very brother ...
The night drave on wi' sangs and clatter and aye the ale was growing better ...
... But pleasures are like poppies spread, You seize the flower, it's bloom is shed . .

At last, it's time to go home. The night is dark and stormy and Tam comes across witches and other ghostly sights.

... Well mounted on his grey mare Meg –
Tam rode on through dub and mire, despising wind and rain and fire –
where ghosts and houlets nightly fly ...
... And vow Tam saw an unco sight –
Warlocks and witches in a dance, and there sat Old Nick in shape of beast –
He screwed the pipes and made them squeal –
Coffins stood round, like open presses, that showed the dead in their last dresses
... a murderer's bones ... a thief just cut from the hanging-rope ...
three priests hearts, rotten, black as muck, lay stinking vile in every nook ...

Tam is taken in by one of the spirits with a short skirt (this is a cutty-sark), and he and Meg, his horse, suffer a bad end.

... Ah Tam, ah Tam, thou'll get they fairin' –
in hell they'll roast thee like a herrin'-
in vain thy Kate awaits thy comin' ...
... Now who this tale of truth shall read –
Each man and mother's son take heed –
Whenever to drink you are inclined or cutty-sarks run in your mind –
Think! You may buy joys overdear – Remember Tam o' Shanter's mare.

Both poems were a bit macabre, but Hasluck told them with such enthusiasm that I quite grew to like them.

My literary relationship with Edie was something gentler. She and I shared a love of books and I was amazed at how many she had, including several of my favourites. She had all the books that I loved written by Frances Hodgson Burnett – "The Secret Garden", "Little Lord Fauntleroy", "A Little Princess" (of which I also had a copy) – and Robert Louis Stevenson's "A Child's Garden of Verses", and some of the others I also knew from school, like "Alice in Wonderland" and "Grimm's Fairy Tales". Edie was kind enough to lend her books to me, so I spent many happy times getting re-acquainted with those I had already come across. I also got to enjoy books by Mark Twain, especially "The Prince and the Pauper"; it reminded me of how I found myself in a different environment to the one I was born to. Louisa May Alcott's story "Little Women" brought me great pleasure and I imagined myself, Minnie, Tillie and Martha as the four sisters Meg, Jo, Beth and Amy, and wondered what it would be like living in America. It's strange that the four of us in fact did go to live on that continent – just a bit further north in Canada.

During my second year in Willesden, my Aunt suggested that I might like the opportunity to earn some money. A friend of hers who lived nearby needed someone in the afternoons to help with the three children and to do some general housekeeping. Pleased at the chance, I agreed, and the next day Auntie and I visited the Groves family to discuss things. Mr Groves was often away on business, and Mrs Groves was very involved with one of the social welfare committees that my Aunt was on. It was agreed that I would start the following Monday and would help on Mondays, Wednesdays and Thursdays, from two o'clock until six. My duties were to look after the children, and any small tasks that needed doing, and to get them their tea and ready for bed when their Mother got home. Bethany would be coming again to help get the dinners at my Aunt's on the days I was out.

Fortunately, the following Monday was fine, so I enjoyed my walk to Mrs Groves' house, and looked forward to making acquaintance with the children. It was some time since I had cared for my own little sisters and brother and I quite missed the fun of it.

The Groves family had a large house, even larger than ours in Strode Road, and the children had their own room in which to play.

My Uncle George and Aunt Mary Ann and my cousins Hasluck, Robert Duke and Edith who I lived with before going to Canada.

Young Bertie was five when I went to work there and a bit shy, and very fond of playing with his wooden trains. His three year old sister, Jane, was a confident little lass with curly blonde hair and a cheeky grin, and she reminded me a bit of our Queenie; she was always up to mischief and the complete opposite to her older brother. Baby Jack had just learned to walk, so he was toddling and wobbling everywhere, and very inquisitive and playful, again quite unlike his brother, Bertie. My first task each afternoon was to make sure that all three children had a nap for about an hour. During their rest time, I saw to any small task that was left for me by Mrs Groves then started to prepare the children's tea. Once the children were rested, it was time for play. If the weather was fine, we went out to the park which was just next to the house, wrapping up warm with coats and hats and scarves and gloves when the weather was cold. Only if it was wet did we stay in the playroom and I found pastimes for the children while we stayed next to the fire. The children had some books in their room, and they much enjoyed the stories of Beatrix Potter, of Peter Rabbit and his friends, and others. After tea it was time for a wash and I'd get the children into their nightwear and dressing gowns, and they would all be sitting by the fire with a warm cup of milk when their mother got in. Sometimes Mr Groves also came in late in the afternoon.

I was delighted to receive my pay from Mrs Groves on that first Thursday. I had never before had any money of my own, and I walked back to my Aunt's with the coins in my pocket, rattling them with my fingers. I had no idea what I would spend the money on, I only knew that, for the first time in my life, someone valued me enough to pay me for my efforts. And I was enjoying the work at the Groves' house. The children were charming and I was not given anything too taxing to do.

But I have to admit that there were some difficulties for me at that time which occurred when Mr Groves arrived home before his wife. I regret that the master of the house tried to make some advances towards me. I was not sure what I should do. I said nothing on the first few occasions, but I knew it was wrong and had to be stopped. Very embarrassed, I tried to explain to my Aunt, and she turned out to be very supportive and agreed that I should leave before anything regrettable occurred. Being from such a large family, I knew something about the birds and the bees, but I had also been brought up to do things in the proper order, and to be aware of the outcome on a young woman's reputation of getting herself into a compromising situation.

As it happened, the very next day after sharing my anguish with my Aunt, we got news from Derrymaquirk that Uncle's father, my Great Uncle Edward, had died and Uncle and Auntie immediately started making plans to return to Ireland for the funeral. It was decided that I should also return home to Coolnagranchy. So it came about that I did not return to the Groves household and there was no need to make a fuss about Mr Groves and his unacceptable behaviour. I was sad to leave my young charges, and never even got the chance to bid them and Mrs Groves farewell.

There was much activity in the house that week. It was February and we needed to take warm clothing. It was with great sadness that I anticipated my farewell to my London cousins, especially Hasluck. Bethany was brought in to do the cooking while my Aunt and Uncle were away, and a new girl, Jane, started work so that she could take over the chores. Jane was much younger than Bethany and me and seemed nice enough. I was sorry that I would be leaving Bethany; she had taught me a lot and had been a good friend.

Bethany and I spent a wonderful evening together, just a couple of days before we were due to leave for Ireland. When she finished her morning chores, she came to see me, very excited. She said that there was a wonderful entertainment at the Lambeth Playhouse and asked if I'd like to go. It sounded good fun so, late that afternoon, we dressed up warm and made our way to Lambeth where we bought tickets to experience the Fred Karno Troupe. It was wonderful, and we laughed till we cried at the entertainers. These included some fresh new acts, Charlie Chaplain and Stan Laurel, both of whom later became world famous. It was a special experience to bring our two years as friends to a close.

It was a Saturday morning when Uncle, Auntie and I set off from Strode Road. I cried, as I had done when leaving Coolnagranchy some two years before, though I was filled with mixed feelings. I was dressed in smarter clothes, and Auntie had bought me a valise, brown leather and second-hand, but I was still overwhelmed with sadness.

As we travelled, back the way we had come previously, I thought about how much I had changed in my two years away. I had learnt much about the world and was returning to a life that I had never wished to leave, but which, in my memory, seemed so strange and almost primitive. It would be wonderful to see my family again, but how would I cope with it now that I knew a different way?

We arrived at Derrymaquirk late on Sunday afternoon and the house was very quiet. Uncle Edward and his wife of two years, Aunt Emily, greeted us on arrival. They said that Aunt Ellen was resting and that she had taken her husband's death very calmly but she was very tired. On the parlour table was the coffin, just sealed up that day. I was glad that it was sealed. If it had not been, I'm sure I would have been asked to bid my Uncle farewell and I would not have wanted to do that. I was tired after the long journey, and just seeing the cask there was hard enough to take. Uncle Edward said that he would take me over to Coolnagranchy and I bade Uncle George and Aunt Mary farewell and we set off on foot. It was a frosty February evening and a clear bright moon was rising as we made our way down the lane. The trees cast dark shadows across our way, but our eyes were soon accustomed to the light from the moon and shortly we arrived back at my home farm.

How strange it was to walk through the yard of my childhood and turn in to the doorway as I had done so many times in the past. As I went in, my family looked up from their meal at the big table. I looked from one to the other and could find no words to express my feelings of belonging, my relief at being back where I belonged. I had worried that the two years away in such a different environment would have changed everything but there it all was, just as I had left it, and everyone was there to greet me. The smiles, the smells, the chatter, my home; everything still existed, and I was part of it all again.

Mother rose first and came to greet me, and everyone else stood and welcomed me home. There they all were – my nearest and dearest friends, Minnie, Martha and Tillie, who had hardly changed at all, and those I thought of as 'the little ones', Kate, Thomas and Queenie, who had grown so much. I looked to my other sisters, Sarah Jane and Eva now fifteen and sixteen and no longer at school and quite the young women, and Lillian and Blanche; they had all grown up while I was away. Only my brother John was missing, and he was replaced by my cousin Duke from Grange who also greeted me warmly. Father got up from his big carver chair at the head of the table and said he was pleased to see me home, then went to talk to Uncle Edward and thanked him for bringing me in. They went off outside and were joined by Duke, no doubt discussing some farm business, or maybe something to do with the funeral arrangements on the following Tuesday.

Mother bade me sit down and brought a dish of food for me. A place had been set for me between Minnie and Martha. I had been expected – I was home again and back with my family.

Conversation and questions flew. Was it a good journey? How were Aunt Mary and Uncle George? How were our London cousins? More importantly, how was Hasluck? I had obviously inspired everyone, particularly Minnie and my bigger sisters, with tales about him. I think everyone knew that I was rather taken with him. What was it like living in England – what was different? And so on, and so on. We sat there chattering for hours. Mother sent the younger siblings off to bed and it left Mother, Minnie, Tillie, Martha and me chattering and laughing. How I loved to see my Mother laugh, rocking back and forth with tears rolling down her cheeks. It was a wonderful time that I shall remember forever. At last, tiredness got the better of me and we all set off for bed. Nothing had changed; I was to share the big bed with my big sisters. As always, it was cold in the bedroom after the warmth of the kitchen, and I snuggled up with the others. At Strode Road, I had a clean, tidy bedroom all to myself but, on this first evening back at Coolnagranchy, I would not have changed anything. I was where I belonged, where I had always belonged, with my beloved family – and it felt just perfect.

The next morning, I was up early with my sisters and we dressed quickly in the cold bedroom and went to the kitchen. I had not registered the night before that there were changes. The clothes drier was there, and the big open fire had gone. Of course, Mother had taken the evening food from the cooking range, but I hadn't really considered the change, probably because we had a range at Auntie's so I was used to cooking on one. Mother told me that they hadn't long had it, and she loved the cooking plates and the oven. She said that it burned turfs, which Father brought in from the land, and it made the kitchen a much cleaner, more comfortable and less smoky place – most of the time!

That evening, after our meal, we sat round chatting in the candle-light. I thought back to the old fireplace with some nostalgia. I missed the flames that had filled the fireplace and which I loved to watch as they licked up around the cooking pots. In those flames I would imagine faces and pictures and magical scenes. I loved to dream as I watched the flames turning and twisting in the blackened hearth. That would be no more; the cooking range was more practical but it certainly didn't have the same magic.

On the Tuesday, it was Great Uncle Edward's funeral and most of us got dressed in our Sunday best. It had been arranged that Kate, Blanche, Lillian, Thomas and Queenie would only go to school for part of that day. It was a cold day, with flurries of snow, and we set off in the cart for Boyle Church, the family Church of the Derrymaquirk Monsons. We dropped the younger children off at Ardsallagh School, then the rest of us continued on towards the church. The snow got heavier as we made our way, but we arrived in good time and huddled together for warmth as it was turning out to be the coldest of days, with a wind from the east. Uncle George and Aunt Mary had already arrived, along with other brothers and sisters of Uncle George who were all there for their Father's funeral. Uncle Duke was there, with his wife, Kathleen, Aunt Elizabeth was there with her husband, John King. Some of Aunt Mary's nieces and nephews were there, and there were several other Grange Monsons. It was quite a turn out.

As I sat in the church with my family around, I thought about the time spent with Uncle George and Aunt Mary. I had learnt so much about the world, and it had given me the opportunity to get to know my cousin Hasluck. Our close friendship is something that we still foster to this day through our letters.

3

From Ireland to Canada

1908-1910

When I arrived back at Coolnagranchy, I found that life had changed very little, apart from the mangle, the washing rack and the cooking range, and the fact that everyone was growing up fast. Good jobs, or any jobs at all, were few and far between. We Coolnagranchy Monsons were all growing older, and the future was certainly looking bleak, particularly on the marriage front. One evening after coming home from market, Father was sitting by the fire, reading the Connaught Telegraph, the local newspaper that he always bought on market day. As usual, he was telling us all about this and that, and we listened with interest at what was being reported – who had died, what little snippets of scandal had been unearthed, which farmer's bull had won the County Show. Then he went quiet for a while before announcing that there was something that maybe we might consider. In the Advertisement Section, he found an item outlining a scheme by the Canadian Government to seek domestic help for farmers in Southern Manitoba. He suggested that maybe this was an idea that we should consider. When I look back, I realise that there was probably also a great shortage in Southern Manitoba of young ladies of marriageable age.

At this time our family was getting quite desperate. What would the future hold for us all? How were we going to manage? After much deliberation, Minnie and I, then aged twenty one and twenty three, answered the call. With no likelihood of jobs and no promise of husbands at that time, it seemed the only way forward. We sent off an application to the address in the advertisement and, a few weeks after, our application was accepted and Father somehow scraped together the necessary funds. We started to make ready for an adventure which turned out to be far greater than we could have ever imagined. It would be a journey the like of which we had never before encountered, and a new life that would be very hard and lonely – far from everything we knew and those we loved. We hadn't considered the possibility that we were jumping out of the frying pan and into the fire.

The day drew near and we packed our few belongings. Paddy O'Rourke arrived early at the farm in his jaunting car. I recall it being a Friday as it was market day in Boyle and Father had a coop of chickens he was hoping to sell. Suddenly, there seemed so little time to say farewell to everyone, from Tillie, now eighteen, down to our baby, little seven year old Queenie, and of course our beloved parents. Mother was tearful and gave us each a great hug, and reminded us to write. Father wished us both well and helped us and our bags up on to the jaunting car. Soon we were off. How we waved and waved as we set off down the rough track, until soon the family and our home were gone from our sight and we were out on the road to Roscommon.

The journey into the unknown had begun. Minnie and I clutched our bags tightly, both unable to speak, both incapable of understanding what was happening and what was to follow. The sound of the pony's hooves on the road was mesmerising, but also seemed to echo an impending doom.

The journey to Roscommon Station should have been fun – we rarely had the opportunity to ride on a jaunting car – but apprehension was getting the better of us. Paddy O'Rourke helped us down and saw us into the station and we bought our tickets to Dublin. A journey by train was also an unusual experience for us, though I had been this way before when I went to London to Aunt Mary's two years before, but then my Aunt and Uncle were there to guide me. We didn't have long to wait and we were soon aboard, struggling to slam the heavy carriage door behind us. Still clinging on to our bags, we found seats by the window and sat staring at each other. I was filled with dread, and I know that Minnie felt the same.

People scurried along the platform, carriage doors slammed, the guard shouted, and then we were off. Snapped out of our stupor by the whistle of the train, we started to chatter nervously, about the family, about the farm, about the ride to the station, a babbling brook of conversation where before we could find no words. We started to relax. We talked about the fields and hills and trees as they passed us by. It was as if we had to take in everything – in case we should never see it all again – which in fact for me was the case. Minnie was to make a visit back home some years later. I told Minnie how I had chanted the poem when I had taken the train before, and it gave us something to laugh about.

The motion of the train lulled us into calmness and a feeling of security. At each station along the way, others came and went. Soon we started to feel like seasoned travellers, on our way to Dublin, the great metropolis. We dared not think about the next part of the journey but, all too soon, it was time to get down from the train and find somewhere to stay for the night. The boarding house was not like home, and we had to share a truckle bed. Neither of us slept a wink. We were pleased to set off early the next morning to find our way to the ferry docks. I had made this journey before, and I did my best to reassure Minnie. Soon we were in the ferry waiting room, about to take to the sea and the next leg of our journey to Liverpool.

The voyage across the Irish Channel was not so bad. We felt it was a rehearsal for the greater voyage to follow. On arrival in Liverpool, once more we had to find shelter for the night and we were advised of a local boarding house. It turned out not to be as grand as the hotel I had stayed in with my Aunt and Uncle, but it was certainly adequate. Ireland already felt far away. The local language was strange to us and the pace of life seemed busier, more chaotic – we certainly felt ourselves to already be in a foreign and dark land. What would be next?

By midday the following day, we had found our way to the docks and the Empress of Ireland – our transport and home for the journey across the Atlantic to our new lives. It seemed right somehow that we should be sailing away on a ship named for our home country. We waited at the bottom of the gangway while paperwork was checked. There were many hundred passengers taking to the seas – more people probably than we had ever before seen at one time. As we made our way on board, we looked back at the warehouses and the busy activity – the comings and goings – the hustle and bustle of the docks at work. There were no friendly faces to bid us farewell, no green hills and fields; already we had left far behind everything and everyone we had always known and loved. The dull, damp day reflected our sadness, our apprehension, our fears of what lay ahead.

On board, we were told the number of our cabin, which was situated low down in the ship in 3rd class. It was all very bewildering;

we had never been on a ship like this before and very quickly lost our way. We were saved by a handsome young sailor who quickly put us right, and gave us a saucy wink as he left us at our cabin door. How we appreciated that gesture, the first sign of friendship we had felt since leaving Coolnagranchy two days before; two days that already felt like an eternity. Once in our cabin, we found that we were to share with four other girls who had also travelled from Dublin the previous day.

We soon became the best of friends and exchanged many tales and much laughter over the days that followed. Ashling, Sorcha, Brigid and Caitlin had grown up together in a village to the north of Dublin, and had followed the call of a new life in Canada much as we had. They all came from Catholic families, but our religious differences never got in the way of our friendship. As I recall, they were to stay near Quebec while we had signed up to venture further to the West, to Manitoba.

We left Liverpool on 8th May and, over the days that followed, we learnt more about the ship and its crew, and met other girls who had answered the call from the Canadian Government. The Empress of Ireland was a new ship, only two years old, and was owned by the Canada Pacific Railway. It would be on the CPR that we would travel across Canada once we'd arrived in Quebec. The ship's captain was Commander Murray, the Purser was Mr Webber, the Surgeon was Dr Gateshead, and there were some other officers – but we rarely ever saw any of them. We saw most of the Steward, Mr Coyle, who told us who was who and what was what. It was he who kept an eye on all of us and sometimes found time for a chat or a funny story. I remember being very seasick for several days, as were the other girls, but once we'd got over it and found our sea-legs, life settled down to a new routine.

As far as I remember, the voyage took just over a week. The day arrived when we at last set foot on Canadian soil. We said a tearful farewell to our four travel companions. Clutching our few belongings, Minnie and I were taken by a tall and somewhat aloof agent to the railway station in Quebec. Most people, including the agent, spoke with an unfamiliar accent; later we learnt that it was French and that this was a language common in this province. Everything was strange to us and we did our best to keep up with the agent as he led us to the main Quebec Railway Station. We had never before been in such a vast building, and felt intimidated by the noise, the people hurrying, and what seemed to be a general chaos. It loomed even larger than Liverpool Station, where I had boarded the train to go south with Uncle and Auntie two years before. We passed black and steaming engines, enormous monsters that seemed so threatening. At last, the agent waved his arms to show that we had found our train and we were whisked along the platform and into a carriage. The Great Pacific Railway would take us onwards to the unknown.

Other girls from the Empress of Ireland came too, and we became better acquainted with some new friends, Siobhan and Clodagh, and talked about our homes and families, so recently left behind but already so far away. We travelled for almost four days on the train, sharing bunks with our new friends. We were amazed that Canada could be so vast. Finally we reached Winnipeg, Minnie and I both tired of travelling and apprehensive of what would come next. Along with several other girls, we were met by another agent of the railway. Several farmers milled about and, as the agent called out names, we were each claimed by one of the farmers and led away to waiting wagons. It had never occurred to me that Minnie and I would be separated, but we were. How we cried in the brief moment we had to bid each other farewell – but there was nothing to be done – we had signed up to this new life and had to see it through.

Minnie went first and I watched her walk away following her new employer, John Morgan. Mine was Nathaniel Jones. He took my bag and gave me his hand as I stepped up on the cart. He tried to make conversation with me but I was so shocked at the separation from Minnie that all I could do was sob as silently as I could, besides it was hard to understand what he was saying. I had never before been apart from someone in my family for more than a short time, and now it felt that I would be separated from them for ever. I felt so homesick.

We travelled some way out of Winnipeg and finally arrived at the wooden farmstead where the Jones family farmed. Nathaniel Jones had three sons, the twins Ernest and Edgar, and baby Ewen. Mrs Jones had died giving birth to Ewen, and I was to take care of the homestead while another girl, Jane, had already been employed as nanny to Mr Jones' young family.

I learned from Jane that Minnie's new home wasn't so far away – only about a mile or two. After church on Sundays, both Minnie and I had some of the day to ourselves, so we arranged to get together on Sunday evenings if we could. Whatever the weather, we would meet at a lonely crossroad, roughly half way between the farms, and comfort each other. How often we cried on each other's shoulder – we were so lonely in this strange land.

My life settled into a new pattern, but I didn't forget Mother's request to write home. I had sent her a letter shortly after arriving in Canada and it was with overwhelming excitement that I received an answer from her. I had watched and hoped for months for news from home, and I was finally rewarded in November 1908. It arrived with the old chap from Dublin who came over from Ireland with his parents during the Potato Famine in the 1850s, and was doing a good business as a travelling postmaster and general stores. With his horse and covered wagon, he was always a welcome sight. He had a sense of humour and turn of phrase that ever reminded me of the old country.

I stand and move slowly across the room to open the lid of my old wooden box and reach in. This carved wooden box was made for me by my dear husband, William, when we needed a box to store the blankets during the summer months. Now, this is the box in which I keep my treasured letters, all carefully filed in date order. Not only do I have the letters Mother has sent me over the years, I also have some of my letters to her, returned to me by Lillie after Mother died in 1926. I never saw my mother again after Minnie and I left in 1908, so any reminiscences of her have always been more than precious. The first letter there is the first I received from Mother almost eight months after Minnie and I had left home.

Coolnagranchy, 4th November 1908

My dearest Lizzie

Thank you for your letter. We have all missed you and Minnie so much and are pleased to hear that you are well. Thank goodness you both arrived safely and that you are now settling into your new lives. I see that your letter was sent in August. I realise that we shall have to get used to long periods without being in touch with each other. When we got your news, we tried to find out where you are. Miss McGahern at school was very helpful and showed us on the globe and in a large atlas - it's strange to us how a world so vast can be recorded in just one small book. Miss McGahern also helped us to understand what your journey was like - you said it took so many days!

I heard in town that some more girls from Boyle have set off for Canada. Do you remember Roisin Kerrigan and Kaitlin O'Hara from your class in school? Also Oona Monson, the nailer's daughter from Boyle. I remember you and she were at school together and tried to find out if you were distant cousins. It may be that our family, the farmers, were once linked with the Monson families in Boyle town who are all nailers by trade, but I've never known how.

It's strange that it's all the girls who are now leaving for America and Canada. In the past, it's only been the men such as your Grandfather's brothers who went to Ohio and Hasluck's brother who went to New Zealand, though I think that he was sent to live with other relatives there after getting up to some mischief. How brave all you girls are.

You may be interested to know that I have news of your brother, John, having heard nothing from him for some months. You may recall that he had little success in Ulster so moved on to Glasgow. Well he got a job as a bartender which is where he got himself into his latest trouble. He says that he was serving a fellow who was being very troublesome, arguing and trying to pick a fight with another patron. Remember that fearful temper of John's? Well he decided to throw the fellow out by the scruff of his neck. There happened to be a horse and cart outside the bar, and your dear brother managed to throw the fellow against the wheel of the cart and he hit his head. The result of this was that the fellow died, there and then. I guess that it must have broken his neck. Of course, a constable came along, and there was a big to-do, and John was hauled off to the station and had to answer a whole load of questions and he was told he would get a summons. I can only imagine. Time went by, and John was called to the High Court in Edinburgh to answer the case. Now this is where John got a stroke of luck - he always was lucky, wasn't he? John's employer hired a good lawyer for him and the case was thrown out of court, and John went back to his job none the worse for the whole affair. Apart from that, John says that Jessie and baby Thomas are all doing well, but I'm sure that the whole affair must have been quite a fright for young Jessie.

Everyone else is fine, though times are still very hard. Tillie and Martha are considering following you and Minnie to Canada. It's Lillie's last year at school. She will be able to give more time around the place, and help Eva if Tillie and Martha do depart the nest. Blanche and Kate and young Thomas are all doing fine. Thomas is nothing like his big brother, John. He's a happy lad and never any trouble. Queenie is now in school, so I have more time to look after the chores. She's always needed keeping an eye on - little miss that she is. I think it's because she was the last baby and you all encouraged her with her laughter and mischief.

Your cousin, Robert Duke, from Grange has been a great help to your Father since John left. He's a hard working lad and a credit to his parents.

That's my news for the moment. Everyone is well and Father and I send you and Minnie our love and best wishes - how we all miss you, and I especially as you have always been my right hand - you are always in our thoughts.

With my love, your Mother

I think back to my dear brothers and sisters, so far away, and chuckle to recall my brother, John, and the trouble he was always in. How tall and handsome he was but, yes, he did have a temper on him, probably born from his frustrations in the classroom. But somehow he was always blessed with good fortune, always found a way to make things right.

Tillie and Martha did leave Ireland and followed in the footsteps of Minnie and me, making much the same journey as we had done two years before, except their ship was the Empress of England. The Canada Pacific Railway brought them to Brandon, Manitoba.

In 1909, Minnie and I decided to leave the Morgan and Jones farms. Mr Jones took a new wife and she would be taking over the household. We'd heard of some vacancies with a farming family called Fallis further West in the Napinka area of Southern Manitoba and thought that we might be nearer each other. We again worked as domestic servants on separate farms – Minnie at Napinka, at the farm of William Fallis Snr, and I worked for William Henry Fallis, known as Yankee, at another of the family farms at Melita about half an hour away.

We learned that old man Fallis was from Harriston, Ontario. Mary Eleanor was the mother of his five children and had died in 1887. He re-married and in 1889 came with his new wife and his three sons and two daughters to homestead in Manitoba in Brenda Municipality. His sons, George, William and John had grown up on the family farm and had all registered their own land near their father's homestead.

It didn't take long for friendships to strike up between Minnie and me and the older two Fallis lads. One thing led to another and soon we both found ourselves promised to be married and talking about plans for the future. We were to be wed in spring of 1910.

George and William felt that they didn't have enough land in Manitoba on which to raise a family so, along with their younger brother John, they headed out to Southwest Saskatchewan where the land had just been opened for homesteading. Land was being taken fast. They took the train from Melita to Gull Lake, then found a fellow with a team and buggy who was taking people out to locate land to homestead. They'd missed their first choice which was south of Gull Lake and north of the White Mud or Frenchman River, so had to be content with land nine miles south of the river in Lone Tree Municipality. They went back to Gull Lake, took the train to Swift Current to file their land and then returned home to Manitoba.

On their return, they explained to us how the homesteading land in Saskatchewan was divided up. First there were Townships, areas measured north of the America/Canada border, and Ranges which defined areas to the west of the 3rd Meridian. Each area was six miles square and was then divided into thirty six Sections, each one mile square, with some allowance for tracks. Then each Section was quartered: North East and North West, South East and South West. That was how each homestead of a half mile by half mile could be defined by which Township, Range, Section and Quarter it was to be found in.

George and William filed on quarter sections adjacent to each other, each a half mile square and John filed on a half section nearby. We started to make plans to build shacks in which to live; and we had to make sure that our plans complied with all the laws of the Homestead Act. George, William and John spent long hours talking about the future as they saw it, and there was much planning to be done, and not much time to do it. They had filed for our homesteads on 11th April and we were planning to set off in the first week of May, only a few days after William and I were to be wed.

Minnie and I also had our say as the men were full of farm talk and we had to look towards the domestic details, and what needed to be procured for everyday living. The men had the plans while we looked to the practicalities. Minnie and I had never had to set up house before so we dug deep into our memories of home back in Ireland and what we would need to run the house. George continually reminded us that space would be limited so we shouldn't go overboard; we would only have two wagons to carry everything for our domestic and farming needs. Minnie and I wondered how we would be able to feed everyone. We would be making a new home on a piece of land marked by a few stakes. We couldn't be sure of what else we would find there. We planned to take some basic foodstuffs, some water, and some chickens, and the men decided what livestock and farm equipment we would need.

Once again, we found ourselves moving towards great changes in our lives. Minnie had married George Fallis on 1st March, a month before the menfolk went on their quest. My marriage to his brother, William Fallis, was on 27th April, seven weeks after Minnie and only a short time after the homesteads had been filed.

At the start of May, our sisters Tillie and Martha arrived in Brandon, the same town where Minnie and I were both married in St. Matthews Anglican Church so shortly before. Their journey from Ireland was much the same as ours. 1910 was a big year for us all, and how we laughed and cried and couldn't get the words out fast enough; our two years apart felt both like an eternity and also an instant. We exclaimed at the changes we saw in each other; Martha had grown taller, Minnie and I had apparently become 'all grown up', and Tillie and I looked more like twins than ever! But the rejoicing was short lived as it was only possible to spend a couple of precious hours together. We were parted almost as soon as we had time to hug and laugh and exchange small items of news; Minnie and I were so tied up in the plans for our departure the next day to our new lives in Saskatchewan, and Tillie and Martha had to get straight back to their new employers to start their new lives in Brandon. We were indeed fortunate that we had found any time at all to make that fleeting reunion.

I wrote home to Mother. Time was of the essence but I had to tell her that Minnie and I had both wed, and that our sisters had arrived safely, and that Minnie and I were preparing to set off to pastures new – and unknown.

Photos taken at Brandon, Manitoba in 1910 shortly after Minnie married George Fallis and I married his brother William. We set off for the homesteads a few days later.

4

Early years on the Prairie

1910-1913

I sit and read my letter I sent to my Mother over seventy years ago, one of the letters my sister Lillie returned to me after Mother's death. I always find it strange to revisit my own words. But it does help to clarify my memories of the time, and often fills in the gaps where things have become hazy or confused.

On the CPR train
between Melita and Gull Lake, Canada
3rd May 1910

Dearest Mother

I have so much to tell you and no time at all for the telling. First I must apologise for my poor handwriting. I am on a train and the ride is not so smooth. We're making our way from our last home in Manitoba to a new life in Saskatchewan.

Minnie and I are so pleased that we left the Morgan and Jones farms and made our way over to the Napinka area in Manitoba. Working on separate farms has not been quite so hard as we are both working for the Fallis family on their homesteads, me at Melita and Minnie at Napinka, about ten miles apart - not too far. Minnie and I have been seeing much more of each other as the whole family gets together for church on Sunday. Things have moved very fast here and many changes are taking place, including marriage into the family for us both and now we're off to pastures new. We set off yesterday from Melita.

And here we are wed to the older two Fallis brothers. So we are now both old married women! It's two months since Minnie became Mrs George Fallis, and only last week, I became Mrs William Fallis. Imagine - your daughters are now very grown up. My William is thirty six and George is five years older. And we're both called Mrs Fallis!

William and George decided that their homestead land in Manitoba was not enough to raise a family. No sooner had Minnie and George wed than they were parted. George set off with William and their younger brother John to register for homesteads in South West Saskatchewan, about 400 miles away from Napinka. It's a new province that has not long been surveyed and thrown open to homesteading.

Our new homes will be about seventy miles south of a town called Gull Lake, which is where we get off this train. We reckon that the journey down from Gull Lake will take best part of a week. Saskatchewan has only been a province for five years, and we've been granted one hundred and sixty acres. We must clear twenty acres and build a residence within three years. This is all under the Dominion Lands Act. We've paid nothing except a $10 registration for the land but must stay there for at least six months each year and improve it, and show peacable possession. I don't imagine that we'll have any time to be anything but peacable ... we'll be so busy building shacks and working the land! Old Mr Fallis, William's father, whose farm Minnie has worked on since we came over to Manitoba, has told us about the hard times that he and his sons went through to set up the farms at Melita and Napinka. I fear that our challenge will be even greater.

What a pity that Tillie and Martha didn't arrive here in time to see either of their big sisters walk down the aisle. We had only a couple of hours with them yesterday. The girls are both well and I'm sure they will be sending you their news, if they haven't done so already. There will be so many letters coming to you that you will hardly have time to read them and get all your work done!

We've been getting our possessions together for the past few days and planning what food we'll need, and so on. Who knows when I shall get the chance to write again, and how I shall get this to the post. I'm hoping that I can send it when we arrive in Gull Lake on Wednesday.

We think it will take the best part of a week to get to the homestead land from Gull Lake. Our new address will be a bit *strange. It's SE'14 - Section 10 - Township 3 - Range 18 W of 3rd Meridian, Saskatchewan, Canada. I'll write again when we've arrived, though expect we'll be a bit busy to start with.*

It's funny to think that the train that brought us here from Quebec 2 years ago is taking us on further towards our next destination.

Send my love to everyone, and Minnie sends her love too.

Your daughter, Lizzie

I recall sealing the letter, and then I addressed it and put it away in my travel bag, hoping to find a post office in Gull Lake. It was two months before I got the chance to put pen to paper again.

As I dozed on the train, I thought about the previous day, when we had taken all our settlers' effects to the train depot. I was going over everything in my mind, hoping that we had packed up all that was needed for setting up our new lives. William and George were running two teams, so we had prepared two wagons, one with some lumber, enough to get us started on the first shack, plenty of rope and stakes and some wire, along with a box with twelve chickens and another crate with a sow pig, already heavy with piglets. The second wagon had some household furniture, and a wooden crate filled with the tools that we thought would be needed. That left space for a stove, a tent, mattresses and blankets, our clothes and personal effects, pots and pans, and a crate of groceries. The wagons were loaded as high as we dared and lashed down with big tarpaulins for protection. William and George were to drive the two wagons, each pulled by a pair of work horses, and we were bringing six cows. These would have to walk along behind the wagons on a rope. Minnie and I were in charge of the horse and buggy, with our brother-in-law, John, riding along.

Early the previous morning, we loaded the equipment into one box car, and the livestock into the stockcar. At last we were on our way. I remember the mixed feeling of anxiety and excitement that Minnie and I both experienced. Yet again we were setting off on a new adventure, with no idea of what lay ahead. The men were taking turns riding in the stockcar and looking after the animals. The rest of us were travelling in the coach with other new homesteaders. Most of the travellers were young men, setting out to seek their fortunes on the prairies. Minnie and I were surprised to find how few women there were. We got chatting with our fellow travellers. Each of them had stories to tell and keen to compare notes and discuss plans.

We lived on the train for three days, making stops along the way for people to leave or join the train, and to alight so we could find food and water. We passed through Swift Current, which William pointed out as the place where he, John and George had come to register our homesteads a few short months before. Apart from one or two small towns and settlements like Swift Current, the views from the train were of endless plains with homesteads dotted here and there. We spent most of the time dozing, which turned out to be a blessing as we needed all our strength for the ordeal ahead.

On Wednesday afternoon, we set down at Gull Lake, and the men unloaded the wagons and animals from the CPR rail cars while Minnie and I went to find water and somewhere for us to have a meal – we hadn't eaten properly for days. I also found a mail office to post my letter to Mother. Gull Lake was bigger than we expected, with a large hotel, The Clarendon. We stopped at Johnston's Dairy for a billy can of milk and some supplies for the journey south, and found out where we could get some water.

Then we came across The Caledonian Restaurant. We ordered some food, and sat to eat our share before taking some back for the menfolk. What a delight it was to meet the owner, a big Scotsman called Peter McLaren. He was entertaining the diners with the story of his life. He fought in the Boer War, and later met Queen Victoria who told him to go home and take a rest when she heard him coughing! Like our brother John in Scotland, he was a member of an Orange Lodge and, to our amazement, it turned out that they had met on one occasion, though Peter McLaren was older than John. Then he started reciting Robbie Burns poems by memory and it so reminded me of Hasluck and his passion for recitals. We couldn't stop for too long as the men were waiting for some food. Minnie and I certainly enjoyed this little interlude and looked forward to meeting Peter McLaren again as we were sure to return to Gull Lake again. We headed back to meet up with William, George and John and found them putting the wagons and buggy together and loading up as we had planned. Once we'd tied the cows behind, we filled up a tank with water and we were ready to go.

Just as we were leaving Gull Lake, a cavalcade of soldiers dressed in wonderful red jackets came galloping into town. I was later to learn that they were the Mounties, the North-West Mounted Police. We heard of their duties across the land, especially in the west where they were engaged in managing illegal alcohol activity and controlling troubles with the tribal peoples. Everyone looked up to see them go. We would come across them again.

The trail south from Gull Lake was clear enough, and John got down from the buggy to read the corner stakes on the homestead sections so we could work out the best way to go. It seemed fairly straightforward to start with. Gull Lake was in Ranges 18 and 19, and our land was also in Range 18. It seemed that we would have to go direct south, from Township 12 down to our homesteads in Township 3. We thought it was going to be easy to follow the Range 18 stakes as we went. The trail was good and we made fair time in the hours left of that day, though it was always slow as we had the two heavily laden wagons and livestock in tow. We stopped at dusk, quite exhausted but excited that we were making good progress. That evening, the men settled the animals and pitched the tent, while Minnie and I lit a fire and brewed coffee, and cooked bacon and tinned tomatoes and bread that we had bought in Gull Lake. The tinned tomatoes were a new and wonderful experience. We slept like logs and rose early the next morning to a breakfast of oatmeal, ready for an early start, optimistic at what lay ahead.

Shortly, the trail from Gull Lake dried up, and the going got harder. Sometimes we had to go through areas that rose in small hills, and there were also ponds and small lakes to contend with. In these places, there were often no stakes, and sometimes the going got so rough that we had to go back on ourselves to seek a better course.

Throughout the day, we could hear the sow in her crate snuffling and complaining away, and all the time the chickens clucked and flapped. Despite their discomfort, they did manage to lay us a few eggs. The cockerel reminded us and his harem of hens that he was in charge! More than once, John threatened to wring the cockerel's neck!

Each day we hoped to do twenty five miles, travelling ten hours if we could manage it. We were constantly on the look out for water - for both the animals, and ourselves – and this sometimes took us out of our way. Minnie and I got up early each morning to make pancakes or oatmeal for breakfast. Each night we lit a fire and made a meal for ourselves, usually beans and eggs and quick bread we made in a pan. Thank goodness for canned food. I'm sure we couldn't have managed without it. We carried grain for the chickens, oats and bran for the horses, and pellets for the cows and sow, and they had to be fed and watered, and tethered and settled for the night.

By Saturday evening, we got to the White Mud Hills, and made our way down the slope to the river north of Stone Pile Crossing. We decided that there wouldn't be time before dark to ford the river and make the top of the hills to the south with all our effects, so we saw to the animals, had a hurried supper, then put up our tent, and got ready to camp for the night on the side of the hills. The clouds were getting ever darker and no sooner had we got our bedrolls down than it started to rain.

In the night, water came through the tent and all our bedrolls got soaked, and by Sunday morning, it was snowing and it was getting colder. While William and George cleared up, hoping that things might clear so they could make the crossing and clear the south hills, John went over to the nearby Ottersons' Ranch and asked if Minnie and I could go over to warm up as we were chilled to the bone. It was crowded already at Ottersons and the storm kept on, so John took Minnie and me in the buggy, with all the wet blankets and personal things, to Quennell's. This was at the suggestion of Harry Otterson, who gave us directions and said that the Quennells would be more likely able to help us out. It was over six miles back the way we'd come but we were at a loss as to what else to do.

Minnie and I shivered all the way and were soaked through and colder than we had ever been before in our lives. John checked the Section markers as we went and finally we reached Township 5 as instructed. We had to go right across the township to find Section 19, where Roy Quennell had a fairly substantial shack. We were so grateful when we reached the Quennell homestead, and were greeted and given a change of clothes and a warm drink. We crouched round the stove, and it took us forever to stop shivering, but gradually we felt ourselves coming back to life. Roy, or Grandpa Quennell as he was known, and his wife Bessie Mae, showed John where he could hang all the wet stuff in the barn and put the horse and buggy for the night. Grandpa Quennell and Bessie Mae were so kind, and insisted that we share supper with them and spend the night. We learnt that the family's holdings occupied a large part of six Sections, and that they had purchased much of their land from Canadian soldiers who had been granted land for their services in the Boer War in South Africa at the turn of the century.

On Monday morning, the weather was much improved, so we bade farewell to our new friends, and thanked them profusely for their lifesaving kindness and generosity. John, Minnie and I set off just after dawn. The weather was much improved, and the journey much easier than the day before. When we got back to meet William and George at the riverside, they too were in better spirits than when we'd left, and had a good fire going and had put up a line to dry their clothes and bedding. They were pleased to see us back, and interested to hear our story as we sat round the fire. But there was no time to waste, and we had soon dowsed the fire and prepared to go on our way again. The sun even came out for us which greatly lifted our spirits, and melted the snow.

We managed to ford the river without too much trouble, though the water level was quite high due to the rain and snow, and the water was fearfully cold. The climb up the hill wasn't easy as it was very muddy and we had to pull the wagons up one at a time using all four horses. The cows were led up the slope one by one, both reluctant and indignant at the whole situation. We looked back to see the Ottersons' house. It was the last one we saw for the rest of the trip.

Along the way, Minnie and I were on the lookout for firewood, just as we had been since leaving Gull Lake. We needed fuel so we could light up as soon as we stopped each night. We needed it for cooking and for warmth, and it was always good for morale. Since there were few trees, firewood was not easy to come by.

We followed the stakes and that evening we finally found the stake at the north-west corner of Section 10, our new home. We looked across the Section with anticipation. That first north-west quarter had a large slough of water. It wasn't one of the quarters that we had filed for and, ever practical, Minnie said that we might consider filing for that as well if it wasn't yet taken. The water would be useful for the animals. We continued on our way, heading across the Section towards the east quarters that William and George had chosen. The land rose slightly to the east of the Section and we went towards the south east quarter as we'd decided to stay together to start with. We chose a spot roughly in the middle of the quarter that was filed by William, and the men tethered the horses and cows with stakes and ropes. They unloaded the wagons and threw tarpaulins over our precious belongings, anchored down with ropes, to keep them safe and dry. The sow and chickens stayed in their boxes.

Minnie and I lit the fire and made supper, and we all sat on the chairs we'd brought with us from Napinka, quite exhausted and looking into the flames with a grateful feeling of relief that we had survived the journey and arrived at last. We also felt overwhelmed by the never-ending prairie around us, and the vastness of the night sky with its millions of stars. We were not only exhausted but also stunned by our apparent insignificance in the endless prairie. We would be reminded again and again over the years of who was master and who was slave. We looked up and for a brief moment our spirits were lifted as a shooting star streaked across the southern sky.

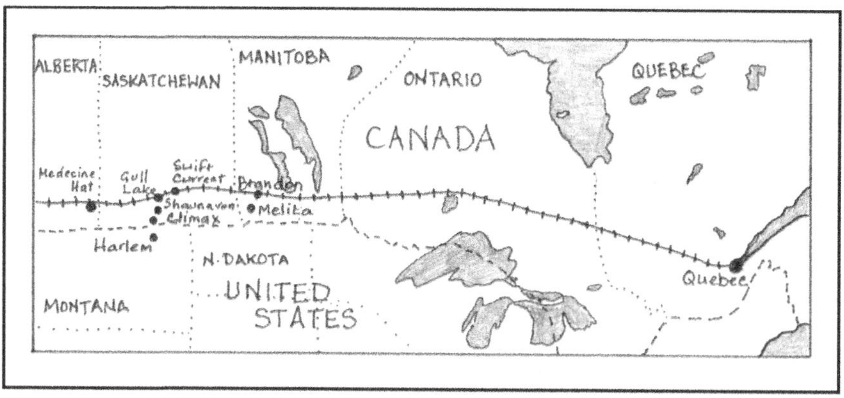

1908 CPR train from Quebec to Brandon (1710 miles) then to Melita
1910 CPR train from Brandon to Gull Lake (410 miles) then overland to Climax (70 miles).

That campfire on our own homestead was the best of all. As the evening drew in, we put up the tent, and fell wearily into our beds. That was the 9th May 1910 – and the start of our new lives. The long journeys were over at last. They had brought us to a new future, whatever it may hold. The next morning dawned bright, with just a cool breeze from the west, and with no sign of the rain or snow we had suffered. We all felt refreshed and ready for anything, and Minnie and I stoked the fire back to life and built it up to cook a breakfast of eggs and beans. While we worked, we laughed together about the new strangeness we found ourselves in. We both admitted that we had somehow expected the new homesteads to be in a lush green land, like our beloved Coolnagranchy that we'd left only a couple of years before. As Minnie was preparing the fried eggs, the pan slipped on the fire and an egg just about missed the pan, and half of it dribbled down the outside of the pan and into the embers. We had but a single thought and both exclaimed that, like the egg, our lives were "Out of the frying pan ... into the fire!" Somehow, the hardships of life back in Ireland seemed as nothing compared to the trials and tribulations we had endured in our journeying to this new place, and where we would have to strive to build our homes and set up everything from nothing. But we were in good spirits and the weather was fair, so optimism reigned that morning.

While Minnie and I chatted and cooked, the menfolk took the cows and horses and led them down by the slough, where they could drink to their heart's content. They brought back water for the sow, and let out our dozen hens, all of them joyful to be free at last, rushing around, pecking and scratching in the rough ground and wild sage. The sow was not quite so pleased, and having stuck her snout into the trough of water, making as much mess as she could, she took a quick look around, snorted at the roughness of the prairie grass, then went back into her crate, flopped on her side and there she stayed till later that day. This was fortuitous as it gave William a chance to get a fenced area set up for her, though she would continue to have her crate as a pig-house for some time yet. Breakfast finished and cleared away, that morning the five of us walked the land together. Our breath was taken away by the vastness of the place, unending views and prairie grass as far as the eye could see.

Views across the homesteads looking North and South.

Everywhere the prairie grass grew thick and impenetrable.
Only a few trees found an existence in that harsh landscape.

Everywhere the prairie grass grew thick and impenetrable, and only a very few small trees found an existence in that harsh landscape. Minnie and I remarked on how different it was to the lush greenness back in Ireland. Though our journeying across Canada never promised anything different, perhaps we had naively expected to find something of the Irish verdure and lushness when we reached out new home on the prairie. But it was what it was, and there was no time for dreaming.

We decided where the first shack would be built, which was in fact there on the land that William had filed on and very close to where we had set down and spent the previous night. We also needed to mark a spot to dig a well so we would have a supply of water for ourselves; the water in the slough was muddy and full of wrigglers and only fit for the animals. We still had some of the water we'd brought with us, but it was important for us to find a new supply. All plans made, John set about digging a hole in the low part of George and Minnie's land, so fresh water could come in. While John did that, William and George set to laying out the timbers to build a one room shack to get us all started. Minnie and I did what we could to help. That evening we were all very tired, but John was probably the most exhausted as the ground was so hard to dig, and the roots of the prairie grass went down several feet in the most impossible tangles and clumps. They called it prairie wool, that knotted twisted grass that held the prairie together. It was something that would challenge us, and the horses and equipment, again and again in the months and years to come, that and the never-ending stones and rocks that just seemed to hatch out of the earth at every turn. At supper, we felt pleased with our efforts as we had made good progress, but we would still need to spend several more nights in the tent.

When they felt that the horses were rested enough, George and John took off early with the two wagons and the four horses to go back to Gull Lake for more lumber for the shacks. During the six days that they were away, Minnie and I took instruction from William to work on the shack. We would all be living in that to start with, until we could get shacks built for Minnie and George, and John also, each on their own land. Once all the timber we had was used, the shack was only about half built. We spent the rest of our time building a house for the chickens, and starting another bigger project to build a barn from sods. It was hard work and we soon found how punishing the land was, as John had already discovered. It was full of stones the size of your fist and bigger, and the prairie grass roots were impossible. Minnie commented that she thought those roots went all the way down to hell!

George and John returned the following Monday, one whole week since we'd arrived. It was a joyful reunion for us all, and they were most pleased to see the progress we had made in their absence. John set off again the next day for Gull Lake and more timber, and the rest of us all worked together for the next three days and completed the first shack, sixteen feet by fifteen feet, and lined with tar paper to keep the rain and snow out.

On 20th May, we moved into our new home – just one room for us all to start with – and we set up the stove so we could cook some hot food, and also for the warmth it would offer during the cold prairie nights. The weather had become unsettled, with chilly winds and showers. We moved as much inside as we could and threw down the straw palliasses, then fixed back the tarpaulins over the items that had to be left outside for the time being, and the farm machinery that would be housed in the sod-built barn once we had completed it.

We were all too tired to be cross or happy, but pleased to get inside from the tent and out of the weather. I exclaimed that if I ever had to sleep in a tent again, that would be too soon! When John returned with the next load of lumber, he was delighted that we now had four walls and a roof to shelter in. He found his sleeping roll and fell fast asleep without even having supper.

The next morning, we hitched up the horses to the plough, and made a firebreak around our new home. Our concern was to do with the prairie fires that caught so easily when lightning struck or homesteaders were careless. Already, we had witnessed where one large area of land was blackened by fire; the dry prairie grass caught light easily and, fanned by the constant breeze across the open plains, burnt everything in its path for many miles. We were not planning to lose what we had toiled so hard to achieve. It was our intention to make firebreaks around all our homesteads and barns.

That night, 24th May, I wrote home to Coolnagranchy. Even though I was so tired, I felt an overwhelming need to let Mother know how things were going. I wrote long into the night.

24th May 1910

Dearest Mother,

I have at last found some time to give you our latest news, and what an adventure we're having, though it's a very hard one. We arrived here on our land two weeks ago. George and Minnie will be going to Gull Lake tomorrow to get some more lumber, so they can get a letter posted for me if I have it ready in the morning. I'm so tired at the moment, and much has happened.

As you know, we started for the homestead the first week in May, after getting everything prepared at Melita in the days before. Minnie had come over from Napinka with George and the buggy, and John, who is William and George's younger brother, came too. The wagons were loaded high and lashed down with big tarpaulins for protection. William and George drove the wagons with two horses each. Minnie and I took the driving horse and buggy, with our brother-in-law, John, riding along. We were also taking half a dozen cows, a pregnant sow, some chickens, and some groceries along with us.

The first part of the journey was by train, which is when I last wrote. We had all our settlers' effects loaded in two immigrant cars at Melita, and then we found places in the coach. The journey was long and uncomfortable, and the men took it in turns to look after the animals. We got chatting to other new settlers, though most of them were young men with no wives in tow. At Gull Lake, the wagons and animals were taken off the train and we got ready for the journey south.

We left Gull Lake and got as far as the White Mud River in the evening of the third day. It was getting late, so we put up our tent and camped for the night in the side of the hills. The next morning it was snow and rain and everything was wet through, so we packed up some of our belongings and John took Minnie and me and our bags in the buggy the six miles back to Grandpa Quennell's. Mother - Minnie and I have never been so cold before in our lives. Our teeth never stopped chattering for hours. At Quennell's, we were able to dry the wet bedding and ourselves and were so grateful to them for taking such good care of us. By morning, the weather had improved and we returned to meet up with William and George.

Crossing the ford with all our load was quite a harrowing experience, but we got on our way and soon climbed up the hill from the river, though it was hard work as the slope was so muddy and we had to use all four horses and our own effort for each wagon. Everything, including ourselves, was caked with mud. We took it in turns to go back to the river to clean up a bit. The water was so cold and there was no warmth in the air. How we hoped that the sun might find its way through the clouds to afford us some comfort.

We got moving again, and followed the stakes and finally found our way to our new lands. We've achieved much since we arrived here on 9th May. We've built our first shack on William's land, using the timber we carried from Melita and more timber that has been brought from Gull Lake. We've also started Minnie's cabin, and built a hen house, and we've set up a paddock for the horses and cows. Our sow has her own little field. We've also built a privy, but here they call them biffys and they're not quite the same as ours at Coolnagranchy - they are liquid rather than dry. We've started a barn built of sods from the ground, but that's an ongoing project, and we're striving to get all the cabins complete.

Before we came here, I was concerned about where we would get fresh water. Well, I shouldn't have fretted. John has dug a water-hole and the water is quite good, so my worries were quite ill-founded. The men are planning to build a proper well and a wind-pump in time, so we can easily bring up the water. We heard that we can get fuel here - there's lignite coal in the hills nearby and it's there for the taking. There are very few trees in these parts, so firewood is not easy to come by.

I send my love to you all, and please send my thoughts to my brother, John, and his young family - I still find it hard to think of him as a father, and you a Grandma too. Perhaps I shall be having babies of my own soon and you will become a Grandma yet again. Minnie and I have been comparing notes and we are both hopeful.

Your loving daughter,

Lizzie (and of course Minnie sends her love too).

PS I think this is the longest letter I have ever written!

Minnie's trip with George to Gull Lake that I mentioned in my letter to Mother was not without its perils. When she got back several days later, Minnie recounted to me that she thought she would drown when they were crossing the White Mud River. The river was running high as a spring flood was on. They proceeded to cross the river and the great depth of the water caused the wagon box to rise up off the running gear and Minnie thought it would float away. She said she was so frightened and that she wanted to jump off into the swirling waters, but George quickly sat on her long black skirt and stopped her. He kept his feet firm against the front of the box and, holding fast to the team with the reins and reassuring them all the while, guided them to the other side. Somehow he managed to keep Minnie safe on board despite her attempts to plunge into the river. He was a skilful horseman and his animals trusted him and were good swimmers, and all was well.

That was the last time that we got our timber from Gull Lake. We heard that there was timber to be had from Harlem, in Montana, just over the border in America. That journey was not much shorter, just sixty five miles, but there were not such steep hills, and only a creek to cross rather than a river. That's where George and John went for the last load of lumber to finish the three family shacks, each little larger than fifteen feet square.

In all, it took all summer to build shacks for everyone and to make some beds to put the mattresses on. In time we looked forward to getting things a bit more organised, including making plans for a barn on George and Minnie's land to house eight head of horses, which became something of an ongoing project. The walls were finished and the loft floor was laid, but the loft was never built. We piled hay on the loft floor to keep the place warm in winter, but it was hopeless when the summer rains came and it seemed to rain longer inside than out. We each built a sod chicken coup so that our precious hens would be safe at night, and we fenced off a corral to include a slough for the horses and cows to drink, so we didn't have to move their stakes and they could roam freely. We were able to purchase some barbed wire, something new to us, which helped to keep the stock in and the wolves and predators out. It was a godsend. The sow gave birth to eight little piglets, and they all snuffled around happily with their mother in the new pen we made for them all. John's well was a great success; the water had come in quite quickly, and that gave us a good supply of fresh, cold, clean spring water right here on our land. He also started a well on his own land on the west side of Section 24; John had filed for the whole of the west side which gave him an area of land one mile long and half mile wide. In time, we developed our well further including a wind-pump, so we could easily bring up the water. The water in this part of Saskatchewn is wonderful, and probably the best part of the prairie! We learned where we could dig the lignite coal in the hills nearby and we felt that everything was falling into place.

We were indeed fortunate to have a house of timber; we knew of other homesteaders nearby who built sod houses. Sod was probably the cheapest way for settlers to make a home and a barn, but definitely not the easiest due to the great toil involved in cutting the ground. Neither did it stand up so well as timber against the ever changing weather conditions. We only used the sod building method for our outhouses. It was hard work but very effective. First we had to cut strips of the sod in about two foot or so lengths, then piled them one on top of the other like bricks. That's how the walls were made. Then lumber was used for the door, door frame, and window frames, and we used the canvas from our old tent to cover the windows until we could get glass. For the roof, logs were placed across the top and covered with sod and hay. The floor was made by packing down the earth. When it rained a lot, the barn and outhouses often leaked, but they were cool in summer and warm in winter. We were glad that we had a wooden house lined with tar paper to keep us dry.

We fast discovered that all journeys on the prairies were long ones. Our initial trek from Gull Lake had been a great test, and, from that day, nothing we needed could ever be obtained by a short and simple journey. For the first three years, all our main trading was in Gull Lake or Harlem, Montana, and going to either place meant an arduous expedition over the scrubby and shaggy prairie grass and wild sage, with a rare rough track full of stones and bumps, marked in places where a homesteader had found time to put down a roadway around part of his plot. Often the land was dried out, and we left a dusty cloud behind us, with the wagon and horses and ourselves all grimy and dirty.

Generally, the weather was kind to us that first year. As well as all our construction work, we had land to clear, not only to fulfil the terms of the Homestead Act but also to provide us with food. We hoped we might also harvest enough to have some grain to barter with. With much help from John, Minnie and I cleared a vegetable patch and set to planting quick growing greens and legumes, and other root crops and pulses to see us through the winter. We'd brought some seeds with us for that first year so, as soon as the land was prepared, we got started as we knew the growing season would be short and the snows would set in by October.

After a few months, both Minnie and I discovered we were pregnant, with our babies expected at much the same time. Life was particularly hard as we strove to add finishing touches to the cabin and start on a second one. Minnie and I were forever tired, and often exhausted. But we were also so happy, the happiest we had been for such a long time. We were grateful to have each other to compare notes, and worked long into the night when we could, making tiny nightdresses and clothes and looking forward together to the day when we would both be mothers. We sang often, and the menfolk laughed with us when they came in from building or working the land. The whole thing lifted everyone's spirits. At this time, we also celebrated the coronation of King George V and Queen Mary back in Britain.

When we first arrived in 1910, not many other homesteaders had settled, so we were delighted to start to get neighbours, most of them young bachelors. Minnie and I were two of the first women in the area, and it meant that we often had company at meal times and would trade a meal for some assistance on the land. We started to get to know Christ Fugelstad, Ed and Abe, the McEwan brothers, and Frank Marritt. Christ said that he would be bringing his wife and four children as soon as the shack was ready and Minnie and I looked forward to some more female company. Christ built them a two roomed shack with a shed and said they would come in the following spring.

Some evenings, we got together to chat and enjoy the music that George and John delighted us with; with George on mouth organ and John on violin. My William didn't play an instrument, though he had a good singing voice so, together the three brothers kept us entertained. Others joined in too. My William was basically a quiet and gentle man, and quite shy, who would never push himself in conversation. But when he was invited to speak, he entertained all and sundry with amusing stories, impressing everyone with his deep joy of life and love for his fellow man. I always felt proud when he spoke.

It is the nature of the prairie that things are forever changing with the need to alter plans and make new decisions. In late September, I started to feel unwell and William said that we should return to Napinka for the harsh winter months. The terms of our homestead only required that we spend six months of each year staying on the land, so it didn't contravene any agreement. George and Minnie decided to move back into Gull Lake and rented a shack for the winter, so we went together with the horses and George arranged livery for them in Gull Lake. The other stock we left in the care of our neighbours. John also decided to find work elsewhere, to make himself a grub stake to carry him over the next year on the homestead, and to provide money for improvements and 'betterment'. We learnt that many people spent the winter months working away so they could 'prove up' their homesteads.

William and I took the train from Gull Lake back to Manitoba where he still had part of a Section in the south of the Fallis land. William's father, Grandpa Fallis, also needed some help with the farm, so it seemed a reasonable idea at the time. Of course, I was sad to leave Minnie and we agreed to write when we could.

The winter months passed quickly and it was soon May and time to return to the land again. I was feeling stronger and I longed to get back to see Minnie and meet her new baby, Herbert, who had been born on the last day of January. His second name was our birth surname, Monson, and I liked the fact that Minnie had named him for our family. My baby was due soon, and I yearned for my dear sister and her company and support, and to resume our lives in our new prairie homes.

William and I left Napinka on the train in high spirits and the journey went well, though I found it very uncomfortable as I was not far off my time. We were bringing some extra stock: four more horses to make our work on the hard land less demanding, and three more cows. This meant that William was constantly away from me, checking the animals in the stock car. I found it almost impossible to sleep, even though I desperately wanted to. My relief was great when we got to Gull Lake, and William settled me on a bench while he got the stock off the train. I watched him proudly; he was fond of the animals, especially the horses, and coaxed them gently off the box car, and tied them up. He always took great care of his animals – it was part of the man that he was. We left the animals in the care of a young lad while we went to find George and Minnie. I was hoping for a rest before we set off back to the homesteads and I felt so much better when I had spent a couple of hours with Minnie and Herbie and had a chance to lie down and relax my heavy body and swollen legs.

William and George saw to the animals and at last all was ready to go, and Minnie, Herbie and I travelled in the buggy, with Minnie at the reins and me cuddling little Herbie. He was about six weeks old by then and a real bonny baby. When I got tired, we put Herbie in a little crib basket between us. He was a happy little lad, and gurgled and fidgeted all the way when he wasn't feeding or fast asleep. We talked about the winter, and Minnie told me how George had gone after any work that was going to help ends meet, and I gave her news of old Grandpa Fallis and the family back in Napinka. We shared dreams about our children, how it would be no time before my baby and Herbie would be playing together. Minnie told me about her experience of childbirth, the pain filled with wonder, and how the midwife had helped her. Although we had both lived in a house in which twelve children had been born, neither of us had any real experience of what was what, and were both fairly sure that no midwife had ever been involved in bringing us all into the world. We knew about things from the animals on the farm, but midwives never came into it. We relived our first nightmare journey from Gull Lake and its trials; we were so relieved that this trip promised more clement weather than that journey only a year before. This winter there had not been much rain and very little snow and we hoped this would mean that the White Mud River would not be swollen and perilous. Minnie reminisced about her dreadful crossing when George had tied her down by her skirts to stop her jumping overboard. How we laughed. Having each other made the journey fairly tolerable, but I was never happy spending the night in a tent, especially not in my heavily pregnant state. The journey passed and we were together and happy again.

We got back to the shacks and life started to resume its old pattern. The weather stayed fair, and Minnie and I had little Herbie to look after. Apart from that I did very little but rest. We all entered into a new found optimism and all seemed well. But the euphoria was not to last; not everything went quite to plan. My world fell apart one night about a week after we'd arrived back from Gull Lake. I started to bleed and it was clear that something was wrong. I'd had certain premonitions for a few days before when I felt no movement inside my belly, and the ache in my back had become almost unbearable. I'd put it down to the long and arduous journey and assumed that, just like me, my baby wanted to rest. The bleeding was telling me otherwise. I woke William and he found blankets and swaddled me and did his best to reassure me. Just before dawn, we set off for Gull Lake; there was no hospital nearer. William and John took me in the buggy and we journeyed without stopping, with the menfolk taking it in turns to drive us. We arrived at the hospital in the evening.

There in the hospital on the night of 9th May 1911 my tiny baby girl was still-born. I was inconsolable and greatly weakened by the ordeal. We stayed there for the rest of the night and, in the morning, the doctors and nurses told me that I could go home. I insisted that we take my baby home, so that she could be buried on our land and near to me. So we set off for home, with me still swaddled in blankets but also clutching a small bundle in my arms which I never released throughout the long journey home. Sometimes I dozed fitfully but overall I recall a feeling of cold numbness, a sensation of being apart from the world as if everything was lost to me and always would be. Once again, William and John took it in turns, one with the reins while the other slumped back in the buggy to sleep.

As we arrived back at the cabin, the light was just fading. I couldn't bring myself to speak, just sobbing quietly inside, and William and John helped me down from the buggy. Minnie came forward and guessed what had happened and took me in her arms, the tiny bundle squashed between us. Our eyes met in a shared agony and she looked from my tear-stained face to the tiny bundle and back. She said nothing, but in that moment we were locked in a sisterly bond that needed no words and bridged eternity.

William stepped forward and said that we must lay her to rest straightaway, and asked where I wished for her to be buried. I could not think my way through my numbness, the all pervading deadness that I was feeling. Minnie came to my rescue and suggested that we make a little grave for her at the side of the cabin, and then later we could make a little garden there for her. John went off to get the shovels and Minnie and I took my poor tiny one indoors to lay her on the bed and dress her in one of the little nightdresses I had so carefully and lovingly made. Minnie and I unwrapped the little parcel; it was the first time I had seen her properly, even though I had clutched her so closely through the long journey back from Gull Lake. She was tiny, with the smallest fingers and toes, each with a perfect little miniature nail at the end. Her head seemed so large compared with her tiny lifeless body, her eyes closed and her lips pursed; she only looked asleep. I touched her cheek, somehow expecting warmth, but she was so cold. It was like touching a china doll. I pulled away and held my two hands together against my chest, staring down at her. I couldn't bring myself to touch her again. How could she be taken from me like this? I had felt her growing and kicking inside me for so long, she and I had been as one. I didn't know how to feel at that moment in time.

Minnie dressed her quickly in one of our carefully made nightdresses with its lovingly fashioned smocking stitches, and gently eased her head into a tiny bonnet. She swaddled her carefully in the blanket in which I had brought her from Gull Lake. She picked her up and went to pass her to me, but I couldn't take her. We walked slowly outside where the men had prepared her grave, a deep hole at the side of the cabin. By then, the sun was just about setting in a blood red cloak across the western sky. William took her from Minnie and, kneeling by the newly dug pit, he put the tiny bundle in an ammunition box he had found and nailed down the lid. He laid her down, deep in the ground. We five stood in silence, just staring down into the earth, with the red light streaming across our land, across the ground, across our anguished faces. John broke the silence with a short prayer to commend her to God, and Minnie took me by the shoulders, turned me away, and led me inside, leaving the men to finish the burial.

I went to my bed, and cried and cried. It felt as if I could never stop. It felt like I cried for days. William and Minnie came and went like ghosts, leaving me tender words, and untouched meals and drinks. I don't know how long it was until one night, a dream suddenly came upon me and I saw my little girl smiling back at me, already grown to youth, her hair curled and a great light around her. I don't know what it was, but that miraculous apparition gave me new heart.

Of course, life went on, and I gradually gained strength. Minnie was always there with a hug and a quiet understanding smile, and everyone let me take things easy for a while. It wasn't so long before I felt a need for something to occupy my time. I set to with the chores and everyday challenges that made up our lives on the prairie: cooking and sewing and cleaning, and when I was stronger I helped again with the digging and building and tending; forever striving to help build our new lives. But whatever was happening and whatever I was doing, I couldn't escape the deep ongoing sadness that I felt; I couldn't see that I would ever be truly happy again. I made a little garden for my lost baby, around the wooden cross and the pile of stones that marked her tiny grave and, as the flowers came into bloom, I eventually felt a new peace and comfort.

I was always ready to give Minnie a hand with young Herbie. He was a happy baby and full of spirit and it gave me a new focus on life. If Minnie accompanied one of the men to Gull Lake, still our nearest centre for mail and groceries and other necessities, I took on her tasks as well as my own, and there were extra jobs around Herbie who was growing fast. It's funny but I never felt any envy, no feeling of unfairness that Minnie was so blessed and I was so damned. I think we were all learning to take what life on the prairie dealt. We all just had to get on with it, come rain or shine, or snow, and there was always plenty of that!

It was at about that time we heard that a Mr and Mrs Huseby had opened a store and post office about twelve miles north-west of us. They called it Amelia. It took us best part of a day for the round trip in the buggy, but it certainly made life easier, and mail days were less few and far between. It prompted me to write home as I hadn't written to Mother for over a year, nor had I heard any news from her. Of course, it was possible that a letter from home could so easily have gone astray. I told her of my great sadness for my lost baby, and the joy I felt helping Minnie with young Herbie.

Life was always about striving to exist. It was our constant burden to keep ourselves fed and watered, sheltered and warm. It was also important to keep the animals safe, and we worked hard to complete our sod-built barn in time to bring our livestock in to shelter them during the months that the weather was too harsh for them to survive outside. There were always so many tasks that had to be seen to, and never enough hours in the day. We were forever on the look-out for fuel for the stove, and soon realised the importance of finding enough wood or lignite coal to see us through the long, cold winter months if we chose to stay on the land all year and were trapped in the house by the blizzards and cold winds. Whenever we could, we purchased lignite coal that had been dug from the nearby hills.

Each spring, Minnie and I prepared our vegetable patch which John had originally dug over for us in the hard ground. We planted seed, some kept from the previous year, some that we traded with a visiting merchant or neighbour for milk and eggs. We toiled hard to ensure that our labours were rewarded with vegetables, watering them when there was no rain, and checking them for blight and disease, picking them the moment they had ripened so they would not be stolen by birds or beasts ever ready to take advantage of our labours the moment our backs were turned. We slowly established fruit bushes as well, and bottled and dried and salted both vegetables and fruits, home-grown and wild, to see us through the year, especially the lean months. Much of our food was stored in a root cellar. We made jams and preserves and were grateful that we had learned these skills back in Ireland and that we had our own supply of Kilner jars, just like those that Mother was so proud of.

Clearing the land in those first years was so hard and we had to chop down trees and pull out stumps using the horses. Our tools came with us from Napinka: axes and hoes and shovels, rakes and scythes and pitchforks. We also added a cradle scythe to our collection, which I soon mastered. It cut the hay and also dropped it in piles. Hay was so important for the animals in the winter. We also traded some goods for a flail, much needed to separate the grains from the rest of the plant. That first year, the men started to plough and till the land so they could grow some crops – wheat and oats in that first season. They had brought a hand ploughshare with them from Napinka, which at first they harnessed up to two of the horses, but soon found that four horses were needed as the prairie wool was so tough and the land filled with small rocks. Having cleared the main rocks and roots, we cut the grass that we could using the scythes and dried it for hay. Then the land was turned and made ready for planting. Not only was the ground hard, making the work of the hand plough a constant struggle for man and horse, also the field work was hampered by hordes of mosquitoes that bred and hatched in the sloughs and grasses. Added to that, there were heal flies that tormented the beasts. We lit smudges in the evening to give some relief to the animals but were not able to afford them any respite while working on the land.

The hand plough was never up to the job so, in the second and for several years after, we hired a sit-on ploughshare and harrow, until finally we bought our own and were able to hire or lend it out to our neighbouring homesteaders. We planted the wheat and barley, rye and oats which we planned to harvest in September each year, as long as it wasn't destroyed by flood or fire, or damaged by drought and dust or hail, or ravaged by grasshoppers or disease. Loss of the harvest was a disaster and meant very hard times in the winter, for us and the animals. Over the years, many homesteaders were beaten by the land and the elements and their quarter section would be returned to the municipality.

Through the growing season we would strive to tend the crop, keeping it weeded so that the young plants wouldn't be choked by the weeds, and doing everything we could to protect it and help it grow strong. When all was ready, we toiled together to harvest the crop, doing our best to cheat the weather and the elements which so often conspired against us. We cut the crop, then bundled the stalks into sheaves which we stood up against each other in stooks so they could dry out in the field.

Later, we hauled the sheaves to the barn, spread them out on the floor and used the flail to separate the seeds, chaff and straw. Once the straw was raked away, we gathered what was left and put the grain and chaff in a winnowing tray, and shook and tossed them to separate the seed. A windy day was good for this as the wind blew the light straw and chaff away and the seed fell back in the tray. Some of the grain we stored for the animals, and some we took in sacks to the mill to be ground into flour. If the season was kind, we had some sacks of flour to trade.

It was a constant fight, a constant challenge, to win the battle for survival, and it took a huge effort to produce only a small amount of grain. We tried in our first year of growing wheat to grind our own flour, but after that we found that flour ground at the mill between mill stones was much better, even though it meant a long journey south. In the early days, the journey to the mill took almost a day in each direction, but that was easier and more efficient than trying to grind by hand.

We also added to our larder when we could by hunting deer, rabbits, wild ducks and prairie chickens, and on occasion caught fish in the creek nearby.

There was always so much to do to make our homestead safe and habitable and to provide for ourselves and our animals. Nothing ever came easily, but with great effort and teamwork and along with support from our neighbours, constantly with the odds stacked against us, we found our way for some years and played our part in taming a small part of the wild prairie.

Many of my memories of the next couple of years are not complete, probably because we were so busy establishing our lives there on the prairie. The time was punctuated with the baptism of baby Herbert in Gull Lake Church, then Minnie's daughter, Florence Mary, was born the next year in mid October. There was no baby for me, but I loved Minnie's babies as if they were my own.

I got little news from Mother, except to tell me that my brother John's son, named John Duke in the family tradition, was growing fast, and she sent me a photograph of my brother. How handsome he had grown.

My brother John Duke in 1910 – born just over a year after me.

Mother told me that my sisters and brothers were one by one leaving school, and that there were no jobs for them as times were still challenging. It was hard to imagine that already Blanche, Kate and my cousin, James, from Grange were growing up so fast. Only Thomas and Queenie still made their way each day to Ardsellagh School.

In the evenings, while we would sit and mend and sew, William often entertained us with items from the newspaper if he got a copy, much as my Father had done back in Ireland. I started to become more aware of what was happening in the political arena in Canada and remember news of the end of the term of office of Wilfred Laurier, the seventh Prime Minister of Canada. He had served since 1896, and had worked to convince the nation that Canada was on the verge of becoming a world power. He declared that the 20th century would 'belong to Canada'. There was quite a fuss when Robert Borden, the Conservative, challenged a treaty with the US intended to lower tariffs in both directions, saying that Canada would get swallowed up by America, and ties with Britain would be threatened. The people of Canada were not convinced by Laurier's arguments, and Robert Borden's party won the Canadian Federal Election in 1911, with Robert Borden as Prime Minister.

Through my life here on the prairies, I am still taken aback by the Saskatchewan climate. Ireland was forever wet, with cold, damp winters and pleasant summers, and always green. I could never have anticipated how it would be on the prairies. Summers here are warm and wet, often hot from June to August, and the wind rarely gives up its constant nagging. Before the land was turned by the plough, the sod was anchored down by the long tangled roots of the prairie grass but, as soon as it was freed for cultivation, the wind could shift it. If the weather is hot and dry, this leads to disaster as the soil gets turned to dust and the wind lifts it and throws it every which way. In summertime, if such conditions prevail, instead of the Land of Plenty once dreamt of, all is enveloped in the great Dust Bowl. Everything is then damped down in the winters which are cold with snow from September to May. We live at an elevation of over three thousand feet, so it's not surprising that it snows so much.

1911 saw the arrival of many more settlers, and we started to feel that we were all part of a blossoming community. Friendships were forged, and there was a wonderful feeling of neighbourliness. Minnie and I were delighted when Christ Fugelstad's wife arrived with the four children, Ella, Agnes, Emil and Cora. They came with the Evensons and Fred Fugelstad and settled in Sections 7 and 12. Other new arrivals in our area were a group of young men who came from Elgin, Ontario, including Sid Minty, who later ran our local Post Office, Bill Goodall, Derek Prosser and his sons Earl and Karl, Geordie Kuhl and Frank Brigden. Frank was a plasterer and cement worker. He impressed us all when he built his house not from sods or timber but from stones and cement. We all marvelled at it and teased him that he would be able to impress a young lady with such a handsome dwelling. Little did we know that it would be our sister, Tillie, a couple of years later!

John Brooks also came from Port Elgin, Ontario, bringing a few animals and the household effects – including a piano. He built his shack and then his wife and two children, Olive and Milton followed in June. When we first invited them for one of our community social evenings, we heard the story of the Brooks family having to wait for a week in Gull Lake because John had not received their arrival details. Reading between the lines, this had caused some difficulties for John as his wife was far from pleased, and it was worse because the children got burnt in the hot sun during the four day journey down from Gull Lake to the homestead. Fortunately the tale took on some hilarity when recounted to the neighbours and even Mrs Brookes was able to laugh about it. She was a very pleasant woman and church services were held at the Brooks' home for some years until Climax Church was built. Ernie Hinkson was the minister, and Mrs Brooks played the hymns on the family's piano. We always wondered at the fact that John had managed to transport the piano all the way from Ontario, first by train and then on a wagon. There were jokes about it being shipped across the White Mud River, with suggestions of 'Water Music' and others. That was the only piano we ever came across while we were at the homesteads.

Whenever someone was planning a trip to Gull Lake, some sixty five miles to the north and still our nearest centre for farm supplies, there was a great kinship amongst neighbours and we all did our best to help each other. I say all but, as in any community, there were those who preferred to keep themselves to themselves, sometimes due to differences in language and nationality. Our neighbours came from many corners of the earth – France, England, Scotland, Ireland, Germany, Finland, Sweden and others – as well as many from Canada, particularly Ontario.

It was our fortune to have our own wagons and transport. There were many who had none, or at least started with none. But there was local help available from the Metis people with their Red River carts. They could be employed to help with the transport of items small and large, from goods to lumber and even small machinery. Their carts were sturdily made from solid oak timbers, tied together with leather string, which they called shagapanni.

Minnie and I made friends with Kathareana, a Metis women of roughly the same age as us. In her broken English, she told us many things about her ancestors, of how they came from marriages between French fur traders and Cree women, of the hardships they suffered at the hands of just about everyone as they were neither European nor Canadian Indians. Shagapanni, she explained to us, was from the Cree word 'piishaakanaapiy' which literally meant 'leather string'. One day, she took the time to tell us one of the Metis folklore tales handed down over the years.

"The Moose Family was sitting in the lodge when a pipe came floating in through the door. It floated past everyone until it reached the youngest Bull Moose who took the pipe and started to smoke it. The Old Moose knew that it would bring the human beings to the lodge, but the young Bull Moose was not afraid, for he thought he could outrun them.

Next day, the Moose People went to the edge of the forest. They caught the scent of the hunters and they started to run but the thin crust on the snow made it hard to move quickly. The young Bull Moose was still sure he could outrun the hunters, but they were wearing snowshoes and they followed him until he tired, and killed him. They thanked him for giving himself to them so they could survive. They treated his body with care and soothed his spirit.

Because the hunters had treated the young Bull Moose with respect, the Moose Family knew that that it was right to allow the human beings to catch them. And so it is to this day. Those hunters who show respect for the moose are always the ones who are successful when they hunt."

Gull Lake retained its particular importance to us for another year, and we continued to endure the arduous expeditions to get supplies which took best part of a week each time, possibly more if the White Mud or Frenchman River was in flood. The journey was a constant source of discussion particularly as, when we had filed on the land, all homesteaders had been promised that the railway would soon come to us, so we could sell our wheat and crops; now it was not clear when this would be. We knew that Shaunavon was in the sights of the railroad men, so that would halve our journey once the town was developed, but there was no clear news of when the line would reach us.

Minnie had become something of a master baker, and provided bread not only for the Fallis family but also for many of the families and bachelors, who would walk or ride for miles for a loaf and perhaps a meal. If they could not pay in money, they would make arrangements to come and help the Fallis effort on the land. Bartering was quite the norm.

1911 Minnie and George outside their homestead.

By the end of summer 1911, we felt that we were starting to make good progress. Our shacks were built, and to the single bedroom, we had each added a lean-to kitchen, and a south-facing porch – all built from timber – and in the yard, we each had a hen house in wood and had completed our barns and other outhouses which were all sod-built. We had toiled together to clear several acres of land and, greatly assisted by a summer that offered both warmth and sufficient rain and no great problems, we had grain and flour and hay, as well as oats and other crops.

Once again, William and I made the decision to return to Napinka for the winter. Minnie and George stayed on the land. John went north to find work.

When William and I returned in the spring of 1912, Minnie announced another pregnancy. She was due in October. I had no such news to offer. Of course, I was happy for Minnie, but it set me wondering if I would ever have a child of my own. Mother had produced a baby almost every year; why was I having such difficulties? But life had to go on, baby or no baby, so I set my mind on our home, and helping Minnie and her growing family.

Later that year there was another great and very relevant excitement. Shaunavon, some thirty miles north of us, was bought by the Canadian Pacific Railway from the original landowners, William and Patrick Ganley and Thomas McNealy. Rumours abounded that the CPR would be establishing their divisional offices there for lines heading west to Lethbridge. Despite the news, nothing much happened that year, and we carried on as before, trekking to Gull Lake and back, or occasionally Harlem, just over the American border. The year was kind and everyone made progress with their betterments, but frustration continued with the lack of transport for getting wheat to market.

A letter came from home.

Coolnagranchy
August 1912

My dear daughters

There are so many problems here in Ireland. Sinn Fein have been shouting for independence, as they have been since before you all were born, and now they've got their way and we've been granted Home Rule by the British Government. You'd think that would have settled things, but in the north they formed the Ulster Volunteers, who are shouting against it, and the Irish Volunteers, who are wanting more. I think I've understood it right. The papers are full of it, and everyone talks of nothing else.

There is very little else to tell you about. We now have a few sheep and Father broke his foot when he kicked one of them. Those animals are so stubborn, and one of them, a ram, was stamping his foot and refusing to move out of the lane and into the field. Well your Father was getting more and more cross, and the ram just refused to go, so that's when it happened. I didn't approve of your Father's action so I feel that it serves him right to some extent. He's hobbling around in a lot of pain at the moment, so I guess I'll need to give him some sympathy and help him out a bit.

Your brothers and sisters are all fine, just the usual coughs and colds. We've all been lucky to avoid most of it. Only Katie, Thomas and Queenie are still at school. We don't hear very often from John in Glasgow, and Sarah Jane, Eva, Lillie and Blanche are all helping out around the farm and the house, always on the look-out for some sort of paid work in town or locally, and all wondering if there will ever be a husband for each of them.

That's my news for now. We all send our love.
Mother

1913 William ploughed while I picked up stones.

That fall, we all packed up and our neighbours, the Dells, agreed to take care of the cows and chickens. William and I returned yet again to Napinka while Minnie and George went to Swift Current with the horses. There Florence was born to Minnie on 16th October, though we didn't get news at Napinka until almost a month later. They stayed in Swift Current for the winter and George worked there in construction, building elevators, along with John and other settlers from our area – all trying to make a grub stake to take back to their homesteads to help make ends meet.

We all returned to the homesteads in early spring of 1913, and set to working the land again. William and I toiled long and hard, me picking up rocks so he could plough the land without breaking the share. The going was always so hard and it took four strong horses to turn the soil to make it ready for planting.

That spring, Minnie was so well and baby Florence was a tiny but strong baby, and very determined. Herbie was fascinated by her, and the little family seemed to be thriving. But it seemed to me that life on the prairie resents success and happiness, and shortly after, when we were all settling into our routines, little Herbie developed some kind of a throat problem. Minnie was at a loss as it was clear he needed some medical treatment, but she was still feeding baby Florence, only a few months old.

It was agreed that I would take Herbie to seek some treatment, and George took us to Amelia in the buggy where we then took the mail coach to Gull Lake. There we went on by train to Brandon and the hospital. Brandon was the town where Minnie and I had been wed only three years before. Throughout the journey, the poor little chap was so pale and obviously in some pain, and I wanted so much for the doctor and nurses to help him in his pathetic plight. We stayed for three days but no-one could say what the problem was. I took Herbie home again by the same route we had come, so aware that nothing could be done, and dreading how to tell Minnie and George that no hope had been offered to help the poor little chap. That summer was hell for us all as we watched our once lively little boy suffer and fade. It seemed that all joy had gone out of things as the cruel illness took further hold; he just lay in his bed in obvious discomfort and often great pain. We tried to coax him with soups and drinks that would not cause him even more distress. Everything seemed so hopeless.

That September, the CPR invited purchasers for plots in Shaunavon. Men queued up in Gull Lake, hoping to buy a prime site near the railway. In eight hours, no less than three hundred and seventy lots were sold to businessmen and prospective residents. Where there had been only wind to claim the land, known as Bone Creek Basin, soon a thriving village was born. Shaunavon had been a stop-off point for spring and fall cattle drives, now there was something more significant, a new interest in the area.

It brought not only a new settlement, but much more. The new local newspaper was excitement in itself; previously news had arrived by chance from a neighbour or passing trader or if we'd brought a newspaper back from Gull Lake or Harlem. Every week, we were enthralled by the news from Shaunavon. By mid-November, the first school was opened, and later that month Shaunavon was incorporated as a village with over sixty businesses and the first work train arrived carrying steel for the new track. Quite soon Shaunavon was nicknamed Boomtown. It was all very exciting and we felt we were part of history in the making, even though we lived some distance away from the great activity.

I still have cuttings from the Shaunavon Standard. This first issue on 18th September 1913 reported that:

"about one hundred and twenty five people were in attendance at Gull Lake. Many had been waiting for the sale to begin for thirteen days and thirteen nights. Within eight hours, three hundred and seventy business and residential plots had been purchased. Early buyers spent $1,000 per residential position number, with some buyers buying multiple plots".

My other cutting is from the end of November that year.

"From this initial purchase approximately three hundred and seventy business and residential lots were bought and by November 27th, Shaunavon was incorporated as a village. Following the initial purchase of land, Shaunavon witnessed incredible construction, within the first few months of its history. Shaunavon expanded and saw the construction of several buildings addressing the needs of its people. These include: Brown-Naismith Hardware, the Kennedy Hotel, Merchants Bank, the First Baptist Church and the Empress Hotel."

William and I returned to Napinka for the winter, John took work in the north, and Minnie and family stayed in their prairie home, caring for the family's livestock, and nursing little Herbie while hoping for a miracle.

5

The First World War

1914-1918

The expansion of Shaunavon brought the railway so much closer, and this improved possibilities for us settlers to sell our wheat and produce, though it was still a long and hard journey to transport goods to the depot. The advance of the railway from Gull Lake to Shaunavon added a new excitement but, more significant to us at that time was that, not long after the coming of the steel to Shaunavon, we had cleared and planted twenty acres as specified by the Homestead and Dominion Lands Act. We were able to obtain title to the full one hundred and sixty acres, though we had been using some of it since our arrival four years earlier. Title was confirmed to us in a document called Letters Patent.

Shortly after getting back from over-wintering at Napinka, William returned to Swift Current to obtain the documents. The date of our title was 17th March 1914, and we celebrated on his return, inviting all our new friends and neighbours. But this also meant more hard work, establishing boundary fences and clearing more land, but a chance to expand our dreams and ambitions. Some of our achievement had been with the help of the family and neighbours, and we owed many debts and promises to those around us who were also striving to succeed. It was a true community with everyone helping his neighbour and a shared sense of determination.

1914 was a year to remember for many reasons, but too many of them were filled with pain and anguish. The first, and probably one of the saddest, occurred before William and I returned from our winter lodgings over in Manitoba. Over the chill and wintry months, little Herbie had been going steadily downhill with no signs of recovery. On 21st January, his little body finally gave up. He was at home with Minnie, George and little Florence when he passed away. It was just one month before his third birthday. When William and I got back,

Minnie told me everything. I was heartbroken that I wasn't there to help her in his final days and to give her comfort when his short life came to an end. George and a neighbour made the wee coffin, and Mrs Cosgrove made a lining. She was a kind lady and tried to offer some comfort to Minnie. She had been a good friend to the family from the time she and her husband arrived back in 1912 and had always been on hand to help Minnie with the children. She was very fond of them partly perhaps because she had no little ones of her own. When it was time for Herbie's funeral, several of the neighbours joined the family at home for a short service, with a reading from the Anglican Prayer Book. Minnie told me that a hymn was sung, but she couldn't remember which one. They lowered his little coffin into the ground on a high spot on the homestead. Before his illness, Herbie had been such a strong and determined little boy; it was impossible to believe that he had been taken from us so young. No sooner had we got to know his character and his delightful ways than he was gone. Now it was my time to give Minnie my sisterly support.

In early June, the Shaunavon Herald carried a report about a ship that had been lost in the St Lawrence River at the end of May. Minnie heard of it first and came running to tell me that the Empress of Ireland, the ship that brought us to Canada, was rammed by a Norwegian ship and had gone down in fourteen minutes. The newspaper reported that 1,012 of the 1,477 persons on board had died. Our shock was so great, and we embraced and cried for some time, thinking of the horror of other young people like us who had been on board and embarking on new opportunities across the seas, with hope and optimism in their hearts. In its time, the lost ship had brought so many people safely to new lives. It was unbearable that such a terrible thing could have happened and with the tragic loss of so many people.

The newspaper included information about the history of the ship, built in 1906, and about that fateful day when she collided in thick fog and went to her watery grave. Minnie and I spent some time reading the news. Somehow it was all very personal to us. We were so thankful that we were not travelling on her when she met her end. How blessed we were that we had been carried safely, as well as our sisters, Tillie and Martha, when they came across the Atlantic to Canada in the Empress of Britain two years after us. Minnie and I pored over the report.

"On May 29th 1914, the Empress of Ireland left Quebec at half past four in the afternoon with a total of 1,477 people on board. Travelling down the St. Lawrence River, the Empress, under the command of Captain Henry Kendall, encountered heavy fog when she was nearing the mouth of the river that same evening. Later that night, when it had already become the 30th of May, the Empress' lookout reported spotting an incoming ship on the ship's starboard side. The rules to be applied when two ships meet in bad visibility were not very complicated: When meeting head on, each ship was to turn to starboard and pass the meeting vessel 'port-to-port'. But if the two ships were on a 'starboard-to-starboard' course, this was to be maintained due to the risk of collision.

When the two ships were approaching in the night, the fog suddenly became much denser. Captain Kendall ordered the Empress of Ireland stopped and her engines put astern to give the meeting ship more manoeuvring space. He then gave three blasts with the ship's whistle to announce his action. Tragically, the crew on board the oncoming ship – which was the Norwegian collier Storstad – had already taken actions to pass 'port-to-port'. Making their starboard turn, the crew of the Storstad put their ship directly across the path of the Empress of Ireland. Emerging from the thick fog, the Storstad's bow crashed into the starboard side of the Empress. Disaster was now a cruel fact.

The Empress of Ireland had been holed above and below the waterline just where the engine room was situated. It took only a short moment before the engine room was flooded, making it impossible for the crew to operate the ship's watertight doors. It also rendered the Empress powerless to move, thus making any plans of beaching the ship unexecutable. In addition, the Empress' electrical power was rapidly fading, and only one S.O.S.-call could be sent before it went out completely.

The whole course of events that followed after the collision occurred during the brief time of only 14 minutes. The Empress of Ireland had taken on a serious list to starboard immediately after the impact, and it grew worse by the minute. Open portholes in the ship's hull made matters even worse – as soon as they went under, more water was rushing in at a horrifying pace. For many of the passengers who were asleep in their cabins, there was barely time to understand what was happening before it was all over. A small number of people, mostly from the first class cabins situated on the upper decks, managed to get out on the boat deck.

But once there, things did not look much brighter. Some ten or eleven minutes after the collision, the Empress of Ireland violently lurched over on her starboard side, throwing hundreds of people – including Captain Kendall – into the freezing waters of the St. Lawrence River. Hundreds of people were clinging to the side of the ship, which was now lying completely on its side in the water. For a short moment, it seemed as if the ship had gone aground and would stay in this position. But suddenly, the Empress of Ireland's stern rose slightly out of the water, and then the ship slipped beneath the cold waves. Hundreds of people were left in the icy waters, and only four lifeboats had managed to escape the sinking vessel.

One of the lucky souls that were pulled into one of these lifeboats was Captain Kendall. Realising his responsibility, he immediately took command of the craft and started organising the rescue operations. Pulling survivors from the water, the lifeboats offloaded them on the ship that had crashed into the Empress. The fog was still very dense, and Captain Kendall did not yet know the name or nationality of the ship that had sunk his command.

After several rescue runs with the lifeboats, no more survivors could be found and Captain Kendall gave up the search. In all, 1,012 of the 1,477 passengers died that terrible night. Only 465 survived."

Later that summer, news came that war had been declared between Britain and Germany. It was August 1914 and Canada was immediately drawn in, being part of the British Empire. Canada was automatically at war with Germany with no possibility of declining. Tens of thousands of young Canadians joined the army in the first few months. We heard that other Empire countries such as Australia and India were also sending their young men to Europe to join the terrible fight. With the war came new challenges and changes. Things were never quite the same again.

Many young men from local homesteads were called to fight, but we were fighting our own battles on the prairies. My brother-in-law John was one who signed up, but he never got to go. If he had gone sooner, he may have been spared a terrible suffering death; who knows what might have happened. In late summer, John bade us farewell, and set off for Weyburn to work on the harvest there, telling his friends that he would meet them to go and fight once it was done. John was a good mechanic and was employed by McTaggart in the south eastern part of the province. His job was to run the separator on a threshing outfit.

He never got to meet up with his buddies as he'd promised as he was involved in a tragic accident. The machine he was working on was designed to pull together twelve bundles to make a stook. The machine had been working for some time when there was a blockage in the process, and it was necessary to make some adjustment while the equipment was still running. John got up on top of the separator to observe what was happening and stepped on a wooden plate which had some rot in it. The plate gave way under his weight and John fell through into the revolving cutters. His legs were torn to pieces and it took some minutes to turn off the separator. They pulled him out screaming from the unbearable pain and laid him on a nearby wagon that was piled with corn. On the journey to Weyburn Hospital, he was in constant agony, though we were told that he mercifully drifted out of consciousness from shock and loss of blood for some of the time. The attempts of his colleagues to try to bind his shredded legs and stem the bleeding only added to his suffering, and, when he was alert, he was tortured by every bump and crater along the way. Those with him knew that it was hopeless. He lost so much blood that the corn was totally saturated by the time they reached the hospital. The doctors there tried to amputate his shattered legs, but their task was impossible. His legs were past saving, and he had lost too much blood. He only lived a short time and died there at Weyburn. It was 21st August, but we did not hear the tragic news until someone from McTaggarts came a few days later to tell us all what had happened. George and William were deeply shocked, as was to be expected, and straight away made arrangements to go to Weyburn and take John's body home to the family in Napinka. There he was buried, with his parents and family, and with childhood friends and neighbours around. John was only thirty one years old and far too young and talented for his life to have ended in such a cruel manner.

In so few years, we had buried three of our Fallis family out there on the prairie – my stillborn baby girl, Minnie's Herbie, and now John. We were not the only family to suffer loss. The prairie was not a kind guardian; she did little to protect her flock, despite their attempts to thrive and to harness her wild nature and bring her lands to fruition.

In September, there was happier news. My sister, Tillie, came to visit earlier in the year and met Frank Brigden at one of our evenings. Minnie and I watched with interest as the couple chatted and laughed together. We had great expectations and were not disappointed. Tillie came to work in Shaunavon and there Frank proposed to her. They were married in Shaunavon on 2nd September. The wonderful thing for Minnie and me was that Frank had built his stone house only about five miles away from our wooden cabins, not so far in prairie terms, so we would be reunited with Tillie and able to make regular visits, especially as we had Bob and the carriage.

The wedding took place quietly, with only the bride and groom and two strangers as witnesses. Minnie and I were disappointed that we were not there in Shaunavon to help our little sister prepare, but it really wasn't practical. But when Tillie and Frank came home, it was a special day for our family, and good to have something to celebrate at a time when so much had been going so wrong. Minnie and I worked together to prepare some food for the few guests. There was not a lot to spare, but we were determined to celebrate as best we could. It went a good way to ease our sorrows and bring a sense of purpose and hope back to our lives.

Despite the war and the shortages, Shaunavon was going from strength to strength. By the end of October, the Shaunavon Herald reported that the village had grown to such a size that it was big enough to be promoted from a village to a town. It had a population of over seven hundred, and was the first town in Canada to grow from a village to a town in less than one year. Within that year, it already had a church, a school and the newspaper, as well as sixty new businesses. It was fast growing from a wild place into something a lot more grown-up.

But there were teething problems and one was to do with the cowboys. Shaunavon had been a stop-off for them when they were driving cattle across the prairie. The new town found it hard to accept their rough manners and this was causing some trouble. Townsfolk needed to find ways to stop them from their boisterous enjoyments, shooting up the town and riding their horses into the bars of the Empress and Kennedy Hotels. This brought about the birth of the first Shaunavon rodeo, and proved to be a great success with not only the cowboys but also townsfolk who flocked to witness this wild entertainment. Sometimes if we were in town to get supplies, we found the time to go along and enjoy the merriment of the occasion and the great daring of the young, and not so young, cowboys. Many stars were born, and the spectacle provided a great diversion to us all whose lives were a constant struggle. It also went some way to lifting our spirits in a time of such terrible world conflict.

The new town took a blow just before Christmas when fire destroyed the Empress Hotel. William had taken me in on a couple of occasions and I had seen what a magnificent building it was, with sixty rooms and a billiard parlour. The fire-fighters couldn't save it or the Savoy Hotel and Café nearby. The story was covered by the Shaunavon Herald and it described the valiant efforts of the firemen with their fire-wagon with its chemical tank and two reels of hose. It took many, many gallons of precious water to extinguish the flames. The firemen worked long and hard into the night and managed to stop the blaze from spreading. They were heralded as heroes. The cost of the damage was eighty five thousand Canadian dollars. But it didn't take long for the area to be cleared and, from the ashes, The Shaunavon Hotel was born.

The new Shaunavon continued to grow, with several more buildings rising from the hard ground and more businesses attracted by the expanding town. The surrounding area was fast being cultivated with wheat. Grain elevators were built to store the grain prior to shipping. Despite life's constant hardship, we felt part of a new optimistic era that was throwing up some possibilities.

The occasional ups were quickly replaced by regular downs, as always seemed to be the case in our endless fight for existence on the prairie. Some of our neighbours decided to leave their homesteads and move closer to the railway, and to the schools and medical facilities that it brought. We were particularly sad to bid farewell to Wes Dells, who had been such a help to us, and to Elmer Movold and his family. Only a short time before, we had felt that our community was growing stronger. With the loss of some of our friends and also so many young bachelors who had signed up to fight, our little township was taking on a changed sadness and emptiness.

One afternoon, we were visited by Joe Francis who had returned injured from the battle front. He broke down on telling us that his brother David had died in the trenches, killed by the terrible mustard gas. Joe managed to put his mask on in time but David was too late and died a miserable and painful death there in the mud, as did too many of our brave young men. Joe and David were originally from England. They were hard working and had already gained title to part of their land back in 1913. We had got to like them very well for their positive attitude and hard work. Poor Joe was never quite the same again and suffered from nightmares and shell shock for some time. It was touch and go for a while as to whether he would go back to his family in England. His neighbour, our friend Ed Kay, did his best to help him with the land and eventually Joe successfully managed and worked five quarters. He never married and was always haunted by the loss of his brother and the terrible scenes he had witnessed in Europe. If he had returned to England and left the land, it would surely have gone back to the municipality; they took back those areas that were abandoned for reasons of war or otherwise. That is what always happened when someone couldn't work their homestead. Sometimes the land was taken again or it lay unmanaged for years.

Everyday life was taking a familiar pattern, ever affected by the weather, but there were always jobs to be done in the cabin. Our small house had only one room with a dirt floor, and with home-made rugs which were always getting wet or muddy or dusty and needed constant beating. But they did make things cosier. The cabin was our home and shelter, where we ate, worked and slept. At one end was a makeshift dresser with hooks where we had all the kitchen equipment, including the meat grinder, the eggbeater, rolling pin, flat iron, coffee grinder, butter mould, candle mould, as well as the cooking pots, mugs, dishes, plates and cutlery. Beside the dresser stood the butter churn, wash tubs, and washboard. My pride and joy was my dutch oven, a cast iron pot which I used all the time for cooking bread, puddings, meat, cakes, stews and casseroles. Soups and stews were our main victuals, with coffee and tea to drink. All our dishes and bowls and cups were made of wood or tin.

Some folks had stone fireplaces in their cabins and that required a large chimney and a lot of fuel. We had an iron stove which we brought from Napinka. It was much cleaner than a fireplace and only needed a small chimney. It stood on four legs along the side wall of the cabin, and next to the kitchen dresser. There were two burners on top and an oven, and it not only provided a stove for cooking but also a source of warmth in the cabin, and we heated hot water in the reservoir. We searched out wood which grew by nearby rivers and sloughs, or bought coal when we could find it. And, if there wasn't enough wood or coal then we used twisted straw and corn stalks. We also gathered cow chips which burned well. We had various tools such as a poker and shovel, and a pail for collecting the ashes, and we saved those for making soap. We always kept a bucket of water near the stove in case of fire. If a spark were to fly it could so easily catch fire to our little wooden shack.

In the evening, we sat round the stove on our chairs, with the homemade rugs on the floor for added warmth. Sometimes, William carved things out of wood, or more likely fell asleep, exhausted after another long day. And I did some knitting or embroidery, but most often there was something that needed mending – a patch on William's breeches, or a sock to darn.

Really there wasn't much furniture in our home – our bed and chairs and the dresser cupboard, and a small table that served us for eating and for just about everything that needed to be prepared or made. Often in the summer months, we moved it outside to make some space in the cabin, and it was good to work in the fresh air if we were skinning rabbits or preparing some other meat that the men had brought home, and especially when we were making soap or candles. The table needed constant scrubbing to keep it clean for preparing and eating our meals. Most of our furniture was handmade, including the chairs we had brought with us from Napinka, and William was a good carpenter so he was always able to do any repairs that were needed. One day we had an idea that the table would serve better if it had hinged ends, both from the point of view of taking up less room in the cabin and also making a larger area to work on when we needed it. Next time he went to town, William took some of our butter and goods to trade and got hinges and screws from the blacksmith and some pieces of flat timber from the yard, and soon we had a much superior table.

At first we had just the one bed, for William and me. It was wooden with ropes stretched across the frame to hold the straw mattress, and covered with a thick homemade feather quilt. William also put shelves on the walls and wooden pegs for hanging up jackets and clothing, and we had a large chest that we brought from Napinka and we used that to store clothing and materials. I still have that chest to this day, filled with my treasures and mementos, and all the precious letters from home and family that I love to read to remind me of times past.

Minnie, Tillie and I were always grateful that we had learnt so much while growing up in Ireland that set us in good stead for our lives on the prairies. Everything we needed for everyday life came either from the land around us and what it yielded, or had to be bought or traded in town, which involved long and uncomfortable, sometimes hazardous, journeys.

To start with, Minnie and I only had the clothes we had brought with us from Napinka: our Sunday best which we had also worn at our weddings in Brandon, some skirts and blouses and underwear, and pinafores to protect them. Once these had worn out and there were mends on mends, we sought out homespun cloth to make our dresses, and hides of animals like deer and rabbit. William and George also had their Sunday wear, and had breeches, shirts and jackets which wore out regularly as their work on the land was so hard. We learnt to fashion their hats and coats and pants from leather to make them harder wearing. When something was too old and worn out to be useable, we tore them into strips and squares for making patchwork quilts or rugs for the floor.

Boots were the only footwear suitable for life on the prairie. Gone were the days of a smart or pretty pair of shoes, though probably the only time I had enjoyed such a luxury was when I lived with my aunt and uncle in London. Footwear had to be practical and strong, and William regularly had to get out his tools to do some resoling or sewing.

Washing and drying clothes was always a major task and took most of a day, often more when the weather was bad. We had no washing machines in those early days, so everything had to be washed by hand. To start, we had to haul water from the well, but thank goodness we had the well, otherwise it would have been a mile to the slough, and that was usually muddied by the animals and full of wrigglers and bugs. If the stove was in, and we had collected enough water from the well and remembered to top up the reservoir, the hot water from there was a godsend. When the weather was good, I could take my wash tubs outside and use a big metal jug to transfer the hot water from the stove. Those were the easiest days. On others, I heated water on the stove in a big metal pot, or lit a fire outside to heat the water for the washing. In the winter months from late September to early May, the well was often frozen so we melted snow for the washing. If the weather was too bad then very little washing got done at all.

Once the water was ready, we soaked the clothes in warm soapy water, first the whites, then the others, and the dirtiest clothes were left until last. The water was used again and again until it got too dirty. Then more hot water was needed. Cleaning the clothes in those days was a matter of rubbing homemade soap over the stains and then scrubbing the clothes up and down on the ridges of the washboard. Next came the rinsing in a second and third tub of cold water. Washing clothes was back breaking work from all the bending, and hard on your hands and arms. I was fortunate to have a wringer, with rollers and a crank, so that helped with the wringing and got a lot of the water out. When the first washing was ready, I fixed the line between the cabin and a post that William had placed for me, so I could hang out the washing, hopefully to dry. We never left the line out when it wasn't in use as it got grimed and dirty when the wind pulled up the whisks of dusty earth in the dry weather, and the rain brought sediment with it in the wet. Of course, the weather had a great affect on the state of the washing itself if it was hung out in bad conditions, so some days there was nothing for it but to stretch lines across the room near the stove to dry the clothes inside. It was never easy. But that was how it was, and we were used to living with such conditions.

Making soap was a skill that I brought with me from Ireland, and I sometimes found myself teaching others how to make the blocks from lard and lye, boiling up animal fat and leftover cooking grease with the lye which was made from ashes soaked in water. I often added wild herbs to take away the rancid smell, and wild sage and lavender added a sweetness to the clothes. We always had to take care with the lye as it could burn your skin, and it gave off a fume that could make you cough and wheeze.

Although we were living on the prairie in such difficult conditions, we always felt it important that we look as smart as possible, and this included clothes, cleaned, well mended and ironed. I usually ironed once a week, and rolled up the damp clothes to keep them from creasing, though it was often necessary to dampen them again to get the wrinkles out when doing the pressing. My iron had been a wedding present from William's parents and was a two-part flat iron. I had two bases, so could heat one on the stove while I used the other, and then just lock the handle on to the heated base when the other had cooled. I liked pressing the clothes as it was the only time in winter that my hands were warmed.

Candle-making was another skill that proved invaluable. At first, candles were the only light we had, besides the glow from the stove if we opened the front. Making candles was always a messy job and took a long time. Some candles were made from beeswax which we traded in town, but most were made from animal fat which we saved from the meat we had killed for food, such as deer, cattle, sheep and pigs. The fat was melted in a large iron kettle which we kept especially for that messy task, then boiled in water and strained into a tub, before the cords were dipped into the hot fat, then cooled, then dipped again. We did this over and over till each candle was thick enough. To be more efficient, we discovered that we could hang several cords on a stick so more candles could be made at one time. We added wild herbs that we collected from the land to overcome the rancid smell. Minnie and I usually made candles at my cabin every few months, and William was never too happy about the awful smell when he came in. But it was an important task, so we all had to make the best of it. At one time, we did try a grease lamp, a metal bowl with animal fat and a strip of twisted cloth as a wick dipped into the melted tallow. We soon gave up on that idea as it did not provide much light and produced an awful lot of smoke. Then a neighbour introduced us to candle moulds to make the candles, and they went on our shopping list next time we went to town. Each mould held six candles. The cords were placed in the moulds and melted tallow was poured in and left to cool and harden. Then the wicks were trimmed. This method was a great advantage and we could make more candles in the time and it was not as messy.

After a couple of years of making and using candles, George came back from getting supplies one day and announced that he had a surprise for us. He presented Minnie and me with an oil lamp each. We were greatly excited and set about taking one of them apart and preparing them to light, even though it was broad daylight! George had also purchased two cans of coal oil for each lamp, and we excitedly unscrewed the stopper on the reservoir and poured in some coal oil and primed the wick. Then we got William to light it and we put the glass chimney in place. The lamp also had a wire and wooden handle, and we held it up in delight. No more candle-making! What a joy!

During those war years, I was often frustrated that I couldn't satisfy my need to write to Mother, or to hear news of the family back in Ireland, but there was no flow of information between us through that long, terrible time while the war raged on in Europe. I couldn't learn how everyone was, nor could I share our sad episodes with them. I imagined that the war would also have a great effect on life back home, and that many of the young men were being dragged into the war, just as the Canadian youth were. Perhaps my dear brother John would also be called up. I thought of my younger brothers and sisters. They would all be finishing school. My youngest sister, Queenie, had her fourteenth birthday in 1915, so that would mean that she and our brother Thomas would be ready to try and find employment and shape their futures. Would times have improved since Minnie, Tillie, Martha and I had left? How I hoped for happiness for them all. It was already six years since I had said goodbye to them all, though it seemed like a lifetime. Would I even ever see them again?

None of us left the homesteads that fall. Although the winter was as harsh as usual, I felt stronger than I had for some time, and I'm sure I benefited from not having to travel long distances back to Napinka by buggy and train as we had so often done before. In February, Minnie gave birth to another son and she named him John Frazer, partly to the memory of our lost brother-in-law, and also for our brother back in Ireland. Baby John was premature and always sickly. The poor little mite struggled from the start and Minnie had so much trouble trying to feed him. He only lived for thirty nine days. Although the winter soil was rock hard, the men managed to dig a tiny grave for him. We all went on the new sleigh that William and George had built that summer, drawn up the hill by one of the horses. There Baby John was laid to rest next to his brother, Herbie.

At last, William and I were blessed with a baby of our own. On 7th April, Martha Irene was born in our shack on the prairie, and William had plenty of time to get Nurse de Lerris. She arrived just as things were starting to happen and swept in, organising what went where and ordering William from the cabin, probably much to his relief. I had felt much stronger during this pregnancy and the baby had never stopped kicking me black and blue. Minnie was there, thank goodness, and was ordered to boil water and get cloths and bring all the things that Nurse de Lerris required. She willingly assisted the midwife and did all the tasks that are needed to be done when a new baby is on the way. It took some hours for my baby to be born, and I think I screamed so loud that the whole prairie could bear witness to my labours. Finally my new daughter was born, also showing great strength in her lungs; she bawled and wailed from the moment she made her way into the world!

Of course, the men were banned from the cabin throughout my ordeal, and William went to stay with George until it was all done. Minnie went for him once the baby's cord was tied and she was swaddled, and I was cleaned and tidied, and our home put back to some semblance of order. He strode into the room with the broadest grin I ever saw on him and he straight way came and took me in his arms and gave me a kiss to end all kisses. It was the happiest of occasions, and William was the proudest man alive, and highly amused by his noisy new daughter.

In fact, I just raced Tillie to motherhood; shortly after, she also gave birth to a daughter, Gladys Lenore, her first child. She had her baby at home and Minnie was on hand, again kept so busy at this time by Nurse de Lerris. Perhaps it helped Minnie to overcome the loss of Baby John. These precious arrivals brought such happiness to us both and the whole family.

The winter that year was kind and life took on a new tempo to accommodate the new additions. I started to become a competent and confident mother and, the following year, my son Clarence William was born in MacKenzie's Nursing Home in Shaunavon on 27th September 1916. I arrived at the nursing home fairly close to term after a rough and uncomfortable ride in the buggy, not sure that William would get me there in time. Mrs MacKenzie managed the place; she was one of those strict but kindly people who immediately took charge, and she soon made me feel confident that all was well. Dr Shares looked after me and, when Clarence was born, seemed to take great pride and interest in him, almost as if he was his own. Later, other new mothers told me that Dr Shares had this same fatherly manner with all the babies he helped into the world. He was a wonderful man.

It wasn't long before Tillie also became a mother again, and her second daughter, Marion Matilda, was born in Gull Lake. She and young Gladys had gone there with Frank a couple of months before as Frank was engaged in some building and plastering work and there was a nursing home in Gull Lake. A couple of weeks after Marion's birth, Frank brought them all back to stay at Minnie's home for a few days rest. Poor Tillie certainly needed it as, not only had she given birth but she had also endured the tortuous seventy mile journey from Gull Lake. Frank was as proud as could be but he had to get back to Gull Lake, though not before inviting William and George to the Brigden residence to share his celebration. William came home a bit worse for wear and only just got his boots off before falling fast asleep, and snoring through the night as only William could.

In fact, Tillie stayed with Minnie for several weeks, longer then the few days planned. Tillie was so weakened by the birth and the journey, and then got milk fever. She had much difficulty in feeding baby Marion because of the pain and high temperature. We brought the nurse to her who gave her some salve for the pain and also a herbal mixture which Tillie said tasted disgusting. But the remedies worked and in a couple of days she was on the mend, and baby Marion took happily to the breast again. Minnie said that the cabin was full to bursting, but Minnie's daughter, Florence, was delighted to have her two cousins to stay. Little Gladys was big enough to be a friend to play with, and they were both enthralled and amused by the new baby and her antics.

It seemed that illness was forever knocking on our door. Minnie was the next to succumb to major health problems. George sent Bert Haddleton, their neighbour, to tell us that she was not at all well, and William went over to collect Florence. George decided that there was nothing for it but to take Minnie to Shaunavon, and Bert agreed to go with him, and that was all the news I had when William came in with little Florence. It was a cold stormy day and the snows had already fallen heavily, and the only way was to take a team and sleigh. Minnie was wrapped up in robes, with a foot warmer. The men had to travel most of the night, taking it in turns to walk ahead of the team to make sure they were on the track. They arrived at Crosswaites' at the river early in the morning, and Mrs Crosswaite made them breakfast and hot tea. The overnight journey had taken it out of the men and horses, but not so badly as poor Minnie, who was chilled to the bone and struck down with a terrible pain in her abdomen. In fact, George told us later that she was begging them to leave her to die. Mrs Crosswaite did her best to raise her spirits and to get her warmed up and, once the team was fed and rested, Minnie rallied a bit and Mrs Crosswaite made sure she was well wrapped up and with the foot warmer reheated on the stove.

At Shaunavon, the doctor could do nothing for her as he couldn't do the operation that he thought was necessary. The only thing for it was for her to go to Weyburn, so George made arrangements for her to travel on the next train to Weyburn which was fortunately the next day. They stayed overnight at the doctor's home then Minnie was carried on to the train on a stretcher and George stayed with her throughout the journey, which took about half the day. Bert returned home with the sleigh and team and came by to report to William and me what was happening. I was so frightened and worried for my beloved sister. Everyday life on the prairie was hard enough, and hospital facilities were so far away both in distance and time. I was devastated that I may never see my sister, my best friend, ever again, and felt so helpless that I couldn't know what was happening. As it was, Minnie did have an operation, which went well, though she had to stay in the hospital for about three weeks, when she was able to return home again.

It was a very worrying time, and while Florence stayed with us, William was brought to his knees caring for all the land and animals. When Minnie returned, it took some time for her to get back to her usual hearty self. We weren't told what had brought her to be so ill, but now I can only think that it was appendicitis, and that we were very lucky not to have lost her.

Over the winter 1916 to 1917, Clarence came down with the whooping cough. He was only a few weeks old and not often did babies so young survive this dreadful disease. William and I took little Irene over to Minnie's, and then we speedily took him by sled to Dr Shares in Shaunavon who told us that the only way for Clarence to survive would be to feed him mare's milk. I was desperate as my darling baby boy was fading away before my eyes, too weak to fight the constant cough that was wracking his tiny frame. William went straight way and bought a mare and he trailed her back home behind the buggy. Many times a day, William was taken from his work with milking the mare. Sometimes she was hard to settle and William sustained some mighty bruises in the quest for Clarence's sustenance, but it all proved worthwhile. We fed Clarence warm mare's milk for many months and, against all fears and expectations, he not only survived but grew hearty and strong. William made us all laugh by suggesting that Clarence was becoming at strong as a horse! I'd never heard of this remedy before, and willingly shared the information with other mothers whose babies and children had succumbed to this frightening illness.

1917 saw a change in the policing of the area. No longer could we look forward to seeing the ranks of red-coated Mounties riding by. On 1st January, there was a new era of law enforcement. The Mounties were formed before I was born, first to deal with problems brought about by the Klondike Gold Rush, and to control the problems with the whisky traders and the local people, then their influence spread to policing the provinces. With the coming of the War, the Mounties were engaged in security and the war effort, so they could not be involved so much in local policing. So the Saskatchewan Provincial Police were formed under the leadership of Commissioner Charles Mahoney and new recruits were signed up. Some of the new policemen came from the Mounties, others had no previous policing experience, so there was always risk of some fairly rough justice. They carried revolvers and handcuffs and nightsticks, and not all wore a uniform. The newspaper carried regular reports of them tracking down criminals, not only common thieves but also cattle rustlers and murderers. Some of the police rode on horses, but they also had automobiles and motorcycles, and dog sleds when the snow lay on the ground.

Over the next two years, we worked hard on the land, ever looking for new ways to keep the wolf from the door. William had also taken on John's two parts of land in Section 24, so we had so much ground requiring betterment. At this time, George and William were hauling grain for McEwans and bringing back coal and supplies for our family and neighbours. The journey to Shaunavon was long and hard, and there was still no sign of the promised railroad coming closer to our land. One warm evening, we sat down for a family pow-wow outside Minnie's cabin and discussed the situation. The men had made a decision to give up the constant struggle of hauling grain over those roads, and the annual fight against the prairie wool and fires and floods and grasshoppers; they were going to try their hand at cattle and give up our dependence on grain farming, at least for the time being. This would provide us with cattle for market, with beef to eat, and could also offer other opportunities to extend the small business we already had in butter and cream.

William and George toiled hard together to add a cattle shed to the end of the big barn, hauling the timber from over the border in Montana, where lumber was plentiful; besides, the going was easier than the tortuous route to Gull Lake, and with the White Mud River to negotiate, so often swollen and the banks either heavily rutted or impossibly slippery and muddy.

We pursued ways of making the most of all possibilities with our new cattle venture. Not only did we have cows for beef and calves, which the men saw to, we also expanded our dairy side and that was up to Minnie and me to manage. George and Minnie bought a new Magnet cream separator so we would not have to bother with the tall milk churns anymore and, shortly after, Minnie also purchased a wooden barrel milk churn out of the butter money. Mr Roycroft claimed that it was the first one he had sold out of his store in

Shaunavon. Minnie was the business woman in all this; in fact she was always the better organised of the two of us, so I was often the one taking instructions from her and following her lead. There were always five or six milking cows in the summer, one or two in the winter months. Everything had to be kept at the right temperature or the cream was wasted. Minnie had a cool room at the end of her cabin, partly underground, to settle the cream. We churned and made the butter, packing it in crocks which we sold to our bachelor neighbours. Some of our butter we made in pound prints that we traded where we could.

As more people settled in the area, a general store was opened up by the Gryde family in Section 34 of our municipality. The new store was called Waldeville and was about five miles away. It stocked many of the basics, things we could not grow such as baking powder, tea and coffee, and things like shoes, hammers, nails, wire, dishes, pots and material for clothing. We rarely used cash as we traded our goods there, including our butter and eggs and some of our vegetables and meat. This saved us having to make so many journeys to Shaunavon. In fact, trips to Shaunavon and Gull Lake were now only for large supplies and for the markets there where we bought and sold livestock and produce.

We got snippets of news about the war in Europe from the newspaper but it all seemed so far away. It wasn't until 1917 that we started to get more information, and we were filled with pride at the exploits and achievements of the lads from Canada, thousands of them, and the nursing sisters who risked everything to go and help the sick and wounded in the battlefields. There were so many tragedies as well - sons of local families and our bachelor neighbours who would never be coming home. We heard about the Canadian flyers, two in particular, whose daring raids were having such an effect on the way the war was going. They were called Billy Barker and Billy Bishop.

Billy Bishop was from Owen Sound, Ontario on the far side of Canada, while Billy Barker was more of a local boy from Manitoba so we took particular interest in him. Minnie, Tillie and I started to look out for news of his exploits into France and Italy. We learnt that he grew up on a farm in Dauphin, about one hundred miles north of

Brandon, where we were both married. He joined the Rifles right at the start of the war, then in 1917 he started his career as a pilot, and that's when we began to hear about his great achievements. We were also entertained by his defiance, often in trouble for disobeying orders, and a bit of a dare-devil. His adventures as an ace flyer inspired and excited the nation, and quite possibly me and Minnie in particular. I recall that after the war he was acclaimed as the most decorated serviceman in the history of Canada, and indeed in the history of the British Empire and Commonwealth of Nations.

His exploits were even more exciting than any adventure story, because they were true. They brought such excitement to our demanding lives, and lifted our spirits and imagination whenever there was a new tale of his daring-do. We read how he was awarded the Military Cross in the Battle of the Somme, breaking up a force of four thousand German infantry. Later he was awarded the Bar to the Military Cross for his involvement in the Arras Offensive. Despite being wounded in the head, he was soon back on successful sorties over France, then later in Italy. We were amused to learn that, having shot up an airfield on Christmas Day 1917, he then dropped a placard wishing the enemy a Happy Christmas! In one of his most daring night-time raids, he flew a bomber to land a spy behind enemy lines.

In 1918, Billy Barker was posted to England, after being awarded the Distinguished Service Order for his great bravery and achievement, along with other French and Italian awards. He was transferred there to command the fighter training school at Hounslow Heath. Minnie, Tillie and I feared that we would hear no more of his exciting missions, but he was soon off to France and was involved in a dog fight with fifteen or more enemy aircraft. He was severely wounded in both legs and had his left elbow blown away, but continued to shoot down enemy aircraft. As a result, he spent several months in hospital in France and England. The next news that we heard of him was that he was awarded the Victoria Cross but was too badly injured to receive it at that time. He was later summoned to Buckingham Palace and there he was presented to the King and honoured for his bravery. How proud we were of this local lad who risked so much for us all, and gave us inspiration, as well as something and someone to focus on in that ghastly war.

I search for and find a newspaper cutting that I have kept from December 1918, after the war was mercifully at an end. The Canadian Daily Record wrote that:

"Lieutenant Colonel William G. Barker of Dauphin, Manitoba was the Canadian holding the record for most fighting decorations in the war. No other Canadian soldier, sailor or airman has surpassed this record. His Sopwith Camel aircraft is to be exhibited in the Canadian War Museum in Ottawa, Ontario. He is one of the legendary aces of the war and remains the most decorated Canadian in military service."

Reading more of the articles that I have kept from that time, I am reminded of battles in France at Arras, Amiens and Mons, and about the Hindenburg Line. One confrontation that made us all so proud was the Battle of Vimy Ridge, when all four divisions of the Canadian Corps operated together as one unit. Vimy Ridge was a strategically important ten mile area of high ground that was often fought over but had always been retained by the Germans. Our Canadian forces trained long and hard in preparation for the assault, including digging tunnels under the German lines filled with explosive ready to detonate immediately before the attack of the infantry took place. Other tunnels were also dug underground for the safety of our troops. We heard from one of our neighbours that their son had written home from the front that some Canadians were not keen on their underground home prior to the Battle as they suffered from claustrophobia.

Before the battle started, German positions were bombarded by one million artillery which, along with the underground explosions, caused great suffering to the enemy troops. When the Germans fired back in retaliation, our men used new optical and acoustic techniques to detect the position of the guns and so knew where to aim to knock out the guns.

Our Canadian lads then attacked the ridge in waves, one following the next, and pushed right through to the ridge itself. It took only three days to take the topmost point of Vimy Ridge, and the Germans retreated. It was a huge achievement and much was written about it, and we, as always, got great excitement from the newspaper accounts.

Everyone we met was talking about it, and greatly inspired by the success of our soldiers, and by those who were honoured with the

Victoria Cross for their bravery. But this was tinged with a huge sadness when we learnt of the thousands of young Canadians who had died. As the weeks went by, we started to hear of more young bachelor neighbours who had been lost. Others we never heard of or saw again but suspected the worst when their land remained unclaimed well after the war had finished. It was eventually taken back by the municipality.

In early September 1917, a letter came from our sister, Martha, who had been running the Post Office in Souris, Manitoba - about sixty miles from the Fallis family farms in Napinka and Melita. It brought some glad news.

Souris, MB
20th September 1917

Dearest Lizzie
(This includes Minnie and Tillie as well)

I have some exciting news. In one week I will be wed to Jack Russell (though everyone knows him as John). I'm sure you'll want to know all about him, and he has quite a tale to tell.

He was born in Scotland in 1901, and his name at that time was Harold Smelt. He was put up for adoption (I don't know why) and grew up as an orphan in the Dr Barnardo's Home in Weir, in Scotland. Then a lot of Barnardo's children, including John (or Harold as he was) were placed in the care of families in Canada. John (Harold) stayed with the Fingland family in Enterprise, Ontario.

As an adult, he changed his name to Jack Russell. (He told me that he wanted to leave his childhood behind and start afresh). He left the Finglands and took a job on the Canadian Pacific Railway. Then it was the War and he signed up and was posted to Europe. He was right in the thick of it and was wounded in the Battle of the Somme in 1916. He received many injuries in the fighting, and walked over 2 miles to get first aid. He was repatriated here to Souris and that's where he was befriended by Alderman Jim Bartlett. It was he who introduced us.

I expect it will be too difficult for you to come over for our wedding. Of course you're invited! I do hope you will get a chance to meet my John before too long. I know you'll like him.

With my love to you all,

Martha

Very sadly, we were not able to go to Martha's wedding, which was on 27th September.

1917 was the year that the first women in Saskatchewan gained the right to vote. It had started in Canada the previous year when all women in Manitoba had been given the vote, as well as the nursing sisters at the Canadian Hospital in France and some others. It wasn't until 1918 that Prime Minister Borden introduced a bill which was unanimously passed to give full suffrage to all Canadian women, though for some reason the women of Quebec were not included. Women's rights advanced quickly and only three years later, the first woman was elected to Parliament in Ontario. She was from Ontario and her name was Agnes Macphail. My sisters and I generally had little time for politics in our lives but we did take up our right to vote.

As in my childhood, I did love to read. That was one pastime that I always tried to find time for. I started to take an interest in the local aboriginal people, and their history in the area. From time to time, we came across them, though they generally kept themselves to themselves, mainly because they were forced to live apart from the homesteaders in areas specially designated to them. My dear neighbour, Elinor Fugelstadt, had come across a book that told their story, and she lent it to me. I was fascinated by the tales and traditions that surrounded these plains people, and felt a certain sadness that their lands had been so changed that their whole way of life was altered forever.

People had lived here on this land for almost eleven thousand years, during which time they established self-sustaining societies. In the 1700s, the Atsina people, also known as "Gros Ventre of the Prairies", lived on these plains. In the late 18th century, they were driven south by the Nehiyawak, or Plains Cree, and the Assiniboine. In 1855, they signed Lame Bull's Treaty and settled on Fort Belknap reservation in Montana in 1888, not far to the south of us, over the border in the United States.

I was fascinated to learn about the Cree and other First Nations people. They were the masters of living on the plains and put our attempts at prairie existence to shame. They were nomadic and relied on the mighty bison herds for their very survival. Not only did they eat the flesh, brains and liver of the bison, they also used every part of the creature to good effect. In summer, they boiled and dried the flesh to make pemmican for the long winter months. They used the tanned hide for tents and bags, and robes and boots, the bones and horns for tools, the fat for soap, the tongues for hairbrushes, the tendons for sewing thread and bowstrings, the rawhide for shields and bags, lassos and harnesses, the fur for blankets, the tail for flywhisks, the hoofs for rattles and glue, the stomach for water buckets and cooking vessels, and the dung for fuel. Nothing was wasted and everything had a use. To the Cree, the bison was the most perfect work of the Maker of All Things. They prayed to the Buffalo Spirit, praised him and asked his forgiveness when they borrowed his flesh and his hide. When there had been a successful hunt, they would leave the animal's heart on the ground, as if to sow the seed of a new animal.

There was other game on the plains in those days of plenty, and the Cree also hunted and ate antelope, deer, elk, moose and gophers, and they gathered berries and wild turnips to add to their diet. The wild prairie sage they used for seasoning, and they made bannock, a sort of bread, which they cooked over a fire. Early hunting had been on foot using spears, then the bow and arrow came into use. One method of killing large numbers of bison involved herding the creatures towards a cliff where they would fall to their deaths below. The women were then responsible for cutting and preparing, and the meat was hauled back to the camp, often on a travois, a sort of sledge made of poles lashed together.

Their tent homes were tipis, and they moved from place to place as the seasons and food dictated. At first they travelled everywhere on foot and dragged their homes and belongings behind sledges, drawn by women and dogs. With the introduction of horses, they used larger travois to move from one area to the next, and also to drag the butchered bison from the hunting grounds back to camp.

Then fur traders came and hunted the bison, greedily taking all they could and casting aside all but their pelts. With the coming of the fur traders and white settlers to southern Saskatchewan, the aboriginal way of life was threatened. Something had to be done to control the growing conflict between the white settlers and the First Nations people who were starving due to the decline of the bison population. In 1874, the Qu'appelle Treaty was signed but did little to solve the problems.

Locally, things got even worse in the late 1870's when the mixed-blood Metis people started moving to Shaunavon when discrimination forced them from Manitoba. They were the descendants of marriages between French fur traders and First Nations women. The Metis were nomadic and also dependant upon the bison for their existence, but there were not enough bison for everyone – the fur traders, the First Nations and now the Metis had come to add to the picture. So, the Metis found a new employment. With their Red River carts, they forged a living freighting goods from Swift Current to Battleford. They worked hard and held their community together, often having gatherings in schools for celebrations and traditional events. But this brought about mistrust and suspicion, and some settlers thought that the Metis were meeting to plot against them, and the Mounties got involved. The mix of economic problems and this new racism brought about great social tension and disharmony.

By 1880, four years before I was born, the once mighty herds of bison were almost completely eradicated; the fur trade had brought such a decline. The Metis and the First Nations Peoples had lost the very thing that they needed for existence. Things were made even worse as the settlers brought with them illnesses that were new to the aboriginal peoples, and many died as a result.

Elinor's book opened my eyes to what great change had come about due to the opening up of the prairies to homesteaders. Many of the Plains Cree and other First Nations people had either gone south, or were given land in one of the reservations that had been set up, deprived of their traditional way of life. I was aware of some makeshift Metis communities, and began to feel sad that the coming of the white man had imposed such a marginal existence upon them. They had no title to the land and so paid no taxes, so that meant that they were not entitled to send their children to school to get an education.

They owned so little and had no privileges, there was poor health and self-esteem, and there were no employment opportunities. But they were proud people and held their communities together as best they could, striving to preserve their traditions and to keep their own language, Michif, whose name amused me as it sounded for all the world like "Mischief"! I had read in the newspaper that many of the young men signed up to fight for Canada, their country, even though they were so poorly treated. Perhaps they hoped for some better acceptance within society, or most probably they looked for an escape from the impossible path that change had brought upon them and which offered them no clear promise for a brighter and fairer future.

With the war coming to an end in 1918, it took some time for things to get back to normal. So many brave young men had been lost, and it was some four years later that the figures were published telling us all how great the loss of Canadian lives had been. More than six hundred thousand Canadians had fought, with sixty thousand killed and one hundred and seventy thousand injured. It was hard to bear. But world peace had been fought for and established, and we all hoped and believed that such an event could never happen again. Of course, this was to prove a false dream.

A significant change came about as a result of the incredible contribution Canada made to the First World War. In recognition of her part in the war, Canada had its own representative at the Treaty of Versailles and was invited to sign the treaty as a separate nation, even though she remained part of the British Empire.

It wasn't long before there was a local post office, much nearer than Mr and Mrs Huseby's at Amelia; that took us a full day to visit. Half a mile from Waldeville Store, Sid Minty set up his business, and sending and receiving of mail became much easier as it was less than five miles away. We didn't have to wait for so long to post and collect our letters to and from Mother in Coolnagranchy, and trips to the post office also meant an opportunity to see Tillie, who lived only a mile from there. I do remember that I felt a bit sad that dear Mrs Huseby had lost our custom. I had always enjoyed a chat with her, but needs must and any shortening of prairie journeys helped to contribute towards an improvement in life and was always welcomed. Time was so precious, with the amount we tried to achieve in such a short season. The striving for betterment of the land, the care of the animals – and ourselves, the constant fight against the cruelty of the elements, all contributed to the need to make the most of every moment of every day. We worked until we dropped, but we still made time to play when we could, and we got great joy from celebrations and home-made entertainment with our neighbours and friends. When anyone left to live elsewhere we all felt a sense of loss, and we welcomed any newcomers heartily into our prairie family. Sometimes language caused a barrier, as settlers came from far and wide. With those from Canada and America, we only had to overcome strange accents, and there was often much amusement at what seemed to be an odd pronunciation. Those from Germany, Holland, Finland and Sweden, all sounded the same to us, though most did their best to learn the language of their adopted new home. There were some settlers from as far away as South Russia, and they seemed to prefer to keep themselves to themselves. I was told that they came to Canada to escape persecution, whereas most had left their home countries to seek their fortunes in the prairies.

With the ending of the War and the coming of the local post office, at last we were able to get letters out to Mother, telling her all our news, and we were also able to announce the birth of yet another grandson, Francis Evelyn, to Martha and John on 26th June 1918. We were overjoyed in the new year when a letter reached us from Coolnagranchy. My letter had not yet reached Mother; our letters had crossed in the post, so she was not aware of our news from the war years. Funnily enough, I had written to her on the same day as her letter to me and sent it almost immediately when the visiting trader called with fare for Christmas that we had not seen for several years.

20th December, 1918

My dear Lizzie

How ghastly life has been over these past five years, with no chance to talk to each other. I hope you will share my letters in future with your sisters if you can. More and more I am troubled with arthritis, and writing is becoming a difficulty - but I shall persevere.

There are no Coolnagranchy Monsons at school anymore. Queenie was the last and finished three years ago. Sarah Jane and Eva have moved to County Down and are both engaged to be married, Sarah Jane to Jim Haire. Do you remember him from over at Carrick-on-Shannon? Eva has met a young man called Thomas Phillips, but we know little about him.

Your brother John came home recently and, as ever, he had a tale to tell! He was called up for the army and after his training he was posted to Perim Island in the Red Sea, which is a hostile place where few white men survive. Usually no-one was posted there for longer than three months, but for some reason they lost track of John and he was there for over two years. They finally caught up with him during a medical inspection and the doctors were amazed that he was still alive. When they asked if he was taking anything special to stay so healthy he said, "drinking all the rum I can get my hands on!" He told stories about fishing for Red Sea snappers as the rations were so meagre, and often non-existent.

Another of his tales concerned an escaped German prisoner who had stowed away on a ship. He was caught and dropped off at Perim Island and locked up in the camp prison cell. One Saturday evening, it was John's turn to be on guard duty and the other soldiers went off to a tavern in a village about a mile away. John didn't want to miss out so he unlocked the prisoner and made it clear to him that if he tried to escape he would shoot him! He marched him to the village and they joined the others in the tavern and spent the evening there. He then marched the prisoner back to camp and locked him up again.

After his long spell on Perim Island, John was posted to Bombay in India where he was quartermaster of a barracks. He remained there until just recently when he came here to Ireland to collect his wife and sons who have stayed with us here at Coolnagranchy during the war. John only stayed for a short visit. How we laughed and laughed at his tales of Perim Island, and his amusing descriptions of the people in Bombay and the funny way they talk. Your brother never ceases to surprise and amuse us all. He and the family have now returned to Scotland and we've heard that John has found a job as a stoker. I shall miss Jessie and the 3 little lads. She has been such good company and it's been good to have some young ones in the house again. Thomas is now 10, James 8 and John Duke already 6. He was only just 2 when they came. Their father can see such a change in them.

You might be interested to hear that your London cousin, Hasluck, was married two years ago to Clara Selena May Walker from Margate in Kent. We received a photograph of the wedding with both their parents and grand-parents, and with several brothers and sisters in attendance. It was nice of them to think of us, perhaps because you spent that time staying with the family before you set off on your travels.

During the war years, there have been further changes in government and so on. Just as the war was starting, the Ulster Unionists introduced the partition of Ireland, but it was postponed due to the war. But problems and differences continued, with different groups wanting different things for Ireland, and the Irish Republican Brotherhood began to prepare for a revolt against British rule.

It all came to a head in Dublin over Easter of 1916. The Republicans seized the government buildings and issued a Proclamation of The Irish Republic. By the end of April, the leaders of the uprising were forced to surrender. Over 400 people died and the newspaper said that the British executed the leaders and arrested thousands of people. We've heard a lot about the British army unit called the Black and Tans. They seem to have no discipline and are brutal and murder innocent civilians. People were outraged and it started a lot of bad feeling.

Then earlier this year, they talked about Home Rule and tried to introduce conscription of our young men to help with the fight in Germany. That was too much, and we had the chance to vote in the General Election. Sinn Fein were victorious, winning 73 of the 105 seats, and pledged not to sit in the British Government.

It's hard to know who to support. The Catholics seem to be driving the call for independence, and obviously we are not

Catholics, but the English do not seem to care much about the Irish people. I think your Uncle George finds things hard as he's an Irishman but also he is a supporter and friend of Mr Lloyd George, the British Prime Minister.

Things are starting to change here. Many folks from the area whose families have always worked the land are now leaving to get jobs in the new factories that are springing up in the bigger towns, and also in the north and in Scotland. With Sarah Jane and Eva going north, that leaves me and your Father at home, with only Lillian, Blanche, Kate, Thomas and Queenie - already seventeen and quite the young lady as I'm sure you won't be surprised! Everyone is quite big enough to look after themselves, so there are no more babies and little ones for me to care for. In ways, it's a relief, but so strange to me as it has been the main industry of my married life. I imagine that you and your sisters are all mothers by now. How I would so love to be able to help you with your little ones, all so far away.

There's not much more to tell really, except we're getting that bit older, and that I get tired quite quickly, and these perishing pains in my bones are slowing me down. I am now fifty three, and your father is sixty four, but of course you're now a woman of thirty four and it's already ten years since you left us! I still miss you, as you were always there to help me out with the children and the chores. Of course I miss your sisters too. Lillian is proving to be a great blessing to me; she's a gentle and caring young woman and always willing.

Don't forget to share this letter with your sisters. I look forward to your news from Saskatchewan - what a funny name it is. I'm sure you will have news of many grand-children for me from my four daughters. I was so sad to hear of the loss of your first baby, and hope that fortune has smiled on you since. I would love to meet Minnie's babies, but that's not likely, is it. Maybe some photographs would be possible.

From all at Coolnagranchy, With love, Mother

While I read this letter, I hoped that Mother had received my news; our letters had crossed in the post. I thought sadly of some of the tragedies I hadn't been able to share with her during the war: the deaths of Minnie's two sons, Herbie, in 1914, and tiny Baby John in 1915, and the tragic accident that had befallen William's brother, John. Mother would have loved to meet our other babies. The war years had seen the births here on the prairie of my two children: my daughter, Martha Irene, who for some reason we always called Irene, and my son, Clarence William, and also Tillie's two little girls, Gladys Lenore and Marion Matilda. Edith Lenore was the name of Hasluck's sister, and I think that had inspired Tillie to choose it as baby Gladys' second name. By the end of the war, Minnie's Florence was already six, and I was pregnant again with my new baby due the following spring. Back in Manitoba, in Souris, Martha's first baby, Francis Evelyn had recently been born, though Minnie, Tillie and I had not been able to visit. It was going to be news to Mother that Tillie and Martha had even got married, let alone having babies!

We started to get more regular bulletins from the rest of the world as well as local news. One of the items that came to our notice was to do with bootleggers. At that time in Saskatchewan, it was illegal to make, sell and buy liquor. A local man, Peter Druar, was known for his home brewed alcohol, and for some time he had served those who wished to buy liquor without getting noticed by the authorities. I know that William and George had been known to slip him some eggs or similar in return for the odd celebratory brew. A new constable came to the

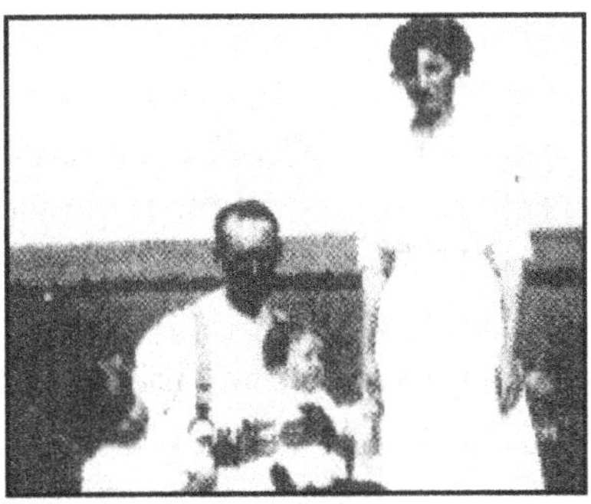

1918 Tillie and Frank Brigden with Gladys and Marion.

district and made it his business to come down hard on the bootleggers. He let it be known that he would reward anyone who brought any illegal activity to his notice. The policeman was not popular and, after all, it wasn't in anyone's interests to end the local supply of alcohol, so we were surprised to hear that Peter Druar's name had come up. No-one came forward as far as we knew, and when the constable chanced upon Peter Druar, the authorities made an example of him. He went to court and was imprisoned for four years. His wife and three children found life very hard while he was away. We were very sad for them and helped them when we could. It was no fault of theirs, and Peter Druar was a likeable man. Prohibition had ended by the time he was a free man again.

In the summer of 1918, we got news from Shaunavon that eighteen businesses, along with The Kennedy Hotel, had been destroyed by fire. The newspaper said it was thought to have started in The Kennedy and then spread rapidly, the flames fanned by the winds whipping off the prairie. No-one was sure if it was by accident or intent. It came at the end of a very dry spell when prairie fires were frequent, so it seemed quite likely that dry timbers may have been victim to a spark and it caught very quickly. Luckily no-one was hurt, but the fire fighters struggled over two days to ensure that the fire didn't spread further into the town. The blaze destroyed a large area of the town, and at the final reckoning it was estimated that it had cost over three hundred and fifty thousand Canadian dollars.

1918 was not a good year on our farms. It was the first of several very dry years, and the summer months presented us with one disaster after another. The lack of rain brought a shortage of grazing grass for the cattle, so we had to fall back on hay and grain to feed them. The few calves that were born were small and weak and needed special attention; two of them were deformed and only lived a few days. Although we had moved to cattle, we still kept some land arable to provide for the animals, and ourselves, and it proved harder than usual to plough the land that year. Everyone's spirits were at a low, and even lower when the grasshoppers struck and stripped everything bare. The optimism brought by the news that the war had ended, was soon damped by the hardships brought about by the weather. We were lucky to still have some foodstuffs for the animals left from the winter's supply.

A long dry summer always means fire, and dust. Once the prairie grass has been ploughed and the earth has nothing to bind it, the prairie wind easily lifts it into clouds of dry choking dust. Late 1918 was a year when the dust was everywhere. The cabins were filled with it, our clothes were covered. It got in our hair and our eyes and the food and water. Our teeth crunched on the gritty grains and wearing a scarf as a gag to help keep it from our faces wasn't really any help. The animals were tormented by it. There was no escape. If it rained, the water just ran off the land, and puddles and lakes and floods were formed. Tillie's husband, Frank, got very sick that winter. At first it was a cough, probably brought about by the relentless dust. But it settled on his chest and turned into pneumonia.

We had heard from Grandpa Fallis that he was to retire that fall, so George and William decided to take Minnie and me and the children back to Manitoba to farm their father's land. We set to packing up and selling most of the stock. George and William decided to take most of the horses with us. We weren't sure when we would be back. In October, we set off on the long and now familiar journey to Napinka, but were able to join the train in Shaunavon, much sooner than the early days before the steel came when we had to make the tedious journey north to Gull Lake. This was a great relief to me as I was expecting another baby in the spring and the pregnancy was proving hard and uncomfortable.

It took some time to arrange adequate accommodation for us all, but gradually life settled and the winter wasn't too bad. Florence started school that winter, aged almost seven. Minnie had intended to get her formal education started sooner, but it wasn't always easy to get things organised. Minnie and I had done our best to teach Florence to read and write, so she was not far behind the other children. School was only a fifteen minutes walk away and she quickly made friends with Molly from the next farm. Minnie or I walked her over to Molly's each morning, then Florence and Molly set off hand in hand and with their little bags on their shoulders, very grown up that they were allowed to walk to school together without a parent. Florence loved her new school and her new friends. Before that, there were few children of her age to play with. She took on a new confidence, and delighted in telling her cousins, my Irene and

Clarence, now three and two, about school and the new things she was learning. It wasn't long before the children were playing at their own imaginary school, with Florence the teacher and the little ones the pupils. I was happy to see them play and to know that school would hold no fears for them. My brother John had suffered such nightmares at Ardsellagh when we were young. Any fears I had that little Clarence would be troubled in the same way were fast dispelled; he already started to know his letters and he was a very confident and easy-going little toddler.

Back at the homesteads, we heard that the winter was as hard as the summer had been. The snow was at its heaviest and we worried for Tillie and Frank and the girls. And we had good reason to be anxious. In the spring, we got news from Tillie about Frank's illness. She thought that the pneumonia would take him from her; it was quite touch and go for two or three weeks. She had never been able to get the doctor to him as it was too cold to venture out and besides the snow was too deep and she couldn't leave the girls. We always thought that Tillie could have been a nurse, and Frank was truly blessed that she took such good care of him. We heard of others that winter who had not survived the pneumonia.

6

Struggling on

1919-1928

My pregnancy improved after Christmas, and I started to get stronger again. I thought my baby would be born in the middle of February, but she hung on and waited till March, but only just! On 1st March, we had another daughter. We called her Lorraine Victoria. She so reminded me of my baby sister Queenie, who's real name was Victoria, so when William and I were looking for a second name for our new arrival, my choice was clear.

Later that spring, Tillie wrote to us in Napinka, greatly relieved that Frank had overcome his illness and was getting stronger. At last he was able to work again. She said that 1919 was starting out to be another very dry year in Saskatchewan and that things were desperate for many back in Lone Tree; that was the name that had been given to our municipality, and it was certainly well chosen as there were very few trees in the area. She and Frank were fortunate that Frank had worked so hard on his land when he first arrived in 1910 and already got title within three years, before he and Tillie had wed. They were not so dependent on the land as Frank's work as a builder and plasterer provided for them and their daughters, Gladys and Marion, now aged four and three. It did mean though that Frank was often away, leaving Tillie and the girls alone on the farm for days or even weeks at a time. Tillie got very lonely and nervous while Frank was away and she would run home and lock herself in the cabin if strangers were passing. It didn't help that Minnie and I were now away in Manitoba and not able to visit regularly or to be on hand in case of problems.

Because of the bad summers, one on another, several people were abandoning their homesteads and moving into town. Tillie wrote to us that she was relieved that their farm was not so far from Waldeville Store and Sid Minty's Post Office where she could go for a chat with the women who served there. She missed female company, and so many of the families had moved away from the land. The only neighbours left were bachelors and, nice as they were, they weren't much interested in woman talk.

Minnie and I so missed Tillie and our outings in the buggy to visit her and the girls. We talked of those happy times, always such fun. When we were at the homesteads, our lives were lifted by those trips, with Bob the horse jogging along and Minnie at the reins, ever more confident than I when it came to so many things. This included driving the buggy. Even the children missed the entertainment that we had, and they all loved Bob, with his black shiny back and the white blaze star on his face. Time spent with Tillie and other neighbours on our little expeditions around Lone Tree and Climax were precious to us all, and we so missed those opportunities. It was a chance to get out of our working clothes and smarten up, and to discuss the great challenges and difficulties that filled our lives, and problems with the children and the various illnesses that forever seemed to trouble them. It was also a time to relax and find something to laugh about together – and there was always something. Life in Napinka didn't seem to offer any of this. We were tied to the family and the farm, and there were few people for us to visit with Bob and the buggy.

Any spare time was spent keeping in touch with the news, both local and international, and we got to rely on the local Napinka newspaper. We looked forward to its weekly news and articles when we could get hold of a copy. 1919 was a significant year in the history of Canada. Convinced that the nation had proven itself on the battlefields of Europe, our Prime Minister Robert Borden demanded that we should have a separate seat at the Paris Peace Conference that year. The British Prime Minister at this time was David Lloyd George, and he opposed the idea.

I always took particular interest in any news that involved Mr Lloyd George as he was a regular visitor to the house when I stayed with my Aunt and Uncle in London. I was always fascinated by his sing-song Welsh voice. Minnie was ever amused at my great pride in announcing that I had met Lloyd George and brought him refreshments at my Uncle's house!

On the Parish Peace Conference, Robert Borden was standing firm, despite the fact that, not only Lloyd-George and Britain were against it, but also the United States for their own reasons. They saw it as an extra British vote. Robert Borden responded by pointing out that Canada had lost a larger proportion of its men than the Americans. Its right to equal status as a nation had been consecrated on the battlefield. Lloyd George eventually relented, and convinced the reluctant Americans to accept the presence of delegations from not only Canada, but also India, Australia, Newfoundland, New Zealand and South Africa. These nations also received their own seats in the League of Nations. As it turned out, Canada only took a modest role at the Paris Conference, which marked the end of the war and the terms for peace, but just having a seat was a matter of pride and the newspapers made a great play on it. However, when it came to its place on the new League of Nations, Canada went on to play an active and independent role. These were the first steps in Canada's independence from the United Kingdom.

There was news from Mother which also involved Mr Lloyd George, but it didn't seem so good. He seemed to have such influence in so many different parts of the world. We were all just getting over the terrible war in Europe, but dreadful things were happening back in Ireland it seemed. The letter took longer than usual to reach us as Mother had sent it to Climax and it was then forwarded to us at Napinka.

30 June 1919

Dearest Lizzie

You can't imagine what's going on here in Ireland. No sooner had the lads returned from the war in Europe than things started happening nearer to home. It's all to do with a determination to be independent from Great Britain. I do support it but I don't like the things that are happening. There is a war here at home and the Irish people are fighting to be free of the English. I'm fairly sure that I told you about the Easter Rising in Dublin in 1916 when the people rose up against the Constabulary. Over four hundred people were killed, and the British Army was brought in. They were cruel and unruly, and murdered several innocent people. People have become more and more determined to get the British out and to have home-rule.

Last year, the British tried to bring in conscription in Ireland, and everything really came to the boil. In December, the Sinn Fein Republicans won the General Election - a huge victory - and in January, the First Dail of the Republic met and issued a declaration of independence from the United Kingdom. Then some Republican soldiers killed two members of the Constabulary, and that set off the trouble. They're calling this the War of Independence. There is an Independent Republican Army and they are fighting the Constabulary and the British, who are fighting back hard. Generally the people have been getting involved only by striking and making trouble where they can and with no appetite for the military approach. But things are changing and we're now hearing that the English and Constabulary approach is likely to lead to more violence because the people are joining the fight. We do our best not to express an opinion, being Church of Ireland as we are. Some of the local Catholic families who have long been our friends, now seem reluctant to pass the time of day. It's all very uncomfortable.

I thought I'd write now as I really don't know where it's all leading to. I'll write again when I can.

Apart from this, we are all well enough, and feeling blessed that not one of us went under with last year's influenza epidemic. So many people died and I've heard that it was mainly quite young folk aged between twenty five and thirty five. We didn't go into town during the worst periods. The newspaper said that 23,000 are dead in Ireland alone. They called it the Black Flu because people turned black, and there was also the Spanish Flu and that was the worst and took people out really quickly. In the morning they could be fine and well, and by night they could be dead. As I said, we feel such relief that we have all been spared.

There was some excitement a couple of weeks ago and it was all reported in the Connacht Tribune - Tom Kenny got the first *interview. Two fliers called Alcock and Brown won a competition to be the first to fly across the Atlantic from America to Ireland in less than seventy two hours. In fact the flight only took about sixteen hours and they landed in a bog in Galway. You can hardly believe it - their prize was £10,000 from an English newspaper and then Tom Kelly reported the next week that they were knighted by King George V. If £10,000 wasn't enough, they were also given another £3,000 from Ardath Tobacco and others. Whatever will they do with so much money?*

Everyone sends their love.

Mother

There was such mixed news from home, but the political troubles were not good. I shared the letter with Minnie that evening and we sat together and wept for our family, trapped in such terrible times. We had been feeling a sense of relief that the war in Europe was over and that, although things had changed, life was settling back into its routine. It seemed that this was not the case back in our homeland.

Although Minnie and I were staying in Manitoba and our sister Martha lived in the same province, her home in Souris was too far away from us in Napinka for regular visits. She seemed happily settled and ran the Post Office there. She and John married there in 1917. They had one son, Francis Evelyn, born in 1918, but at that time Minnie and I had never seen him. We made plans to visit them in September, but the weather changed suddenly with torrential rain and floods and that put paid to the trip, at least for the time being.

The whole of that 1919 to 1920 winter was stormy and wet. William and George called a pow-wow for us all to discuss whether we would stay in Napinka or return to the homesteads in Saskatchewan. Really, the Napinka farm was not big enough for our expanding families, and besides we had made a commitment to better our Saskatchewan land. Minnie and George wanted to get back to the homestead and decided that they would leave in the spring. William and I took some more time to make up our minds; after all we had three young children and Lorraine was still only a baby. Finally, we talked with Grandpa Fallis and it was decided that we would let out the Fallis lands in Napinka and Melita to a neighbouring farmer. Grandpa Fallis and William's stepmother would stay in the farmhouse but would be relieved of the main responsibility of the land. This agreed, we made plans to get back to the homesteads.

Just before we set off at the beginning of April 1920, we heard from Martha that she had a new baby daughter, Kathleen Louise. Our family seemed good at producing daughters. Mother and Father had ten daughters and two sons. Now we girls were keeping with the tradition. Martha, Tillie, Minnie and I had between us six daughters and only two sons.

The journey back to the homesteads was uneventful, if travelling with four children and a demanding baby can ever be so, not to mention the horses and livestock that we were taking back to the land with us. Florence was just eight by then, and we all used to say that she was born sensible! She was certainly a great help to me with the little ones. While we were on the train, we celebrated Irene's fifth birthday, just a couple of days after Easter. It was quite a thrill for her as her only previous rail trip was when we came to stay at Grandpa Fallis' in Napinka two years before and she really was not well at the time so it had been quite an ordeal for her. That time she had not been old enough to enjoy the adventure. But most excited of anyone was Clarence, then aged nearly three and a half, who loved trains more than anything in the world even though he had rarely seen them. He couldn't contain his happiness, and he was a constant worry, rushing here and there to look out the window or see what was happening in other parts of the carriage. During the journey, which took best of four days, George and William took it in turns to check the animals in the stock car, and sometimes took Clarence with them, much to his great joy. You can imagine Clarence's delight when one of the passengers whittled him a little model engine. Once Clarence was aware of the young man with his sharp knife and block of wood, he sat patiently, watching the little engine take shape, enthralled by the industry of the craftsman, and politely asking him questions. He told the young settler, whose name was Jim, that the train would soon be coming to Climax, near our home. When the last trimming and smoothing was completed, Clarence must have been the happiest little boy in the whole of Canada. From then on, he drove his little train over everything he could: the seats, the floor, the walls, the windows, the bags, the family, making train noises as he went.

I thanked the young man, and learned that he had registered land near Shaunavon and had just been to Swift Current to get the title as he had achieved the required betterment. He told me that he had fought in the war and seen some horrible things, and now he just wanted to work hard and put that all behind him. Now that he had title on his land, he hoped to find himself a wife and have a family. I wished him well, and thanked him for his kindness to Clarence. While the children slept, we talked with him for some time about the challenges of life on the prairie and how hard George and Minnie, William and I had so often found things since our arrival in 1910. He spoke of his family back in Ontario, which interested me as that was where the Fallis family originally farmed and Frank Brigden, Tillie's husband, also came from there. He wouldn't be drawn to talk about his experiences in the war; it was obvious that he had suffered greatly and wouldn't, or probably couldn't, bring himself to talk of it. He noticed that Minnie and I had an Irish accent and asked us about that, and we related tales of our childhood and the reasons that we, and two others of our sisters, had left our homeland for new opportunities here in Canada. We also told him of our recent news from Ireland and about the terrible times there. We laughed together when I said that it was a case of 'out of the frying pan, into the fire'.

Once the train had reached Gull Lake, some of the wagons, including ours, split off to go down the Shaunavon spur drawn by a new locomotive. There was always so much noise and clamour at stations, with much shouting and frantic activity. William and George went off to check that our goods and stock were heading the right way, then we were ready for the last leg of our journey, signalled by the blast from the locomotive's horns. The mighty engine pulled away, with the long slow whoof of the first steam, building and building to set the train in motion, the wagons and trucks and carriages taking up the slack with a clatter, and then the whole thing clicking and clacking, engine and wagons and steel rails working together to carry us on our way again. Clarence was enrapt at the whole proceedings, dashing across from one side to the other, regardless of whose toes he stepped on, and pressing his little nose against the windows.

Finally we arrived at Shaunavon, and George dashed off to see to the stock and our wagon while William gave Minnie and me a hand with the children and the baggage, and Jim was also a great help getting the bags off. We bade him farewell and wished him luck.

We all met up with George at the stockyard, then made ready for the trek back to the homesteads, which was about thirty miles. We didn't expect to get home until late into the evening. Minnie took me, Clarence and baby Lorraine in the buggy drawn by Bob. The two older children, Florence and Irene, sat between George and William in the wagon, pulled by four horses. The wagon was piled high as there were four crates on board, one with twenty chickens, another with two pigs, one full of household wares, and the last containing farm machinery. We had also shipped twenty cattle with us from Napinka, and George had arranged with the local stockman that they would be herded for us to the land. Irene was happy to travel with the pigs; she had a special love of pigs for some reason and chatted away to them and they seemed to snort and chatter back.

We made good time and arrived at George and Minnie's cabin and decided to get the children bedded down; we would then see to things in the morning. The cabin was cold and damp, which wasn't surprising as there had been no-one there for such a time and the winter weather had been so wet. Minnie and I got the stove going while William and George saw to the animals. They put the horses in the big barn, and left the pigs and chickens in their crates.

Life soon settled down again and it was time for Irene to start school. Minnie's daughter Florence had been attending the school in Napinka while we were away at Grandpa Fallis' farm, but she would now be starting at Glenedyth School which was about two miles away in Climax. Irene was also old enough to start school and Minnie and I arranged to share the task between us of getting the girls to school in the buggy. Tillie also brought her daughter, Gladys, down to Glenedyth, about three miles distance. This was a happy time as we sometimes had a chance for a chat with Tillie before heading back to tackle the daily chores.

On the first day, Minnie, Tillie and I all went with the girls to their new school. I left Clarence and baby Lorraine with our neighbour, Mrs Movold, and Tillie left Marion in the care of William Dell's sister. There was always a will amongst homesteaders to help each other out.

We were invited to take a look around the school and to meet the teachers. I remember comparing Glenedyth to Ardsallagh School, where my sisters and brothers and I had attended all those years ago when Coolnagranchy was our home. I felt that, in many ways, our children were so much luckier.

1920 Glenedyth School, Climax.

Glenedyth School was a grand building, built in stone and two storeys high. It had a central doorway. In the entrance hall to the school, there were hooks so the students could hang up their outdoor clothing, and shelves for the lunch pails. There was a stand with a washbasin and a pail of water where the children could wash their hands with soap and water. One hand towel was shared by everyone, so it got very wet. The water was brought in pails from the well at the back of the school and the older students took turns collecting it. Drinking water was kept in a separate pail on a table and everyone could take a drink using the metal dipper that hung on a hook beside.

Leading from the entrance hall, there were two large classrooms downstairs, and the stairway led to two more large classrooms upstairs. All the classrooms had windows all along the back and front of the building to let in the light. At the back of each classroom there was a wood-burning stove, with a tidy pile of logs stacked beside. Large overhead stove-pipes ran from the stove to the main stone chimney and helped to warm up the classrooms. This was so different from Ardsallagh School, where the stove was fuelled by turf, not wood, with mucky piles of turf stored in the front hall. It's hard to forget that pungent smoke that filled the air and our clothes with a lasting smokiness.

The downstairs classrooms at Glenedyth were for the younger children, and the older children aged ten to fourteen had their lessons upstairs. There was plenty of ground outside the school surrounded by a boundary fence, and entry was at the boundary gate with a wide path leading to the main door. In the grounds were outhouses which contained the toilets, a separate one for boys and girls, and a store for wood and coal. Each term, we parents would bring wood and coal to fill the store and this went towards paying the school fee. At the side of the school building, there was also a play area with swings and a teeter-totter which had been built by some of the parents. We were all very proud of the school and happy to help with jobs and maintenance.

Just outside the boundary fence was the teacherage, a cabin where the teachers could live during the school terms. We were lucky to have four teachers at Glenedyth, and in turn they were lucky to have somewhere to stay that was close to their place of work.

As well as four teachers, there were also four assistants, who lived in the area. Some of them were not much older than the senior students. The classrooms were bright, lit by natural light and oil lamps mounted on the walls; they were draught free and warm, so different from the chilled and smoky two rooms at Ardsallagh. The classrooms had the usual desk and chair for the teacher, but on a slightly raised platform so she could keep an eye on everyone, and there were desks for the students that were bolted to the floor, not the mighty tables and hard benches that we had back in our childhood school.

Irene and Gladys started school in the same downstairs classroom, while Florence was in the other room downstairs. As well as the desks and chairs, each room had three blackboards, and bookshelves with school books and slates. In Florence's classroom, there was also a large bottle of ink and a pot of quill pens. The teacher explained to us that the younger children learnt their letters using slates and chalk, with rags for rubbing out, then the older children were taught to use pen and ink once they progressed to the fourth form at the age of eight. The school subjects were reading, writing, arithmetic, spelling and geography, much the same as when we were growing up. Each classroom had a few books. These included primers which contained the letters of the alphabet, numbers, some spelling words, simple stories and poems. Then there were readers, at different levels. They contained poems, stories and lessons in nature and history. Aesop's Fables were popular because the stories were short and each story taught a moral lesson. There was also a Bible which was not only used for bible teaching but also for reading.

In each upstairs classroom, there was a globe of the world for teaching geography, an abacus for counting, and a yardstick ruler. Every classroom had a pointer stick for pointing to the blackboard, and on the wall by the door was a list of rules. Minnie, Tillie and I stood and read the page and we were pleased at the level of discipline set down for our girls and the other children.

Respect and obey the teacher
Accept the punishments the teacher gives you
Do not call the classmates names or fight
Do not disturb others as they are working
Be silent; do not talk unless necessary
Feet flat on the floor, hands on the desk
Raise your hand if you wish to speak
When given permission to speak, stand up by your desk, then speak
Do not leave your seat without permission
No more than one student may go to the washroom
Go quietly in and out of the classroom
Do your duties if told to

Little Gladys was such a chatterbox, we feared that she might at first have some difficulties with keeping silent, or going quietly about the school, but all in all we felt that the rules were fair and about right. We hoped none of our children would be singled out for the strap which hung by the teacher's desk.

At home each morning, there were chores to be done before we set off for school, and the children had their fair share of doing the dishes, shaking the mats and sweeping the floor, collecting eggs, and making sure that they had everything prepared. When we got to school, they were to wait outside. Some children came to school by horse, and they had to tie them up at the back of the school. When the teacher came out with the hand bell, the students were to line up in size order, smallest to tallest with girls on one side, boys on the other. Once the bell rang, they entered the school in silence, hung up their coats and went straight to their classrooms, putting their lunch pails on the shelf provided. Our girls had lunch pails that we made from lard pots and added a handle, and lunch was whatever was available at the time, perhaps a sandwich or some hard-boiled eggs, maybe some pancakes or dried meat. If we had any potatoes, we cooked them in the morning and the children had them for lunch, and if the weather was cold they carried them in their hands to keep them warm, or we gave them warmed rocks wrapped in a cloth.

The only children who didn't have to wait outside were some of the older students who came earlier to help the teachers with preparation. The older girls were tasked with doing errands for the teachers while the boys brought in wood from the woodpile and pails of water from the well for drinking and hand-washing, and they filled the oil lamps. The toilets were checked and the girls were responsible for tearing squares of newspaper and threading them on to strings to hang on a hook on the back of the door, and making sure that there was a rag available for wiping hands. The teachers or some of the older students lit the stove before school began so the rooms had time to warm up, and they lit the oil lamps if it was dark. If it was too cold indoors everyone wore their coats till it warmed up, which was sometimes all day if the stove would not light or the weather was particularly bitter.

School followed a similar pattern each day, with prayers and songs to start, and the morning was taken up with reading, penmanship, arithmetic, and spelling. Then it was time to wash hands and have lunch, followed by the part of the day that the children liked best which was recess and they could play outside. The children who rode to school were responsible for the care of the animals during the lunchtime recess, and they joined the other children for games as soon as they could. Our girls reported to us each evening about what they had learnt, and also about any rough and tumble that the boys had engaged in, which often led to trouble and punishments and the use of the strap. Lunch recess was time for games and they loved to play hopscotch, and jump-rope, Follow the Leader, Blind Man's Bluff, Red Rover, Mother May I, and Hide and Seek. They also played circle games like Duck-Duck-Goose, and Drop the Handkerchief, tag games like Freeze Tag, Elbow Tag, Pom-pom-pull Away, and Mr. Wolf. When the teacher rang the bell, students rushed to the door of the school and lined up. In the winter they built snow forts or slid down snow banks, and when the yard was covered with freshly fallen snow, Fox and Geese was a favourite. Afternoon lessons varied with history and geography and some other main subjects.

Each day, the bell rang at the end of afternoon school, and all children collected their coats and pails and waited outside, whatever the weather. The only exception to this was again the older students, who were tasked to sweep, dust and tidy the classrooms, clean the blackboards, clean the windows, and empty the ash from the wood stoves. They were joined by those who misbehaved who were given extra chores before they were allowed home. From time to time, the chimneys needed sweeping, and this was a task that was taken on by some of the older boys, and some of the fathers traded their time against school fees for this and other maintenance tasks.

Minnie and I took it in turns to collect Florence and Irene, and sometimes there was time to chat with Tillie when she came for Gladys. There never seemed enough hours in the day, and we all had to get home to finish the day's chores and to get the dinner. Sometimes the children would have some instruction to pass on to us from their teacher, or announced that they had nits in their hair; it seemed that nits were universal and would be around for all time. There was never much time to spare, a snatched hello or a wave. We hurried the girls into the buggy which we used when we could, otherwise we brought the sleigh when the snow was on the ground.

But there were days when the girls didn't get to school. From time to time they were ill and couldn't go. During harvesting and planting seasons, there were days when we just couldn't spare the time to take the girls to school. Also severe weather conditions, either snow or torrential rains that made the tracks so muddy that they were impassable, sometimes forced us to keep the girls at home. There were even times when Glenedyth was closed for part of the winter. Little Clarence always liked these days best as he had his sister, and often his cousin, to play with. He couldn't wait to start school with the others, and longed to have other little boys to play with. It wasn't so long before his turn came.

When they first started school, many of the children could speak very little English as their families had come from Finland or Germany or other countries, and they spoke their mother tongue at home. The classroom assistants worked hard to help them, and it was probably through their learning that their parents also learnt. At the store, I sometimes saw children helping their mother to ask for goods. In school, there were only a few books available so children shared readers, and they were all in English.

Glenedyth School also doubled up as a centre of activities in the Climax community. Religious services were held there before the church was built. The school was also used for meetings, parties, dances, weddings, picnics and other get-togethers. We were all very proud of our school.

Early in 1921, we heard from Martha over in Souris that she and Jack had a new baby. This was their third child and they called her Vivian Grace. At much the same time, Minnie and I were sad to learn that Tillie and her family were about to leave. Because most of his building work was in Shaunavon, Frank had decided to move the family there. It was a tearful day when we bade farewell to Tillie and her two little daughters, Gladys and Marion. Shaunavon wasn't a million miles away, but there would be no more meetings at Glenedyth and outings in the buggy to her home in our municipality. Once she had left, we heard from Tillie that they were waiting for Stone School to be built, and a temporary school had been set up in someone's home with the children being taught by a young teacher who lodged there. This was a step backwards for Gladys as she had loved Glenedyth where she was a bright student. She also had many friends and was sad to say goodbye. As for little Marion, she was going to have to wait to start her education.

Rumours of the railway continued. Then one day, George rode over with an official from the railway. The railwayman was telling us that the new line would be routed through the middle of our land – across the middle of Section 10. William and George hoped this might be an opportunity to lift our fortunes and haggled on price, but nothing much came of it as the CPR knew that they had the upper hand as everyone wanted the railway to come. In fact, only George had to sign any papers agreeing to the railway going through the middle of his farm, and only George was paid. William didn't have to sign as the line would only border our land, and we weren't paid anything. The railway was scheduled to arrive in Climax the following year, and then the line east and through our land would be laid the year after that.

That year, Canada had a new prime minister, but not a change of political party. The Liberals were voted in again, and William Lyon Mackenzie King was our new first minister.

I was delighted to receive a letter from Mother, the first from her for almost two years. I noticed how spidery her handwriting had become; in fact much of it was not in her hand at all. As I read, it became clear why.

Cavetown Farm
12th May 1921

My dear Lizzie

The last time I wrote, I didn't mean to alarm you. It really was a worrying time. To be honest, there is some good news, but everything seems far from settled.

You'll see from the address that we have left Coolnagranchy. Father sold it and Lecarrow Farm to your Uncle George. George has retired from his work in the Civil Service in London, and he and your Aunt Mary Ann are now back home in Ireland and have moved into Coolnagranchy. George has a wish to be free of the strict rationing they have back in England and to return to the land and do some farming. It's odd as he's never before had the opportunity in his adult life to be his own master on his own farm. When he was growing up, he helped his parents, Edward and Ellen at Derrymaquirk, but there was no chance for him to inherit so he went off to Dublin to start a new career there.

So we're now at Cavetown Farm, which is very much larger than Coolnagranchy. It's a shame that we didn't come here sooner. It would have been grand when we had twelve of you to care for. Now there are only five of your sisters and brothers at home, and all quite grown up. Lillian is 26 next month,

Blanche is 24, Katie 22, Thomas 20 and Queenie 19. Poor Lillian despairs of ever finding a young man to wed. Just a few days ago, she announced that she's resigned to the idea of always being a spinster, and Blanche, Katie and Queenie said that they would never give up hope, and neither should she. They have discussed the idea of joining you and your sisters in Canada, but they've been put off by your news of the great hardships you suffer.

Blanche has recently managed to get a job in an office in Sligo. She has to travel an hour to get there, but she likes it well enough, and she is pleased to be able to contribute something to the housekeeping. Lillian still hasn't found any permanent work, but she is my helpmate and I'm not sure that I could manage without her. My arthritis is so painful and I can hardly walk some days, let alone get all the chores done. My poor hands have made knitting so difficult, and Lillian has taken over from me the knitting of cardigans and socks, but that's only possible when we can get hold of some wool. Otherwise it's the old unravelling to make something new. Katie and Queenie sometimes help at Ardsallagh School, so that gives them some interest and a few pennies in their pockets.

Father has a lot of work to do, mending fences and working on the farm, and he and Thomas are off all day long. Auntie Kate's son, Robert Duke, stays with us from time to time to help on the farm. We often don't see the three of them from dawn till dusk. Your Father also gets called to help Uncle Edward at Derrymaquirk. We usually see your Uncle Duke and Aunt Kate at Croghan Church on Sundays, and sometimes we go back to Grange with them so Father can help out there. We're lucky that we have family nearby and can all help each other when needed.

Cavetown Lough is not so far from here, and a favourite hideout for Thomas and his fishing rod when Father lets him off the work. He's always very proud of himself when he brings in some fish for the table, and the rest of us are very pleased as it means a change from our usual diet.

You'll have more news of Minnie, Tillie and Martha than me. Do let me know how everyone is doing - I love to hear about my big grown-up daughters so far away. Nearer to home, John is still in Glasgow with Jessie, and their three boys are getting big. Thomas is 13, James 11, and little John Duke is already 9 - and not really little at all! How quickly they all grow up. I haven't seen any of them for 5 years, though John sent me a photograph of the family last year. Sarah Jane and Eva both live in County Down now. As you know, Sarah Jane married her cousin, Jim Haire, and I get news of them through Jim's sister Molly at Killukin. Molly's a very good letter writer and I often hear from her, and also we get to see her occasionally when we go over to Carrick-on-Shannon. The news from Eva is not so good. She has been in County Down for about 3 years, with her husband Thomas Philips. I've heard from Sarah Jane that there's a problem. Eva has given birth to a daughter but she and Thomas Philips are no longer together and Eva has put her baby up for adoption. How I wish I could have helped and surely the little girl could have come here, but it's all done now, so I hope Eva can find a happy way forward. I only know this from Sarah Jane. I must drop Eva a line with my love and support.

How much news do you get of what's been happening here in Ireland? Times have been desperate with the War of Independence. Last November was the worst time. They called it Bloody Sunday. Fourteen British intelligence officers were assassinated by the Republicans, and the Constabulary retaliated that afternoon by opening fire on the crowd at a football match at Croke Park, the sports ground in Dublin. They killed 14 and wounded another 65. Then a week later, the Republicans ambushed and killed 17 Auxiliaries in County Cork. The UK government declared martial law throughout Ireland. And that was the start of it, and it's been going on since with the main troubles in Cork and Dublin and Belfast, with at least 1,000 killed and many more imprisoned. They've spoken of dividing Ireland into 2 parts, with the 6 northern counties staying under the rule of Britain, and the south, which includes us, having its own rule. I wish that things can soon be resolved. I so hope that there can be an end to all the strife and that we can start to live in peace. It's been a ghastly time with the war.

As you can see, Lillian has helped write much of this letter for me. She's a blessing. I don't know what I'd do without her.

Your father and Thomas will be in for dinner soon, so I'll finish now. I look forward to hearing your news. Please share this letter with your sisters, and don't worry about us - I'm sure it can't go on forever. At least it isn't happening right on our doorstep.

With my love,
Your Mother

I recall reading the letter several times, sad that my Mother was struggling so and that times were so difficult. I wondered if I would ever see any of them again. I doubted it as I could never imagine how I could possibly leave my family for the amount of time that it would take to travel all the way back to Ireland and stay for long enough to get to see everyone, or at least those still left in Boyle. It would have been wonderful to take my children to meet their grandparents and aunties and uncles, and my cousins, but the expense would have been impossible. Perhaps things might change and I could go and see Mother, probably just one last time, but I really felt that it was impossible and that my place was to remain here on the prairie with William and our children. William and I decided to send a photograph of us all to Mother and the others. They had never seen our little family, so a photograph would be the next best thing, and it might go some way to cheering Mother up a bit.

1921 Outside our cabin on the homestead. Clarence, William, Lorraine, me and Irene. (SE'14 Section 10 Township 3 Range 18 W.3rd).

It felt strange to think that my parents had left our family home, where all my brothers and sisters had been born, where we had played together and knew all the land and trees and streams and secret places around, where we watched foxes playing and badgers snuffling around. We knew the best places to fish, and pick berries, and collect firewood, and dig turf, and where the longest slopes were for sledging when the winter snows came.

I was to be forty in a couple of years and my youth was far behind, and somehow the fact that my childhood home had been forsaken underlined how the years were passing. I think I imagined that Coolnagranchy would stay, locked in time, with members of my family keeping it as it was when I was growing up there. At least my Aunt and Uncle who I knew well would be taking over. I was fairly sure that my Aunt had lived there before, in fact was born there, and stayed until she married my Uncle in the year her father died when she was about twenty six. So she had lived there more than I had as I'd left when I was twenty three.

I wondered how Aunt Mary Ann and Uncle George were managing in our tumbledown cottage at Coolnagranchy. It was such a change for them as the house in Willesden where I stayed with them was so grand and comfortable. I remembered my amazement when I first arrived there; it was so, so different from my Irish home. But Uncle and Auntie were accustomed to the family homes where they had grown up, Uncle George at Grange and Aunt Mary at Coolnagranchy, so life wouldn't be so strange for them.

1922 was one of those unforgettable years, not for any good reason though the first unusual thing to happen was quite memorable. One April morning, six men arrived at Minnie's door. They came in trucks piled high with timber and equipment and tents and announced that they would be doing a land survey and would be based on the high ground on our land. It turns out that this was to do with making better maps of the border with the United States, and also Saskatchewan and the surrounding provinces. They set up camp and, over the following months, they lived and worked there. They also brought their own cook so they really didn't trouble us at all, except for drawing drinking water from our well. We watched their progress, and over the weeks they built a mighty wooden tower, with long rope lines fixed with large metal stakes to steady it to the ground. Once the tower was complete, they hauled a huge electric lamp up to the top of the tower and fixed it firmly there. Then they were ready to start their work, and the lamp shone, on and off, during the dark hours of the night. They told us that this was the first time that the new automatic lamps were being used. There must also have been more towers some distance away as we could see lights flashing from other places. It was as if they were having a conversation. Sometimes the lamp was set in a different direction. When the survey was complete, they packed up, taking the lamp with them. They left the tower behind. The local lads saw this as a good place to play, and there were several bumps and bruises when someone took a tumble from the tower.

1922 was also the year that the railway roadbed for the branch line to Climax was completed which promised to make a great difference when it came to selling the wheat and other grains. However, many hopes were dashed as the harvest was ruined due to the weather.

I remember that summer well as that was the year of the biggest cyclone we ever experienced. In late July, there was a powerful tornado up in the north-east at Crystal Springs and we had felt the brunt of that. We read in the newspaper that it had lifted a house and dropped it in a field nearby. Minnie and I thought it sounded quite funny, but we soon changed our minds the next month when we got our own cyclone which turned out to be a greater beast – a Force 3 tornado. We were used to constant winds and dust on the prairies and made our houses as strong as we could to withstand the constant buffeting, but this was something else. The centre of it hit at Eastend, only about fifty miles away, and we didn't find it funny at all.

If you have never experienced a cyclone or tornado then you probably have no idea of how terrifying it can be. Anything that is not fixed will be sent flying away and never be found again, or not in one piece anyway. The noise of the wind is like a mighty roar, crashing and bashing everything in its path; and it seems never-ending. It comes suddenly, and you must shout above the din if you want to be heard; and outside it sounds as if you are under attack from a mighty demon that is trying to get in and will not leave you in peace, even for a moment. During that cyclone of August 1922, I was convinced that we would all be dead by the morning. I tried hard to reassure the children, but I was terrified myself. And then it left as suddenly as it had come and we timidly made our way outside. There was such devastation. The fences were all down, the crops and vegetables were flattened. We were so relieved that we managed to get the animals away in the barn in good time. We headed over to see how Minnie and George had fared.

We were shocked to see that Minnie's homestead was so badly damaged. The lean-to kitchen was completely torn off the house, and some farm buildings had been destroyed, along with the new binder that George and William had just bought. Minnie was in a terrible state, not her usual capable self, and I toiled long and hard with her to get everything tidy and back in place, or as much as we could, while the men did their best to patch up the damage to buildings and fences. It was a blessing that the lamp had been taken down from the survey tower; it would surely have smashed down in the high winds. The tower itself stood up quite well, probably as there was room for the wind to rush through between the struts and beams. The Shaunavon Standard reported that many people lost their homes and outbuildings altogether, and that two people were dead and four injured. I'm sure many more people than that were injured by flying debris, so I guess that the paper meant that four were seriously injured. Both Minnie and I were terrified of high winds after that, and it took several weeks to get new timbers and remake what had been destroyed.

Not so long after the tornado, Irene was the victim of the lack of good medical facilities. She needed to have her tonsils out and the doctor who was in Climax at the time set about it in his office, which was a lean-to on the old drug store on Main Street. There were problems and, as a result, she haemorrhaged and almost died. But, praise the Lord, the doctor managed to stop the bleeding and she pulled through, though it was months before she got her full strength back. We were so frightened that we would lose her. When we took her back home, she was much weakened for some time and could only manage soups and thin porridge. Her little brother, Clarence, was so sweet and did his best to help her and cheer her up.

We decided that Florence, who was ten by then, was old enough to walk with Irene and Clarence to and from school. They set off each morning at about half past seven and it was about two and a half miles to Glenedyth. The path took them past Climax Graveyard and it wasn't long before we started hearing tales of ghosts and howling, and poor Irene often came home quite upset. We looked into it and it turned out to be one of the lads from the area who was inventing stories. William decided that enough was enough and confronted the boy and he soon gave up his wicked ways.

It seemed to me that no year went by without something happening and 1923 was no exception. In the spring, the mighty wooden survey tower was taken down, much to the dismay of the local lads who had made it their playground. The men came and dismantled it and all the timbers and cables were loaded on the trucks. It took a few days, but finally it was gone. But they left a mark of their work that will probably last forever. On the spot where the tower had once stood, they built a solid stone block about waist high, and on the top was a brass plate that recorded that measurements for the survey had been taken from there. It said, "GEODETIC SURVEY OF CANADA" and "TRIANGULATION STATION". The children lost their climbing tower and the stone in its place became their new target for climbing and jumping off – and frequent grazed knees!

1923 The plate on the top of Geodetic Survey marker.

In March, the railroad finally arrived in Climax. The coming of the steel was seen as a great opportunity to all the homesteaders, and everyone planted as much wheat as possible because the train would now be close by for taking it to market. Farmers had been busy all the past fall hauling their grain to Climax to sell it to the buyers who were there. The town was piled high with grain. Every day, long strings of teams and sleighs loaded with grain passed close by Minnie's house. A newly arrived neighbour, George Sweeney, hauled his cook car to town and served meals to the haulers.

Now it was time for the new leg east to be built. The line had reached Shaunavon ten years earlier, and the track west to Eastend and Consul was complete. It was next scheduled to go east via Climax and as far as Val Marie. Part of it was to go across our land. The railway contractor, Donald Grant, arrived with scores of men and horses to set up camp down on Minnie's land by the big slough, as had been agreed before. There were big strings of horses, a cook tent, bunk houses, a pay office, a large elevating machine and other big railroad building equipment. It was like a small town had come to our land. It took six weeks to get the equipment from Climax to our Fallis land, and it was cruel work for the horses and some perished under the heavy loads. The countryside became a hive of activity, with huge teams of men laying the steel tracks. Our initial fascination soon wore off, especially as the men were not always disciplined and it started to impact on our lives. Liquor played a great part in the unruliness, and we often heard rowdy brawls going on long into the night, with horses being ridden around the place at breakneck speeds. We heard of men being dismissed for their undisciplined behaviour, and replaced by others who were only too pleased at the chance of paid work. But if we adults found it tiresome, the children certainly did not, especially Clarence. They took great amusement in the activity, and always saw great excitement in the comings and goings, which they delightedly reported back to us at mealtimes.

When I wrote to Mother in the summer, my news included the announcement that she had two new grandchildren due that year. Martha and I were both expecting babies. Only a short time after, Martha wrote announcing the birth of yet another daughter, Barbara Joyce. I would have to wait a few more months as I was not due until December. I was pleased to hear back from Mother so quickly; the postal service was improving.

Cavetown 1st August 1923

My dear

Thank you for the photograph of your beautiful family, and you and William have another baby coming - how wonderful. I'm sorry I didn't write sooner, but there's always something to be done, and the house here at Cavetown is much bigger than Coolnagranchy, and the rheumatism troubles me more and more. Please send my love to Martha. The railway coming across your land sounds as if it's causing you some problems, but it will surely be a godsend once it's all finished and you can get around more easily and get your produce to market.

We've been blighted by civil war across the whole of Ireland. It all got worse when the 6 counties of Northern Ireland were established and the 20 counties in the south got their freedom from British rule and became the Irish Free State, but still within the British Empire. The war has been between the two groups of Republicans. One supported the Anglo-Irish Agreement while the others saw it as a betrayal of the Irish Republic as it was proclaimed in the Easter Rising. The fighting and murdering has been horrible, and we have tried to keep quiet and not even go to church as we don't want to be branded as anti-Catholic. Many of the railway tracks and bridges have been blown up and it has meant that it has been hazardous to travel anywhere over the past two years. There have been times when threats have been left on our doorstep. Father always keeps a gun at his side, especially at night.

The war has now ended - mainly because the British government supported and assisted the Free State forces. Peace was declared on 24th April, a day that had another meaning to our family. My dear sister lost her husband of 43 years; yes, your Uncle John Duke died that very day that peace was declared. He was 69 years old. We buried him in Boyle Churchyard and most of the family were there, and all his sons and daughters except for Abraham, who is away in America seeking his fortune. Your uncle has been unwell for some time and William and James have been looking after things; they will now be seeing to the farm business and taking care of their mother.

On that sad note I will say farewell. All the family send their good wishes and ask to be remembered to you.

My love to you and your sisters and families,

Mother

I was saddened to hear of the death of my Uncle and imagined that my Aunt Kathleen would be looking to Mother for support. The Civil War in Ireland also brought great sadness to me. I had read a little about it in the newspaper and wondered how my family were faring. We were Church of Ireland and the troubles all seemed to be tied up with the Catholics and Republicans. How relieved I was to hear that the hostilities had ended, though the loss of many, many lives was terrible. However, Ireland was not the only place blighted by war. The newspapers at home were full of a threatened war between Britain and Turkey called the Chanak Crisis. My old acquaintance, the British Prime Minister, David Lloyd George, appealed repeatedly for Canada to support by sending its soldiers, but Canada refused. I was beginning to feel quite uncomfortable about Mr Lloyd George and wondered how my Uncle George was taking it all since he had been such a supporter of him and his policies.

Winter came with its usual harshness and William rushed me off to the new hospital in Climax – the first in the town. Minnie came over and looked after the children, and William and I sped off in the sleigh, a considerably more comfortable journey than if we'd been bumping along in the buggy. On arrival, we were greeted by Nurse Sinclair who was Matron at the hospital, who we knew as Ed Hickson's wife. I was made ready, then she and Dr Nicolle attended the birth. All went smoothly and on 11th December 1923, Lois Sylvia was born – another daughter. After a few days rest, we set off back home where the other children were all delighted to have a tiny new sister. Little Lois started out well, but over the winter she got very ill with the whooping cough and we had to take her to the hospital for treatment. I was terrified that we might lose her, but she rallied and we were overjoyed when she came back home again, much better but in need of several weeks of careful nursing. We remembered Clarence's whooping cough and Dr Shares' marvellous remedy of mare's milk, so we got another good mare and William was in charge of providing milk several times a day. As with Clarence, it did the trick and we could see Lois getting stronger by the day.

Once the winter was over, work started once more on the land. Minnie and George had their cabin right by the prairie trail and many travellers passed their door on their way to and from Shaunavon. Some stopped to chat and rest the horses. Some sheltered from storms and bad weather. I was often over at Minnie's helping with the dairy and it was good to talk to passers-by and get their news, and sometimes a newspaper.

With the railway nearby, more grain was grown which meant more threshing machines. Some were steam driven, and made wonderful noises as they toiled away, and the whistles as they started up each morning could be heard for miles. With the new machinery, new settlers came and bought the vacant farms. There was much activity on the land; the prairie seemed to have come alive. Soon five great grain elevators were built by the railway track in Climax.

The expansion of industry brought new opportunities of work, and George went to haul bundles, and Minnie sometimes helped out with the cooking on a cook car. At harvest time, everyone worked hard together, and we womenfolk were hard pressed to prepare enough food for the farmers and the many itinerant workers who turned up to help with the effort. Needless to say, the children all loved harvest-time.

Fall was the time when Jim Wright came to help butcher the beef – some we kept for ourselves, some we sold or traded, including with neighbours who had no cattle. Buyers started to come over the border from the USA, and we sold two or three or more head to them each year. Once they had bought what they wanted from the local farmers, they herded them south across the line then took them to Chicago for shipping. They didn't pay us much, but it gave us a market that we wouldn't have had otherwise.

I think it was about 1924 that George's eyesight began to fail and reading became a great problem for him. More and more he had to rely on Minnie to read the papers and notices to him. He was always so interested in what was happening so this was a great frustration to him.

1923 Grain elevator by the railway track in Climax.

1924 was the year that they consecrated the ground for the new Climax Cemetery. They planted caragana bushes around which in time grew up and made a good wind break for the graveyard. We got talking about it and Minnie expressed a wish to move the coffins of Herbie and Baby John. They had been buried out on the land since their deaths in 1911 and 1915, and Minnie wanted them to be brought to this new safe place where they could stay long after we left the land; this so often seemed a possibility when things were conspiring against us. We made an arrangement late that summer and George and William went together to take the coffins from the ground. They were simple boxes and made in good hard wood, so they were still strong. Minnie and I stayed away and visited Minnie's babies in their new resting place in the cemetery once it was done.

1924 Herbie and John were moved to the newly consecrated Climax Cemetery.

Early in 1925, there was a letter from home.

Cavetown, 6th November 1924

Dearest Sisters

We have such sad news for you. Yesterday morning, our sister Blanche passed away.

Did Mother tell you that Blanche was working in an office in Sligo? She was so pleased to have found a job at last. But there was a problem there. Someone else who worked in the office had consumption and was always spitting into the wastepaper basket. They let him go a while back, but the damage was already done and our poor dear Blanche had already caught the disease.

It has been some months now since she became ill with it. The doctor came a couple of times and said we must make sure she gets plenty to drink, and that we must cover our mouths when we see her, lest we catch the dreaded disease. She has been going downhill for some time now, and has had such difficulty with her breathing near the end. Several times we thought she was gone, then yesterday morning she sat up and smiled at us all and we thought she was suddenly better. Then she slept and we left her to rest. She slipped quietly and peacefully away in the morning. When we took her some soup for her lunch, she was gone.

Mother asked us to write. She is quite distraught - Blanche just had her twenty eighth birthday two days before. She was always so well before she got the consumption.

You are all in our thoughts.

With love from us all

Lillie, Katie, Thomas and Queenie.

I felt so homesick, so helpless and unable to be with my younger siblings. I had such a hollow feeling that I could not be there to help dear Mother. Being the oldest, I had helped to bring up all my younger sisters and brothers, especially those who were still at home at Coolnacranchy, who I thought of as the little ones. Blanche had always been such a sweet girl and full of fun and good humour and energy. She was the first of our family to leave us and far too young. How unfair life could be.

I thought again, as I often did, about the possibility of visiting my family back in Ireland, but I always came back to the conclusion that my life was now here in Canada and that I would probably never return to Coolnagranchy, never see that branch of my family ever again.

The next week there was news from Martha in Souris. She and Jack Russell had a new son, Richard Henderson – a son at last after four daughters. There was new life where so shortly before one had been lost.

As well as the constant work on the land and with the animals, and the daily household chores, we were also kept busy with the children's education and the materials they needed. They needed copybooks for school which we made ourselves. We bought or traded sheet paper, folded it into pages and then sewed them together, adding brown wrapping paper to serve as a cover to protect the pages. Then the children were made to draw lines to create ruled paper so they could write their letters. These books were very precious, not only for the effort it took to make them but also for the precious learning they contained. As the children got older, they no longer worked on slates and we had to make quill pens for them. We collected large goose feathers and these were sharpened so they could be dipped in ink for handwriting. Ink was made by mixing ink powder with water. Later, lead pencils were available, which were a godsend as the children didn't come home so often with inky fingers and clothes.

During the summer of 1926, another letter came from Ireland. I was still getting over Blanche's death and feared that maybe another member of the family had succumbed to consumption. But it was much worse than that.

Cavetown, 20th June 1926

Dearest Lizzie

Our Mother has died. Last week she took to her bed saying that she was so tired, and yesterday evening she just passed away. We sat with her and held her hand and she kept saying

"I'm so tired, so very tired". Gradually her breaths were slower and shallower, and then she was gone. At least she had no suffering but still we cannot believe it. We have never known our life without her.

Father and Thomas have gone to Croghan Church to talk to the minister about her burial, and Kate and I have been making her ready for her final rest.

Please pass this to Minnie, Tillie and Martha. I'm sure they will find it as hard to take in as we have.

Your sister

Lillian.

My Mother was dead. How could that be? I worked out that she must have been sixty one and it was nearly twenty years since I had left her. I sat quietly, clutching Lillian's letter in my hand. My Mother would never see my babies, and they would never get the chance to know their grandmother. Irene, Clarence and Lorraine were all in school, and I picked up little Lois and started to walk the half mile to Minnie's to tell her the news. I walked slowly, dragging my feet across the tangled grass that grew along the edge of the track. I never realised how hard this would be, how empty my world had suddenly become. My Mother, my dearest Mother, was gone forever, gone from all of us who had loved her and so depended upon her. Although I was far from home, I always pictured her there at our family home, doing the same old things in the same old places. I was thousands of miles away, but I had always felt rooted to my childhood home, and to my Mother. I felt overwhelmed by my sadness, my insignificance and emptiness. She had taught me so much, and I had been her help-mate for so many years. Somehow I felt deserted, incomplete, detached from everything around me.

I hardly remember that walk to Minnie's, or the heaviness of carrying little Lois, now three years old and no lightweight. Minnie was working outside, doing some washing I think. The dog beside her looked up at my approach and came towards me, tail wagging on recognising a friend, expecting a greeting. But he got none, and Minnie too called a greeting but got no response. She quickly sensed my anguish and came to me, drying her hands and asking what was wrong. I had no words. She took Lois from me and stood her down, then saw the page in my hand. She gently took it from me and started to read its contents. She too was lost for words, and we stood locked in each others' arms, sharing that unexpected news that we never wanted to hear. Seeing that I had come over, George and William came from the cow barn where they were working. They found us locked in this sisterly embrace. Minnie passed the letter to William and immediately he understood. He and George were wonderful. William brought a bench for us to sit, and both our dear husbands went off into the cabin to make us some tea. William caught Lois up in his arms and took her inside for a rest, then we all sat together. William offered a prayer and it opened the way for us to talk, and share our sorrow.

But, as it is said, life must go on, though it seemed to go slowly for some weeks. We got another letter from Lillie, confirming Mother's funeral and adding some other family news.

Cavetown - 1st September 1926

Dear Lizzie, Minnie, Tillie and Martha

I thought you would all like to know that Mother's funeral was on a beautiful sunny day. She now lies at rest in Croghan Graveyard, next to Blanche. We feel that they can take care of each other now they are together. There were lots of family members there, and Eva and Sarah Jane came down from County Down, and John and his family came from Glasgow for a few days, so we were all together and able to give Father our support.

Our Grange cousin, Abraham, was also there. He has just returned from America where he went to seek his fortune. He's now back and has been able to purchase Grange Farm, which is just down from Grange where he grew up. He sends his best wishes. He says that there's a lot of work to do there and hopes to build up the place and then find himself a wife.

Our brother Thomas has recently built some impressive concrete steps leading up to the front entrance of Cavetown House. A short while ago, he started courting Delia Casserly who is 19, that's 6 years younger than he is. She was raised on a little farm near here called Glooria. When her mother and only sister died, her father Mr Casserly sent her to stay with Mrs Rose, then later she went back to Glooria and became the domestic servant for her father and four or five brothers. That's all very well, but the main problem with her seeing our Thomas is that she's Roman Catholic, and Father isn't having any of that.

Father has offered to sell the Cavetown house and farm to Thomas for £1200 providing he ends his relationship with Delia Casserly. Now Delia has become pregnant and her father has ordered her out of the house. So she's back with Mrs Rose at Boyle and her father has completely disowned her for committing such a mortal sin. Thomas has vowed to stand by her, so that's put an end to his aspirations of buying Cavetown Farm as Father's sticking to his point of view.

Maybe if Thomas had ended the relationship and bought the farm, then he could have taken up with her later on and there would be nothing that Father could do about it. But it could never have worked out anyway.

Please keep sending us your news. It seems more important now than ever that we keep in touch with each other.

The others send their love, as do I.

Your sister Lillian

How pleased I was to hear from Lillie, and I was heartened by her wish that we keep in touch with each other. I forwarded her news on to my other sisters, and they too were pleased that Lillie would be writing to us, in place of the letters from Mother that we had received over the years.

It was at about this time that there was something of a constitutional crisis here in Canada, and it brought about a change that stopped Britain interfering in Canadian political affairs. Mackenzie King was our Prime Minister and it was time for him to dissolve Parliament and call another election, and he had to ask the Governor General, Lord Byng to make arrangements for this. But Byng refused and took it upon himself to call upon the Conservative Party leader, Meighan, to form a government. Meighan tried but failed as he couldn't get the required Commons majority, so he advised dissolution of Parliament, which this time was accepted. There was much rejoicing in the newspapers as it had long been an issue of national concern that Britain had such a hold on our Canadian affairs.

1927 was a year for local celebration when Climax was declared a village. Although times were hard, and often cruel, we had some very happy times too, and there was a strong spirit of co-operation. We had some wonderful friends and acquaintances. Differences of nationality and language sometimes got in the way, but generally you knew that you could call on your neighbour, especially in times of difficulty. Picnics, dances and card parties were an important part of our social life. George was also popular at dances and gatherings with his mouth-organ. Ever since his death some years before, we still missed John; he could always strike up a merry tune on his violin.

More news came from Lillie; her letters were more regular than mine and she was starting to keep us right up to date with news from home.

1927 George, Florence and Minnie.

Cavetown Farm, October 1927

Dear Lizzie

Just to keep you up to date with the Thomas and Delia story. Father and John will never see eye to eye, so Thomas has left home and gone to Scotland to join our brother, John. He says that he has promised to send for Delia once he is settled up there. The whole affair has weighed heavily on Father and he says he doesn't care if he never sees Thomas again. He says that he is a fool and that he is the master of his own destruction. We are all very upset about the whole thing. I'm sure Mother would have been able to make him see sense.

Father has made a decision to sell the Cavetown house and he put it up for public auction in April. We're pleased to say that it did not sell, times being hard as they are. So we still have a roof over our heads, and don't have to leave our home just yet. But it's sure to come and then we'll have to move on. I think that Father is considering going to Scotland with John, and don't know what Kate, Queenie and I will do, perhaps go up to the north and join Sarah Jane and Eva.

I have sent you a copy of the Advertisement from the newspaper which might be of interest to you, even though you never lived there.

We've heard from John that he found Thomas a job on a farm in Barrhead, south-west of Glasgow, and Thomas was working 16 hours a day, saving to bring Delia to Scotland. In early September, Delia joined him. She was already 8 months pregnant by then. The farmer Thomas worked for allowed her to stay in the bothy with Thomas till the baby was born. They were married just in time in Barrhead and Levern Registry Office, and one week later, on 21st September, their daughter Blanche Mary was born in Rottenrow Maternity Hospital in Glasgow. That was 3 days before Thomas' 27th birthday.

After Blanche was born, John arranged for Delia to rent a room from a Mrs. McMillan in Inchinnan where he was living, while Thomas remained at the bothy close to his place of work. The McMillans are a Catholic family so it's working out well. Every Saturday evening, Thomas cycles from the farm in

Barrhead 8 miles away and stays with Delia and the baby until Sunday night, when he cycles back to the farm and works 10 hours a day for 6 days. As agreed with a Catholic priest, Blanche has been baptized in St James' Catholic Church in nearby Renfrew and Mrs. McMillan is her godmother. Thomas has accepted all this, and accepts it that Delia attends Catholic Mass each Sunday with Mrs. McMillan and her many children. Thomas must love his wife and baby so much. I hope he does anyway as he's given up such an opportunity for them. In ways I admire him for his loyalty to them.

It's taken us some time to sort out Mother's affairs. In her papers, we came across letters from you in Canada. We've sent some of them to you in this parcel. We've also sent Mother's green necklace that she inherited from Grandmother to you so you have something that she was fond of.

That's all my news for now. Love from us all to all of you,

Lillian

ADVERTISEMENT

Cavetown House

Very Attractive Sale of a Valuable Residential Holding of Land

At the Courthouse, Boyle

On SATURDAY, the 9th April, 1927 At 2 o'clock, p.m

I have been instructed by Mr Thos Monson, of Cavetown, Croghan, to Sell by Public Auction, on above date, his Farm of Land in the Townland of Cavetown, containing 102 Acres of very good land, held subject to £45 yearly interest in lieu of rent under 1923 Land Act, Poor Law Valuation, £87. This Farm is within one mile of Croghan, and four miles from Boyle and Carrick-on-Shannon. There is a plentiful supply of water on the land, and a turf bank attached. The Dwellinghouse is a very substantial one, and contains large Kitchen and eight rooms and the Out-offices consist of cow-house, stable, car-house, piggery, fowl-house and hay loft all slated, besides other sheds. There is a good kitchen garden attached to the house, well stocked with fruit trees. For further particulars apply to Dermot, Mac Dermot, Boyle, Solicitor having carriage of the sale; or to Lewis D. McLean; Auctioneer, Boyle.

I shed a tear for my Mother. I was so grateful that Lillie had thought of sending me the necklace. It remains a precious keepsake to me to this day

I spent some time enjoying Lillie's letter. Although I had never lived at the Cavetown House, I was interested to see the advertisement. It was much bigger than Coolnagranchy. What a shame that we didn't have the chance to live there when we were all young and growing up. I realised that I knew which house it was as we passed it each Sunday on our way to Croghan Church.

Life continued, and times got harder and harder. Crops failed due to too much rain, or too much sun, or too much wind, or too many grasshoppers. The children were growing fast, and my Irene was almost at the end of her schooling, with little Lois due to start at Glenedyth in 1928. Lillie and I continued to exchange news regularly, and I heard from her over the next two years that Uncle George and Aunt Mary Ann had left Coolnagranchy and sold it on to my cousin George from Grange, who was just six months older than me. In 1929, my sisters Kate and Queenie left the Cavetown House and moved to County Down. It seemed strange to me that there had been so many in our family home when Minnie and I left for Canada, and now only Lillie and Father were left there.

In 1928 we read of another change in the policing of the province, and it was back to the Mounties again, though they had changed their name to the Royal Canadian Mounted Police. Commissioner Mahoney and the Provincials had done a fair enough job, but they were always undermanned due to shortage of funds. There was some concern that the headquarters of the force would be far away in Ottawa, and we were all assured that we would have a senior Mountie in Sakatchewan who would make sure that local concerns were taken into account, and this turned out to work well. Once more, it was a welcome sight when the Mounties came by in their red coats and dark blue breeches.

7

Hard times

1929-1938

Bartering was the lifeblood of the prairies. We traded everything – our time and labour, our butter and eggs and cheese and milk. We shared our skills, our animals and equipment, even our children. One thing that the children could do to help their families was to pick up stones off the land. So we sometimes lent the children to other settlers to help with this task when they were preparing the land. It was hard work. Rarely did anyone use their grain to trade as that represented hard cash when it was taken to market. But when there was nothing left to barter, that's when you went under.

1929 saw the beginning of the worldwide Great Depression. Canada was hit hard, but none harder than those of us in the west.

There was yet another mouth to feed in our family. Our daughter, Jean Louise, was born in February, and I had gone to Eastend for her birth. It was getting harder to keep ourselves and five children. Minnie was also finding it hard to make ends meet, and that spring she and Florence went to run the Canuk Hotel for Mrs Hazelton. We got news that Martha had given birth to another son, John Dennison, who they all called Denny.

From Scotland came a card announcing the birth of another son to my brother Thomas.

Announcing the birth of
James William Monson
On 22nd October 1929
The proud parents are Thomas
and Delia Monson

A few days later, a letter from my sister, Lillie, confirmed the news:

Cavetown, November 1929

Dear Lizzie

This is just a quick note to let you know the latest twists and turns in the lives of our brother Thomas and Delia Casserly. I gather from Thomas that he has sent you an announcement card of the birth of his second child, James William, on 22nd October last. I'm fairly sure that he won't have told you everything.

The baby had been born in the house of their landlady, Mrs McMillan, and Mrs McMillan herself was the midwife. Thomas then announced that his two children were now to be brought up as Protestants, which was something of a change from before, and that his new son, James, was to be baptized in St Margaret's Episcopal Church in Renfrew with our brother, John, and his wife, Jessie, as godparents. This wasn't the end of it though.

Delia had other ideas, and discussed things with the Priest. He told her that baby James would end up in purgatory unless he was baptized in a Catholic Church, and that she could not attend mass again until James was properly baptized in a Catholic Church. Despite Delia's concerns, Thomas got his way and baby James was baptized at St. Margaret's and the Minister authenticated the baptism on the back of the birth certificate.

I haven't heard whether Delia and Thomas are still speaking to each other. As you can imagine, Father is quite pleased that his grandchildren are not to be Papists! I'll let you know what else I hear.

I don't know - our brothers!

Your loving sister

Lillie.

I must say that this news did amuse me, and we certainly needed something to raise our spirits. By the end of 1929, times were getting worse, and when the thirties hit, things hit rock bottom. The "Dirty

Thirties" they called it. Harvests failed year in year out due to hot dry summers. Nothing could grow, there was no feed for the animals, and everyone was near starvation. Never a week went by without news of a suicide. It was mainly the men. Somehow the women dug deeper and showed a greater resilience, but there was no-one and no living thing that didn't suffer. The hardship that struck the plains didn't leave our neighbourhood unscathed, nor did it pass us by. We were surrounded by the tragedies of so many of our neighbours, but the bottomless on-going sadness lay deep within us all. We could give it no time as we too were facing the same life-threatening impossibilities.

With the constant cloud of dust over the parched land and the failing of the crops, even the grasshoppers left us alone.

By Summer 1930, it was the end for us. Due to the Great Depression and drought, our farm failed for the second year. Most of the animals were lost; even the chickens had stopped laying. If we didn't leave the homestead and find a new way forward, we would all perish. William left to find work to help support us all, but jobs were hard to come by. I moved into Climax with the children, now aged from fifteen down to one. William did his best to send money home, and visited when he could, and I looked out for some house work for families in Climax. It was so hard to make ends meet. One good thing was that it was a much shorter walk for the children to get to Glenedyth School. Irene was fifteen by then and had left school, and she was a great help to me in looking after the younger ones.

The land had driven us away, but even those who relied less on the land were going under. The problems were having a knock-on effect and many were forced to abandon their farms and move into the towns or back to where they had originally come from. Tillie and Frank had already moved to Shaunavon back in 1921 and that had worked out for a while, but by 1930 Frank could get very little work so he decided there was nothing for it but to sell the farm in Climax, with the beautiful stone-built shack, so the family would have some money to live. Our neighbours, the Goodall's bought it from him. Life was at rock bottom, and it was hard to see any way out.

Even our heroes were falling by the wayside. We didn't hear till quite late that our famous flier, Billy Barker had died in March. I don't know how we missed it. Minnie came across the newspaper that announced the sad news. The article said that he had suffered greatly from the physical effects of his 1918 gunshot wounds when his legs had been permanently damaged, and he also experienced severely limited movement in his left arm. In the last years of his life, he struggled with alcoholism. He took his last flight on 12th March 1930 when he lost control of the biplane he was flying during a demonstration, and plummeted to his death near the Rockcliffe Air Station near Ottowa. He was only thirty five. The newspaper went on to describe his funeral, the largest national state event in Toronto's history. Over fifty thousand people lined the streets to show their respects, and his coffin was escorted by an honour guard of two thousand Canadian soldiers as well as soldiers from the United States Army. The cortege included many high ranking people and it stretched for more than a mile and a half. Again Minnie and I felt such pride in this courageous young man, who had so inspired us in those dark war years. How sad that his bravery and daring had dealt him such a hard blow in his later life. It was sort of a consolation that he had died doing what he most loved, better that than wasting away as a sickly and sad old man in an armchair.

The house in Climax was a little bigger than we'd been used to on the prairie, so that was one blessing, but it was so hard to make ends meet. We quickly established a vegetable garden and the hens started laying again – thank goodness. Most weekends, Clarence went fishing with some of the village lads and almost always brought something back. The White Mud River was just under four miles distant, so he and his friends would set out early morning and get to the river in good time for a full day's fishing. He brought us carp, perch, burbot, sometimes an evil looking pike of some size, also red-horse and white sucker, but my favourite was walleye. Whatever Clarence brought we either fried or it went into the pot or was salted or dried. The White Mud River was also a source in late summer of the plump juicy purple berries of the saskatoons, and we ate as we picked fruits from the shrubs and small trees that grew around. Collecting saskatoons was quite an outing, and people took a picnic and made a day of it. With them we made pies and jams, and the children just liked to eat them as a sweet treat. We dried them so they would last through the year, much as the local indigenous people had dried them with bison meat to make pemmican. In fact, the Saskatoon plants were always a joy to us if we were passing near the White Mud River. Early in the year, they were festooned with fragrant white flowers which we picked to bring some joy and sweetness to our homes, and just before winter they displayed brilliant autumn foliage which we took home to brighten our cabins. In winter, they stood bare and all but dead. Come spring, new life emerged with promise of the summertime fruit harvest.

When we could get meat, some we stewed, some we salted, or smoked with herbs in the way we learnt from the Metis and local aboriginal peoples. Another favourite was black pudding, which we bought from the slaughterer. Of the Metis people, they generally kept themselves to themselves, but still carried goods on their Red River carts for a small charge for those who needed their help.

Life in Climax was so different to the time out on our prairie land. We could walk in town when we wished, and the streets were full of automobiles. We heard that the municipality was considering the introduction of 'silent policemen'. These had been installed in Shaunavon, because there had been so many accidents with pedestrians being knocked down. The newspaper showed pictures of posts positioned down the centre of the main street to slow down the traffic, but there were also tales of vehicles hitting the posts with the drivers or passengers being hurt, so they were something of a mixed blessing. In fact, the 'silent policemen' never did come to Climax. I was ever fascinated by the cars and trucks in town. They seemed to drift around, silent and never in a hurry, unlike the horse drawn vehicles which threw up the muck and dust and noisily announced themselves. You couldn't hear the trucks coming, so were often stopped in your tracks when you suddenly found them upon you. I felt that the Shaunavon traffic problem was more to do with people not paying attention and stepping out in the way of a truck, rather than drivers being reckless.

We rarely got to Shaunavon those days, but the newspaper still brought us the news of life there. We liked to hear about the Shaunavon Rodeo, which continued to flourish, and about its famous cowboy stars such as Slippers, Buck Murphy, Alex la Frambois and Buck Hardin.

I took to keeping clippings from the newspapers before using the rest for firelighting. It is my scrapbook of newspaper cuttings that has helped me recall those years and the terrible times and changes that had such effect on our lives; that and my collection of letters from my family back in Ireland.

The Prime Minister, Mackenzie King, along with the Liberal Government, seemed blind to the troubles of the people. It was reported that he believed that the crisis was only temporary and that everything would soon recover without government intervention. He refused to provide any aid to those in difficulties and said that, if Conservative provincial governments demanded federal dollars, they would not be given "a five cent piece". This statement didn't go down too well and, in the election late in 1930, the Liberals were defeated. The nation felt that Mackenzie King and his ministers were out of touch with the hardships of ordinary people.

One thing that almost passed us by in 1931 was something called the Statute of Westminster, and it amounted to the British Parliament offering independence to Canada. The British Prime Minister by that time was Ramsay MacDonald – no longer 'my' Mr Lloyd George who had been gone from government for some nine years.

It's strange that the government didn't see the disaster coming. Over the previous four years, wheat prices plummeted from seventy eight cents a bushel to twenty nine cents. Many people saw most or all of their assets disappear. It was a time of terrible suffering with two thirds of the prairie farmers on relief.

The gross national product dropped 40%, and by 1933, unemployment reached 27% and a fifth of the population became dependent on government assistance. Many businesses closed as profits turned into huge losses, and Canadian exports shrank by 50%. Construction all but stopped, and wholesale prices dropped 30%. Each week, the newspapers brought us an increasingly pessimistic story. I remember well the news of the uprising of so many unemployed men in Western Canada at this time. They decided to protest against the dismal conditions in the federal relief camps scattered in the remote areas. The Great Depression had left one in nine citizens on relief, but the relief did not come free. The Bennett Government ordered the Department of National Defence to set up work camps for single unemployed men and they were tasked to construct roads and other public works. This could have been a good solution to the problems, but the men were treated more like animals. They lived and worked in the camps at a rate of only twenty cents a day and conditions were desperate. This led to general unrest and a union was formed followed by strikes. In late 1934, many men made their way to Vancouver to protest. They only returned to the camps when the government promised to look into their complaints. But nothing happened, so a second strike was approved by the union members and a walkout was called early in April 1935. About 1,600 strikers headed for Vancouver. Their demands were for wages of fifty cents an hour for unskilled work, union wages for those with skills, and at least a hundred and twenty hours of work a month. Their demands also included the provision of adequate first aid equipment in the camps, fair compensation for all, recognition of democratically elected workers' committees, and rights for all workers to vote in elections.

Public support for the men was enormous, and every week the newspapers were full of reports and stories. But the municipal, provincial and federal governments passed responsibility between themselves and no clear decisions were made. The workers decided that their only course of action was to take their grievances to the federal government. On June 3, 1935, hundreds of men began boarding boxcars headed east in what was known as the "On-to-Ottawa Trek."

First they went to Regina and met two government ministers, Manion and Weir I think, and a meeting was arranged between eight of the protesters and Prime Minister Bennett to be held in Ottowa a few days later. The other protesters were to stay in Regina, supervised by the Mounties. The meeting in Ottowa went on for several days and ended in a shouting match, with the Prime Minister accusing the protesters of being a group of radicals and embezzlers. The delegation was then escorted out of the building and on to the street.

On 1st July, the eight delegates met with the protesters back in a large square in Regina to update them on the outcome of the talks in Ottowa. On three sides of the square were large trucks concealing riot squads, and the police station was nearby on the fourth side. There were up to 2,000 people at the meeting, unaware of what was about to happen. Shortly after 8pm, a whistle was blown and the police charged the crowd with batons from all sides. The people fought back with sticks and stones and anything they could lay their hands on. Then the Mounties charged in on their horses and started to use tear gas and guns. The battle continued in the square and the streets for several hours, with buildings damaged and burned, and many people injured. They were taken to hospital or people took them into their homes. There were about one hundred and twenty arrests, and it was reported that a policeman and a protester died though the police denied this and it was said that hospital records were altered to conceal the cause of death.

Many of the protesters returned to the exhibition grounds where they were camped, and a barbed wire stockade was erected around this area and police with pistols and machine guns stood guard. According to our local newspaper, reports were front page news across the whole of Canada. Our Saskatchewan Premier, Gardiner, took up the cause of the protesters and accused Prime Minister Bennett of precipitating a riot when he should have been negotiating a settlement with the workers. The outcome was that the protesters were fed and watered and sent home, and Premier Gardiner arranged for this to take place. The Saskatchewan government provided free transportation for the protestors. The camps were soon dismantled and replaced by seasonal relief camps, with slightly better pay. Bennett was convinced that he had brought down a communist revolt.

Things didn't get any better under the Conservatives and, despite their promises and attempts to make things better, the depression was getting even worse. Gasoline prices were raised again and again, and so auto owners started to pull their cars by using horses. These got to be known as Bennett Buggies.

So the Conservatives failed and Mackenzie King and the Liberals were voted in again in the 1935 election. People voted for them when they used the slogan "King or Chaos", convincing us all that all would be lost under the Conservatives. It was a landslide victory. Bennett's Conservative government lost almost one hundred seats, dropping to only thirty nine seats. We heard that there was some false reporting, aimed at discrediting the Conservatives, but I think that the main thing that swung people's view was the promise of a trade treaty with the USA. That turned out to be the turning point and marked the passing of the worst of the Depression. Everyone was feeling more optimistic, and the state started to help the people with new relief programs such as the National Housing Act and the National Employment Commission.

Between 1936 and 1939, many new and improved initiatives came about. The Canadian Radio Broadcasting Corporation was nationalised, Trans-Canada Airlines and also the National Film Board of Canada were formed. Parliament also transformed the Bank of Canada from a private entity to a crown corporation. New political parties were formed, including the Social Credit Movement, the Co-operative Commonwealth Federation and the On-to-Ottawa Trek Party which brought about many improvements in the aftermath of the whole affair surrounding the Regina Riot.

At this time, a strict immigration policy was introduced, and there was a rise in political awareness of the Aboriginal peoples. We had been reading for some time about a man called John Baptiste Tootoosis. He came from the Cree Reserve called Poundmaker, near Cut Knife, about 300 miles north of us in the north of Saskatchewan. We read about his travels across Canada since 1930, receiving no salary and relying on donations. His vision was to bring the Aboriginal peoples and organisations together so they could have a single voice to get themselves and their treaty rights heard. This was the start of a long fight which eventually would achieve some success and turn over some of the injustices of the past.

Throughout the thirties, the troubles had a great effect on our family, but life still went on, and there were celebrations and sadnesses. In 1931, my first daughter, Irene, married Mathew Jalmar Maki, and together they set up their farm in Ridgeley District. He was nine years older than Irene and had come with his father, Elias, and family to Many Berries in South East Alberta in 1918, then moved to Climax in 1924 and that's where they met a few years later. My happiness at my daughter's wedding was short-lived. That year also brought tragic news from Ireland, as well as the final migration of our family from County Roscommon. This time the news came from the hand of my youngest sister, Queenie.

1931

Dearest Sister

I can hardly bear to tell you the saddest news. Our beloved sister, Lillie, has died in the most horrible way. She was complaining of a bad toothache for some time, and eventually plucked up the courage to go to the dentist in Boyle. He said that she must have two teeth pulled, so she was put to sleep so it could be done. Something went badly wrong because she never woke up again. I got a message from Father and I went down straightaway to Cavetown to help with arrangements. Lillie has been Father's only company since Kate and I moved up to Bangor. Our sister is now laid to rest at Croghan with Mother. She was thirty six when she died.

Aunt Kathleen came to the church with our cousins, William and Fred, and our sisters Sarah Jane, Eva and Kate were all there for Lillie. Father was pleased to have us all there. We couldn't get news in time to John and Thomas. We have written letters but heard nothing back.

Father has decided to come back to Bangor with me. Kate and I both married this year and live in Bangor, County Down. Kate's husband is Joe McCaugherty, and I am married to Chris Fildes. Sarah Jane now has three children, Florence, Muriel and Jackie. Up in Scotland, Thomas and Delia have two little ones, Blanche and James, and John and Jessie have Thomas, James and John, who are all now quite grown up and have families of their own. There are no other nephews and nieces for you, apart of course from your Canada sisters' children.

I'm sorry to bring you the sad news of Lillie. I know she has been good at keeping you up to date with the family. I'll try to do the same from now on.

Your 'baby' sister Queenie.

How sad I was and, when I shared the news with Minnie, we cried for our dear sister. She was always such a help to our parents, and much loved by us all.

1932 Irene's cabin, near the railway in Climax.

1932 also brought its own share of troubles. Irene was carrying my first grandchild and I went to stay with her in her cabin in Climax, near the railway track, to give her my help. Everything was going well and, on 11th October, she had a baby boy, a little brother for her daughter, Hilda Irene, born the year before. Our happiness and excitement was cut short the very next day when the poor wee thing just slipped silently away. We never knew the reason, though he was a very small baby. It brought back to me my own tragic loss of my first baby girl all those years ago. Just two days later, there was more news from Queenie.

Dearest Lizzie

I seem only to bring you sad news. Father has passed away. He was over at Newtownards visiting Sarah Jane and the children and he just sat back in the chair and died. He was seventy eight years old.

Sarah Jane, Eva, Kate and I were at the church. We got a

letter from Aunt Mary Ann and Uncle George, Father's only existing sister and his cousin.

No other news for the time being. I hope it will be better next time I write.

Queenie

So, now Father was gone too, I only had memories and two photographs left of my parents, though there was little chance that I would ever have seen either of them again. Once more, Minnie and I had a great sadness to share.

At last we had some happy family news in 1933. Minnie and George's daughter, Florence, was to wed a handsome Scotsman, James John Brown. He was known to everyone as JJ. We all got together in Climax on what turned out to be a beautiful day at the end of June. That day seemed to mark a turning point in life as a whole. The Depression was reaching an end, the sun was shining, and everyone's spirits were lifted.

Then came more news from Ireland. My Uncle Edward of Derrymaquirk had died, aged sixty three. My cousin, William, and his wife, Muriel, were to take over the farm, and Aunt Emily would stay and help with the housekeeping.

1934 brought new babies. In Northern Ireland, I heard from my sister Kate that she and Joe McCaugherty had their first son, Jackie. Nearer to home, Minnie's Florence had a daughter Helen Margaret on 2nd April. It was lovely to be able to visit Florence and her new baby in Climax. Florence looked so happy, and we had all taken to her handsome Scots husband, Jim Brown. Minnie came to stay for a couple of weeks to give Florence some help, and it was lovely to spend some time together, just chatting and reminiscing.

We hadn't heard from Ireland for some time, then a note, this time from Eva.

Portavogie, Co. Down
27th May 1936

Dear Lizzie

I saw Queenie yesterday and she suggested that I drop you a line. We've just got the news from Grange that our cousin, William, passed away on 13th May. It was just one week before his forty third birthday, no age really. I feel so shocked as I'm only four months younger. Fred will take over the Grange. William never married, and neither has Fred, so Aunt Kathleen is still running the house. She's seventy six now and has a girl from town to help with things.

My marriage to Thomas Philips in 1918 ended about two years later, not in the happiest of circumstances. I asked the others not to mention this to you, but now I am ready to tell you the whole story. I was not well for a long time, especially after having the baby. We lived in Newtownards and my beautiful baby girl was born late in 1919. I loved her dearly and called her Mary. But I could not cope with anything, and Thomas could not cope with me! Finally he walked out leaving me and my baby, and in a terrible state. There was nothing for it but to put Mary to foster parents, and I did my best while she was growing up to give something to help support her in her new family. After some years, Thomas and I were divorced. Sarah Jane has been such a help to me and I've also needed help from the doctor. Now I'm feeling much better and last year I met a wonderful man, twenty years older than me, called George Mahood and we will be married next month. My daughter is now sixteen, seventeen in October, and she comes to see me from time to time and tells me about her life - she's a very sweet girl. She is in service in Bangor.

I feel better settled than I have in many years. George has a beautiful little country farmhouse called Benown Farm in Glastry, near Portavogie, with a dairy business which he inherited from his father some years ago. And it will be my home shortly. We have together set up a small business in Bangor, called Tangent Buses, and I am in charge of things, which I am enjoying very much. If that isn't enough, we've also bought a movie theatre and named it Tangent Theatre, the same as the buses. It's very popular and is proving to be a good business. My life is so full of excitement, and I'm coping very well. George is such a good friend and so encouraging.

Well, dear sister, I'm sorry it's taken me so long to write. But my news for so many years has been far from good, and now

I'm sure you're pleased to know that I am so fulfilled at last. I'll try to write more frequently - but no promises as my life is now becoming so busy and full.

With my love

Your 'little' sister Eva (now 42!).

Well, that was a turn up for the books. Mother had told me long ago of Eva's hardships, but I had never mentioned it to her that I knew. And now she wanted me to know it all. While those of our family here in Canada were facing continuous challenges, I had never thought that Eva was suffering so. I was sad that she had known such difficulties in her time, but rejoiced that she was now so well settled with a good husband and a full life.

Our families were growing up fast, and soon it was time for my Lorraine to marry Leonard Hardy, a young man from Quebec about ten years her senior. They married in Turner, Montana – I wasn't sure why so far away. It was possibly to do with Leonard's work.

In March, Minnie's daughter, Florence, had her second child, James Milton, a little brother for Helen, born three years before. It was lovely to have the little ones here in Climax, and to see them growing up.

And there was news from Kate back in Ireland announcing that she too had a second child, a daughter who she and Joe named Evelyn. Yes, it felt good to have the little ones here in Climax, but it would have been wonderful to meet all my other nephews and nieces. When we were growing up, we knew all our cousins, played with them, knew so much about them. Our prairie babies would as like as not never get to meet their aunts and uncles and cousins back in the old country.

1937 was the year of the terrible 'Sleeping Sickness' horse disease. Bob Balfour went to Shaunavon and brought back vaccines for the horses of Climax, but it was too late for our dear Bob, who had served us so faithfully, pulling the buggy when we went visiting, though not so much since he was getting older. He had been part of the family for so long, and a great favourite with the children. We had managed to keep him going, even through the hard times.

More babies followed the next year – on both sides of the Atlantic. Over at Frontier, baby Ernest Mathew was born to Irene and Mathew,

1936 Climax Main Street.

a brother for Hilda who was already seven and overjoyed to have a baby in the house. She was always in attendance, helping Irene and laughing and singing with her new brother. Lorraine and Leonard had their first child, Rochelle Lorraine, also over at Frontier. When she was older, Rochelle was always a great comfort to me.

Back home, Kate and Joe's family was also growing. I got news that they had another son, Desmond. Sometimes I daydreamed about going back to see them all, but the thought of another journey on land and sea soon brought me down to earth. Then there was an announcement in the newspaper of the new possibilities for passenger flying on the new Trans-Canada Airlines, and Minnie said she'd go if it wasn't so expensive. I wasn't so sure. Despite being so inspired by the exploits of our hero, Billy Bishop, the idea of flying myself was far from tempting.

My husband, William, came home from time to time, when he was able. He took work wherever he could find it, but it was hard. Sometimes it felt as if he had lost his happy joy for life. He brought us what he could to help support the family, and little trinkets for Lois and Jean, now in their teens. Lois was our prize student, and her dream was to be a teacher. 1938 was a good year for him, and there was enough for us to buy a refrigerator and, to my joy, a washing machine. In previous years, a water heater and a wireless had been possible, so by then I felt that our home had all the modern conveniences that we could ever need. I loved the radio with its news and music. Little did I know that it would soon bring us news of yet another world war.

8

Another war

1939-1945

1939 started with another new baby for Florence – a son, Barry John, born on 9th February. He was a strong and healthy baby and Minnie was delighted to have yet another grandson. Florence and James were living in Climax, so I saw them most days, and it meant that Minnie often came into town to visit. It gave us an opportunity to get together and catch up with each others' news. Throughout our lives, Minnie and I were never parted for long. She and George were still working their homestead, including our quarter as well, and Minnie would take advantage of coming to town to get a good bath and shed herself and her clothes of the eternal dust that blew off the prairies.

The summer was fair. Wheat and grain production was good, we had a bumper crop of vegetables and fruit, the chickens were laying. Everything was going well, too well. It was all to change.

In no time, another war was upon us, with all its horrors and wretchedness. We had been told that the 1914-18 conflict was the war to end all wars. But it all began again in 1939, first in Europe, but then it quickly escalated into a global fight that included even more countries than the First World War had done. It started when Hitler, angry and dissatisfied at the way Germany had been treated in the previous war, started his attempt at world dominance when his Nazi soldiers invaded Poland in the first days of September. The newspapers and radio were full of the news, and everyone was talking about it and dreading what would follow.

On 10th September, Canada declared war on Germany and joined the terrible fray, one week after Britain. The papers suggested that Canada had delayed as a symbolic demonstration of independence. Clarence was twenty three, and it frightened me to think that he might get involved. I couldn't bear the thought of losing my only son in some far away field of conflict.

Unlike the previous war, Canada did well and it went some way towards restoring our economy and national confidence. Industry and agricultural output were increased as the government mobilized the economy for war. Not only did Canada play a major role in the Atlantic and in Europe, but closer links were forged with the United States, and major airbases were established across the land. Mackenzie King's government negotiated aid for Britain, supplying food, raw materials, munitions and money. Building up of our Royal Canadian Air Force, independent from Britain's Royal Air Force, was a high priority. Canada trained airmen for the Commonwealth, and guarded against German U-boats in the Atlantic. Our troops fought in Italy, Germany and France.

Late in 1941, Japan came in to the war, and there started a time of great suspicion of those of Japanese descent living in our land. There was intense public demand for their removal, and thousands were relocated in internment camps far from the coast despite the fact that most of them were law-abiding and not a threat, and had been living and working in our communities for many years. It must have been very unsettling for those families torn from their homes and cast into camps, far from home and their livelihoods.

We got accustomed to the war around us and its effects, and life went on as usual, though much more comfortable as a result of the improvement in the economy. The marriage of my Clarence to Helen Fizzell was a joyous time. The Fizzells were homesteaders like us, from the next municipality. Clarence looked so handsome and my heart was filled with pride. They set up home in Frontier, about seven miles from Climax. It wasn't long before Helen, four years Clarence's junior, announced her pregnancy, and in no time at all, their son Gordon Clarence was born.

My joy in 1941 was also tinged with sadness. We rarely saw Tillie these days since she and Frank had moved away. We got news that their two daughters, Gladys and Marion, were now grown up and setting up homes of their own, and Frank decided that it was time to return to his home town of Port Elgin, Ontario, where he grew up, so Tillie would be moving far away. There would be more opportunities for Frank to get work, and his parents were ailing and in need of help. Tillie came to visit one last time, and we spent a happy few days together, she, Minnie and I, reminiscing and laughing together. Then she was gone, a thousand miles away.

News of the war early in December filled us all with horror. Japan attacked the US navy base at Pearl Harbour in Hawaii. The Japanese managed to destroy nearly twenty American naval vessels, including eight enormous battleships, and more than three hundred airplanes. More than two thousand American soldiers and sailors died in the attack, and another one thousand were wounded. The newspaper was full of the story. We and all our neighbours could talk of nothing else; we were all so shocked with the awfulness.

A new baby in the family was always uplifting and helped us to forget the horrors of the war for a while. Early in 1942, Clarence and Helen had another son, young Wayne Ernest, and we got together to wet the baby's head. But, as ever, there was a trade to be made for new happiness. At the end of May, poor Helen was left to care for a toddler and a new baby when Clarence made the decision to join up with the Canadian Active Army. On 27th May, he was posted overseas with the 2nd Canadian Armoured Division, also known as Lord Strathcona's Horse – Royal Canadians. Clarence was never one to put pen to paper,

1941 Martha and me at Climax.

so neither Helen nor I got news from him. We neither knew where he was, nor how he was, or even if he was dead or alive. We assumed that no news was good news as the Canadian authorities would surely keep us informed of anything we needed to know. It was very hard.

My daughters were all doing well, and I was delighted when Lois, by now aged twenty, went over to Souris to holiday with Martha and her family. Lois became great friends with Martha's daughter, Kathleen (known as Kay), and they started up a correspondence from that time. It prompted Martha to come and see Minnie and me in Climax, the first time she visited us. We had such happy times catching up, and also a chance to share so many sorrows.

We had another war baby. On 21st October 1943, my daughter Lorraine gave birth to a second daughter, Shaaron Sylvia. They were here in Climax so I was able to lend a hand with little Rochelle, now five and a happy and spirited little girl, and it went some way to taking my thoughts off my concern for Clarence.

The hostilities wore on, and the battles came closer to home than in the 1914-1918 War. German U-boats operated in Canadian waters, and many naval and merchant ships were sunk. This was known as the Battle of the Atlantic, and Canada took charge of defences in the Western Atlantic. Many thousand Canadians served in the Canadian Merchant Navy as well as those in the armed forces. Canada's contribution to the combat was great; of a population of about eleven and a half million, well over one million served in the armed forces. We read the papers with interest, especially news of the Canadian Army, ever wondering where Clarence might be. With dismay, we read of early failures in Hong Kong and Dieppe in 1942, of the allied invasion of Italy, and we were heartened by news of the highly successful invasion of France and the Netherlands between 1944 and 1945.

News started to reach us of something they were calling The Holocaust. Hitler and the Nazis were attempting to kill every person in certain ethnic, religious and political groups. The Jews of Europe were the main victims and they were taken from their homes and killed in gas chambers. At the end of the War, we learned that around six million Jews were murdered, as well as about five million other people that the Nazis targeted such as Poles, Communists, homosexuals and gypsies. We all found this information abhorrent.

Nazi Germany surrendered in May, but Japan refused to accept the terms and the War in the Pacific continued. The allies were determined to stop the Japanese. With the United States and Britain, Canada had been involved in something called the Manhattan Project which had successfully developed the atomic bomb. In mid 1945, the United States carried out a firebombing campaign that obliterated many Japanese cities, and then in August, atomic bombs were dropped on Hiroshima and then three days later on Nagasaki. The papers showed pictures of two huge mushroom shaped clouds, and brought news that at least one hundred and twenty nine thousand people were dead. This helped to end the war, but at what human cost?

Throughout the war, those of us left at home did our best to hold things together and to support each other. We prayed for those who had joined the call to arms, for those who were injured or lost. The worst thing was not knowing if our loved ones were safe, and when and if they would be returned to us. Of course, we were proud of them all, but it was so hard.

That terrible World War ended on 15th August 1945, a date that none of us will forget. Our hearts were filled with relief that all we had witnessed had at last come to an end. Helen and I cried together, longing for news of Clarence and his home-coming. But more than fifty million people lost their lives; thirty million of them were civilians. In Canada alone, more than forty five thousand died, and another fifty five thousand were wounded. We all hoped that there would be no more wars. The forming of the United Nations to prevent future strife seemed a promising solution. Some countries were divided such as Germany and Korea - to keep the different factions apart. It seemed that some good decisions were being made in the right direction, but nothing is ever perfect. Families were divided, and in the United States and the Soviet Union new hostilities were born. At least this didn't lead to armed conflict; it was known as the Cold War.

9

Retirement years

1946-1979

Over the thirty years since World War II, my life has settled into a patchwork that seems less punctuated with landmarks. Whereas our everyday existence bridged from one significant episode to the next, later years seem to have become more gentle, more easy to cope with. The foundation of the years' traumas and events makes all else pale into relative insignificance. Everything in my life that has happened in the past three decades seems tinged with the inevitable, though not without its tragedies. My expectations are diminished to an extent that I expect nothing and accept everything.

It so often seems to me that a door opens on a new life, to then let out one that is departing, before it closes again. That was in my thoughts when my daughter Irene gave birth to a second daughter, Fay Loretta, at Frontier, and then almost the same day, Minnie's husband, George Fallis, died of pneumonia. We had seen both events coming. The new baby had been making Irene's life uncomfortable throughout her pregnancy and she had reached her time. George was struck down with the flu, which he, like so many, couldn't shake off. He died at home on the prairie. It was the last day of April, the year after the war had ended, and just over a month after Clarence came home, safe and sound, and honourably discharged from the Army.

How relieved and happy I was that my son had been spared. I knew many mothers who had not been so fortunate; their sons had perished on the battlefields of Europe. They would never see them again, never hear their laughter, and cruelly denied the joy of their sons and daughters, the grandchildren who they would never see born and growing up. Of course, I felt a certain guilt that my Clarence was unharmed, while so many others had lost their boys who they had nurtured and loved, experiencing all the challenges and pride of their formative years only for it all to be terminated in some ghastly foreign place far from home.

With great pride, I read again the newspaper article I have cherished all these years.

"Clarence Fallis was born at Shaunavon, Sask. on September 27, 1916. He enlisted at Regina, Sask. with the Royal Canadian Engineers on May 27, 1942. He embarked for Britain on March 10, 1943. Clarence transferred to the Royal Canadian Army Service Corps on July 6, 1943 and proceeded to the Central Mediterranean area on November 12, 1943 and Northwest Europe on February 18, 1945. Clarence returned to Britain on December 3, 1945 and sailed for Canada on January 26, 1946. Clarence was discharged on March 20 1946. He received Service Awards: 1939-45 Star, Italy Star, France and Germany Star, Canadian Volunteer Service Medal with Clasp and War Medal 1939-45."

George Herbert Fallis 1869-1946, Climax Cemetery.

Besides the article was a full length photo of him in his uniform, looking his ever smiling and relaxed self. I've always felt grateful to the news reporter who managed to bring together all this information about my son's movements during the war. Helen and I never knew where he was, or if he was safe. When he returned, Clarence never discussed it with any of us, apart from later showing his medals to his children.

Clarence took up residence with Helen and the two boys in Shaunavon, and his life settled down. He became a member of the Canadian Legion, and took up curling with a passion. He and the family often came over, especially on a Sunday when we would all go to church together then enjoy a family lunch. I was blessed to have him and the children living nearby, and Clarence was always there to help out with any small jobs that needed to be done around the house. He also looked after my vegetable garden so, weather and grasshoppers permitting, we had fresh vegetables to eat each year.

With George gone, Minnie found the homestead too much to look after on her own and she asked everyone she met if they'd like to buy her farm, which she called Hungry Dog Ranch. She even wrote to Scotland to our brother, Thomas, to see if he would like to come and run the farm. He declined, unsurprisingly as he had his home and family and friends and a good enough standard of life where he was. So Minnie just had to do the best she could. It was almost two years before she found a buyer.

News came from Glasgow in a note from our other brother, John.

Dear Lizzy
Summer 1946

I have recently been widowed. My dear Jessie took a brain haemorrhage and died on the doorstep of our youngest son, John. It was extra hard because John was away, and his wife, Cissie, had to let me know.

John is often away these days. Things have been going badly between him and Cissie since he came home from the Army. They will shortly be divorced, and John is moving to Hazlemere in Surrey where he is planning to remarry. It is possible that I may join him in his new home. Cissie has been such a great help with many of the funeral arrangements. I'm sorry that things have gone wrong for them. It may be of interest to you that Cissie plans to emigrate to Canada with Jackie and

Ronnie, her two sons. Maybe they'll be near you and you can help them settle. I'll let you know where everyone ends up.

Best wishes from your brother John Duke.

I was, of course, sad for John, but I chuckled at his naïveté. Did he have any idea of the hugeness of Canada? It would be a coincidence indeed if Cissie and the boys moved to Climax! I never heard any more so have no inkling when they came or where they finished up.

The ever-opening door let in another son for Clarence, little Leonard John, while it closed for Mathew Maki, Irene's husband. He was away visiting family in Wisconsin when he was struck down. They brought him home to Climax and he was buried in our little cemetery, close to where Minnie had buried George the year before. The funeral was attended by so many of the Maki family who farmed in Lone Tree Municipality. There were ten of them in Range 18 in those early years of our homesteading, all come from Finland with so many others to make a new life for themselves. Things were hard for Irene, left on her own with three children, including Baby Fay who was only just one. Hilda was sixteen and a great help to her mother with the two younger ones, Fay still so little, and Ernest not yet eight.

My daughter, Lois, trained as a teacher. She got a very good position at McNutt and loved her work. After the war, she met a young man called Willard Johann Kendel, born in Shaunavon in 1923 to an immigrant family, but then we were all immigrants. Only the First Nations, the Plains Indian tribes, were originally of this land, and they were all marginalized and moved to reservations. Willard's father was Adolph, a German from Russia, and his mother was Margaret Becker Kendel. I was very fond of her, though we could not exchange much more than a word or two due to our language differences.

The wedding was in Shaunavon on a dull July day. In attendance were Willard's parents, with Irene, Clarence, Lorraine and all their families, and Jean, my youngest daughter, as yet unmarried. It was a happy occasion, especially as my William was able to join us. Lois was twenty four, and I felt so proud to see her wed, and her father there to give her away. It was six years since we had last come together in a family wedding. Lois and Willard set up home in Shaunavon, so not too far from us.

1946 With my third daughter, Lois, a teacher at McNutt.

In September, I got a letter from my cousin Mollie, from Carrick-on-Shannon announcing the sad death of my Aunt Mary Ann, who I had stayed with in London before coming to Canada.

Killukin
24th Sep 1947

My dear Cousin Lizzie

I am writing to let you know that our dear Auntie passed away on the 5th. Uncle wrote to me a few times telling me that she was not well. I thought I'd let you know, you being fond of her, and in case no one else has written.

Uncle kept us up to date. Some days she seemed to be recovering, others it seemed she might linger out for days or weeks. I wish I could have been near; both to see her and to give a little assistance in caring for her. But by the time all routines for permits, etc was done, I fear that it would be all over. Uncle sent us a wire to say that she was gone and that it was a gentle passing, so that's a blessing. Her funeral was attended by many people and Uncle said that he received over 30 letters of sympathy from far and wide. Auntie was so well known and respected for her good works.

Mind you, we are so busy here, it would have been a great difficulty getting away. Harvesting means so much work, especially not having a steady man; we are rather handicapped. We are very fortunate to have all hay saved (216 cocks) & all in shed and a pike; only 20 cocks we hope to get any day, its raining last night & today but S & A are busy in the garden now. Since 1st Aug its continual rush, I was out every day. We got casual man every day we c'd, we finished cutting the oats on Tuesday last. Wheat is not ready yet. I never worked so hard out doors or done so much & I feel fine now, the hot sun & outdoors is great. Winnie Clifford, next door, came up almost every day & she is a great worker at hay. I did what I thought was impossible. Geo made the foundations for a pike out in the 4 acre field & he and A. had 2 carts & filled both & then brought in loads & pitched them to Winnie, she pitched it over to me & I built the pike (35 cocks in it). Geo put the last 2 cocks on top &

roped it, we had it roped at dinner time next day & She and I were very proud it has kept up & straight too.

We borrowed Len Smith's single machine & reaper attachment for the oats, G & Arthur both sat up to work it when I got tired, tying the sheaves. I took Geo place on machine & drove the horse & A tipped up the sheaves. I enjoyed every day.

Now it's near dinner time & I want to get this posted & Excuse writing & mistakes.

Much love to you & yours from all here
Yours very affectionately
Mollie

I thought back to times at Killukin and imagined that S and A must be Sarah and Archibald, Mollie's sister and brother. I was sad to hear that my Aunt had died, but also amused to get such a rambling letter from Mollie. She always was such a chatterbox, and this little story from her reflected that and reminded me of how she always was.

It was a couple of months before I heard from Hasluck. He wrote to tell me of his mother and to find out how I was. This was the start of several letters between us, later taken on by his daughter, Joan, who became a firm friend over the miles.

Ridgedale,
Dawlish Road,
Teignmouth,
Devon

(The address was impressed into the paper, which I found rather fascinating).

1st November 1947

Dear Cousin Elizabeth

I often wonder how you and your sisters are faring in Canada. I find it hard to believe that it's almost forty years since you lived with us in Willesden, and we are now both in our sixties. My wife, May, and I have five children, Joan, Pat, Cis, Mick and Ted, though all except Ted have fled the nest and now starting families of their own. Joan and Cis each have daughters, Susan and Rosemary. Ted is much younger than the others, only 11, and is still at school and not likely to be leaving home for some time.

I am writing to let you know that my mother passed away in September. She was 88. She led a good and useful life, devoted to commendable works for the poor and needy. We were overwhelmed by the letters of sympathy and admiration for all her achievements. My father is 86 and going strong, and adjusting to life without Mother. He sends you his regards. He still recalls the time that you stayed with us in Willesden before you and Mary Ann set off on your travels.

My sister, Edie, still lives at home, so she will be able to give our Father a hand. She has never married. She works in London and has a full social life. She says she doesn't have time to find a husband! Our brother, Robert Duke, lives in New Zealand and his wife is called Alma. We rarely hear from them. I don't think that they have any children.

Perhaps you might find some time to drop me a line. I would be very interested to hear how things have worked out for you.

With fond wishes
Your cousin
Hasluck

Hasluck always called me Elizabeth, when I lived with them and since, and referred to any of my sisters that he knew by their given names, not our father's short names for us. So, his letter reminded me that Minnie was really Mary Ann; we hadn't called her that for over fifty years! I read the letter over and over, and mused upon the fact that, like me, Hasluck had five children (my first baby, stillborn, I didn't include). It was good to hear from him, but sad, of course, to hear that my Aunt Mary Ann had died. I set to straight away that evening to write back. It took me several evenings to tell him of our life on the Saskatchewan prairie.

It was a couple of years later in Climax that Irene's daughter, Hilda, my first grandchild, was married. She was eighteen. Her new husband, Richard Anthony Beaume, was working in Climax, but it was not so long after that he and Hilda moved away to Chatham, Ontario. Irene put on a brave face but it was as if she'd lost a friend as Hilda had been such a help after Mathew had died. She was left to care for young Ernie, now ten, and Fay, who was a three year old full of mischief. I too was sad to bid farewell to my grand-daughter.

Minnie decided to sell up all but the land. She had been finding her 'Hungry Dog Ranch' too much for a woman alone, and so far no-one had come forward to take it off her hands. So she sold the stock and all the equipment and decided to take a trip back home to Ireland. She tried hard to convince me to go along too, but my mind was made up that I could not leave my home and the family, so she made arrangements without me. Perhaps if Mother was still there, I might have thought differently, but both she and Father were gone, and all my brothers and sisters either in Scotland, in the north of Ireland, or here in Canada, and Lillie and Blanche had passed away.

So I bade Minnie farewell on her journey back to the home we had left some forty one years before. We were both in our early twenties then, now Minnie was sixty, and we had never been very far apart in all those years, except for the time that I had been in England with my Aunt and Uncle. I thought her quite brave to make the journey, but Minnie was always the more capable and determined of the two of us. Once there, she stayed at Coolnagranchy with our cousin, George Robert, who had been away working in the north for many years to earn the money to buy our old home farm.

As was the way, George's parents, Edward and Emily, had left the Derrymaquirk farm and all their possessions to their oldest son William, leaving the other three children with nothing. So now George had bought his way back to the family lands. He was now at Coolnagranchy where he married Irene Sleator in Sligo in Spring 1949. His sister Ruby married Len Smyth and moved to England where I heard they had eight children in all, and his older brother Eddie with wife Mary Murray went to Michigan, USA, where they had three sons. It was only several years later that I learned these facts and many others about my Monson cousins and relatives back in Ireland.

Minnie was away for over a year, and while there she was able to help Irene Monson at the birth of her first child, Emily Olive. Irene was almost forty by then, quite an age to be having her first child and she was very grateful to have Minnie there to help, and to give a hand with the new baby. Minnie spent some of her time visiting other relatives, over at Carrick-on-Shannon and Leitrim. She went north for a while to see our sisters, Sarah, Eva, Kate and Queenie, and to meet their families who we had never met.

On her return, Minnie told me how wonderful it was to hear the sound of a child again in our old Coolnagranchy home, and that there would soon be another as Irene was already expecting again. There were many changes to report back and Minnie and I spent several happy times with her telling me about this one and that, what had changed, what was the same, and the people she had met on her travels including so many who had been born since we had left.

Minnie returned with a new resolve to work her land, and she got Jim McNaught to break some of the homestead ground. She took domestic work with a neighbour so she could pay Jim, and to keep her head above water.

I became a grandmother again and again – and all grand-daughters it seemed. In the early 1950's, Hilda gave birth to Gail Patricia, Clarence and Helen had Lenore Helene, who I'm fairly sure was named after my cousin Hasluck's sister, Edith Lenore, who I had lived with back in London. Lois had her first baby, also a daughter who she called Pamela Jean. And Minnie heard from Coolnagranchy the news that George and Irene had a second daughter, Helen Alexandra.

It's funny how things go in waves. After grand-daughters, there were grandsons. Minnie's daughter, Florence, had a son, Warren Dennis, then my youngest daughter, Jean, after her wedding to Otto Vogel in Medicine Hat, also had a son Terence Dale the next year. They had settled over at Moose Jaw. News came from Chatham that Hilda's second child was yet another boy, John Robert.

Then it was the turn of the girls again. Jean and Otto, lately moved to Regina, had another daughter, Margo Jean, and Hilda's new baby, her third, was named Debra Lee. The variety of new names amused me as I had grown up in a family where the same names were used over and over. Family names for boys included John Duke, Robert Duke, George, William, Frederick, Thomas, John and Edward, and for the girls there was Elizabeth (like me), Mary Ann (like Minnie and two of my aunts), Sarah, Kathleen, Emily, Ellen and Alice.

In about 1952, there was great excitement in our area as oil was found in the Bone Creek Basin. They called it "black gold", and we were told that it would bring great wealth to our land. That was joy to the ears of all those that had struggled for so many years. In August, the first drilling rig of any magnitude moved on to the south west section of Minnie's land. The sudden activity brought great interest, and a small reward for Minnie. People came from all around to see what was going on, and to watch the equipment being erected. The well on Minnie's land didn't strike lucky but it, and other drilling, did bring business and new employment to the area for a while, though none of the great riches we'd hope for. Any prizes went to the oil production companies. Once some of the rigs started producing oil, the coal digs up in the hills that we had all relied on for fuel up to that time were abandoned.

In March 1953, we received sad news from Tillie that Frank had passed away. He was buried near their home in Port Elgin, over in Ontario. Tillie then came back west to Calgary, Alberta to be closer to her daughters, Gladys and Marion, who were married and having children of their own. Her new home was still some way away but, with the buses and the improved roads that were now making transport so much easier, it made it possible for her to get over to see Minnie and me, and it meant that we were able to meet up from time to time. It was always a happy occasion for us all, and gave an opportunity to bring many of the younger ones together. Tillie took a job as a seamstress in a clothing store, modifying dresses to suit customers and worked there for many years. She was always good with a needle and thread.

I found that I was content with my life in town, with the greater security and companionship that it offered. In that way, Minnie and I were quite different. She was always happiest on the land and finding ways to make the best of it so, at the ripe old age of sixty eight, Minnie remarried a homesteader she had met at one of the evenings at a friend's cabin. Edner Skalbeck farmed over in the Canuck area, some eighteen miles away. He was the same age as me and three years older than Minnie. His parents were Edwin and Mary Skalbeck, both born in Sweden. They migrated to Minnesota in the US and had eight children. In 1911, Edner's father settled in Maple Creek, and Edner came the next year at the age of seventeen to help his father. The rest of Edner's family joined their father in 1913, and Edner and two of his brothers worked the land together just south of Bracken, in the Canuck area. None of them ever married, that was until Edner and Minnie joined forces, and Minnie moved over to his farm at Canuck.

In the time leading up to Christmas each year, I took great pleasure in preparing letters and cards for my family, both near and far. That always set off wonderful Christmas exchanges that went on into the New Year. I particularly enjoyed hearing from Hasluck's daughter, Joan. She lived in Devon where she farmed with her husband Tom. We always had so much to talk about. I search out her letter from December 1955.

East Underdown Farm,
Drewsteignton,
Nr Exeter Devon
England
1st December 1955

Dear Lizzie and family

I received your news in November and I was so pleased to hear from you and to see the picture of you with Auntie Minnie and Auntie Tillie. Your description of the weather couldn't be more different from here. We have some snow from time to time, but nothing like several feet from November to April as you have. Our growing season is so much longer than yours. I shall do my best never to complain about our weather again.

My daughters, Sue and Jenny, are doing well at their new school. I take them each morning in the Land Rover, and then bring them home in the afternoon. It does take a bit of time out of my day but it's fun to chat to the other mothers while I wait for the girls to come out. The farm and garden keep me so busy. This part of England is mainly sheep farming, so we have sheep, and just one cow for dairy. I do my best to grow as much of our fruit and vegs as possible, and make jams and chutneys.

I enclose a small gift for you and hope you will like it. I saw it in a shop in Chagford and it reminded me that you said that you always like to have an apron on. The little flowers embroidered on it are like the flowers in my garden at different times of the year - violets, primroses, forget-me-nots, poppies. I do hope you like it.

My best wishes to you and your family

Joan

I was so pleased to receive such a pretty apron and wrote straight back to Joan to thank her.

By 1956, I had five more grandchildren. Lois' daughter Pamela was delighted to have a baby brother, Kyle, and Hilda had two more daughters, Susan Margaret and Wendy Lillian Irene. Jean had a son, Dennis Lorne, over at Biggar, Clarence and Helen had a daughter Marcia Louise.

I often had some of the older grandchildren over: two of mine, Fay and Ernie, and Minnie's Barrie. They all seemed to enjoy a meal with their Gram Fallis and often asked for more. Sometimes they would stay for a few days, or more in the holidays, except for young Ernie who was fine in the day but would never stay the night. One day, when I asked his mother why, she said that he was frightened of staying. I admit that I was always very firm with the youngsters, but I hoped that I was fair. As they got older, they got up to all sorts of tricks, including smoking in the bedroom. If they thought I didn't know what they were up to, they were wrong! In fact, I had fun at their expense, creeping up to the bedroom door and then knocking abruptly and calling them to come to tea. I could only laugh at their panic!

One weekend, Minnie arrived unannounced on my doorstep. At last, someone had bought Hungry Dog Ranch from her. She had sold her farm to Don Rapley and his son for $10,000 and couldn't take the money to the bank as it was closed for the weekend. She was very excited and asked if she could stay until the bank in Climax opened on Monday morning. In she came and dropped a large brown valise at my feet. I told her to come into the sitting room and in she came and opened up the bag to show me it was stuffed full of bank notes. I had never seen so much money before and I asked her if she had robbed a bank or something! She explained about the sale of the land and wanted me to help her to count the money, which we did, laughing all the while like a couple of schoolgirls. Then we packed it away and pushed it under a bed. That bag of money distracted us from all the daily chores. Neither of us had ever seen so many bank notes before, and we began to fret that somehow it would be stolen or magically disappear. Several times, we pulled out the bag and counted the money again and again to check that none of it had gone astray, putting it in piles around us to help keep tally. We hardly slept at all that weekend and, when Monday morning came, Minnie and I moved the valise from under the bed and on to Minnie's buggy, guarding the bag between us as we set off into town. At the bank, Minnie handed the bag to the manager, and we watched intently as he got a teller to count it out. The manager then arranged for the deposit documents for Minnie, and gave back the valise. We set off for home in the buggy, laughing all the way about Minnie's new good fortune. She had wanted to sell up for so many years and, at last, it was done and the money was in the bank.

Minnie stayed for a few more days before heading back to her Canuck home. It was while she was staying that we got the news that our dear sister, Martha, had died in Brandon, Manitoba. About ten days before, on July 19th, 1956, she passed away in hospital after a stroke. She was sixty five, and the third of our siblings to depart this life. She was widowed some nine years before, and the news of her death reached us from her youngest son, Denny, who lived near her in Souris with his wife and two children. A few days later, we got news that Martha's funeral had taken place. Really this was something of a blessing as I had been distressing about the long and arduous journey over. Even Minnie, our seasoned traveller, was not sure if she could manage it. I was almost seventy two and Minnie was about to have her sixty ninth birthday, so it would not have been an easy journey for either of us. Denny told us that not all his five brothers and sisters had been able to get to the funeral as they were spread far and wide, in Ontario, Alberta and Winnipeg. He sent us a lovely letter, telling us where everyone lived and all about Martha's eight grand-children. Of the four of us Monson girls who had come to Canada, it had been hardest over the years to keep up with all Martha's news as she lived so much further away. We were so grateful to Denny for his kind thoughts.

The flow of additions to my family continued. Hilda and Richard, in Chatham, had a fifth daughter, Cindy Lou. The pattern of their family seemed to be following that of the Coolnagranchy Monsons; first a girl (like me), then a boy (like John Duke), a girl (Minnie) and so on. I wondered if the pattern would follow all the way through with ten girls and two boys. I hoped that Hilda would not have the struggles that Mother had with so many children to feed and clothe. Shortly after Hilda's new baby, my youngest daughter Jean and husband Otto had a third daughter, Trudy Lorna, over at Biggar.

1958 was a year of personal tragedy for me, and felt like it was the start of many heartbreaks. I got news that, on 8th June, my dear William, my husband of forty eight years, was dead. He had worked so hard for me and our family, and when the land had failed us, he did not give up but took work wherever he could, so that the children and I could be sustained. He always showed great optimism with life and people. At his death, he was eighty three, ten years older than me. I was sad that I was not with him; he was away at Fort McLeod where he often found work, when he suffered a stroke. I can only feel that it was a blessing that it took him straight away. He could not have borne a partial death that would leave him impaired or without speech. As any widow will know, this loss takes a part of you away. Even though William had been forced to work away for so many years, I still found it hard to believe that I wouldn't see him again – my life's partner, the father of my children, and we had toiled together against such odds to build our life on the prairie. His interment was held at Trinity United Church in Fort McLeod and Clarence took me in his truck so I could bid him farewell. It was a long journey, but I was pleased that I could be there.

But life goes and, and there was always something to keep me busy. Now I was a widow, and my children all grown and gone their own ways, I felt as if I was allowed to slow down. I had served my time and now life was giving me its consent to take things very much easier. There was more time for letter-writing, and receiving news from my family, far and wide, brought me great joy. I was surprised in 1960 to get post from Ireland, and it was from Tillie. I never knew she was going over the water, and here was communication from her, and a picture of her with Eva, John, Tom and Sarah. I remember feeling just a bit jealous that I wasn't there with them to enjoy the occasion, but happy too for the opportunity to see them all together and to see how they had changed.

Ireland !
July 1960

Dear Sister

I'm sure this will come as a surprise to you. It's a long time now that I've been wanting to visit our old home before I get too old to do it. Now that I'm alone (I can't believe it's already 7 years that I've been a widow) and the girls have got their own lives, I've taken the plunge. Eva's the one who has been egging me on, so I've done it - and here I am, and having a wonderful time.

Eva lives in County Down, in the North, with Kate and Queenie nearby. John and Tom came on a visit from Scotland. We've had such a merry time. This picture is taken in Eva's garden, where she lives at Benown Farm. Eva's husband, George, took the photo. It was such a bright sunny day, you can see his shadow in front of John! Queenie's not so well at the moment, so we all went on a short visit. She and everyone send their love.

We spent a couple of days down south visiting Coolnagranchy and Derrymaquirk and the old places of our childhood. The second photo is from Croghan Church of Mother and Blanche's gravestone - it's grand, isn't it. None of us is sure where Lillian is buried.

Much love
Tillie

My Canada family all call me Gram Fallis, which always makes me chuckle. News from any of them is always welcome, and I rejoice in my children and grandchildren, and am always delighted when they come to visit.

Hilda was still having babies, but the Coolnagranchy pattern didn't last. Next was a son, James Mathew, and the next year a daughter, Belinda Gay. That was 1961.

It was yet another year of tragedy, but whereas my William's death was in the proper order of things, the loss of my beloved daughter Irene was almost too hard to bear. Early one evening, I got a call from Ernie, her son, over at Frontier telling me that she was involved in a

July 1960 – Eva, John, Tillie, Thomas, Sarah
Benown Farm.

Mary Monson (nee McMaster) 1865-1926
and Blanche Florence Monson 1896-1924
Croghan Graveyard.

car accident and died of her injuries. She was fifty eight, and she was my first born. She came into this world in our homestead cabin after that first winter we stayed on the land through those cold dark months. Life had so often been cruel to us, but this seemed the cruellest, and not in the right order of things at all. No parent should have to grieve for their child in this way. My family was a wonderful comfort to me, and gathered round to give me ease and share my pain, but of course they were feeling it too.

The following year marked the beginning of several health scares for Minnie. It started with a stroke and she was rushed to hospital. We were blessed that she recovered, but four years later, the day before Christmas, she fell and broke her hip. After that she always walked with a stick.

In 1964, Jean's first son, Terence, died. He was only just twelve. I also got sad news from Northern Ireland from my sister Queenie.

Bangor, Co. Down
January 1965

Dear Lizzie

Thanks you for your last letter. I'm sorry I haven't written for so long, and now it's with more sad news I regret to say. This time it's Sarah Jane. She died last month at her little farmhouse at Newtownards, just about four miles from us. She caught the pneumonia and never got better. It's only a short time ago that her husband Jim Haire died. Do you remember him from over at Carrick-on-Shannon - Molly's big brother? Sarah was seventy two and left behind her two daughters, Florence and Muriel, and a son, Jackie.

Her burial was at Comber, just down the coast from Newtownards - such a beautiful little town. Everyone was there who could be. Sarah's family came: Florence and Hugh and their daughter Angela, Jackie was there with his three daughters, and of course Sarah's youngest, Muriel. She's never married. She's been such a blessing to Sarah, helping to care for her as she has. Eva and George came over from Portavogie, and arranged for one of their Tangent Buses to bring some of us from Bangor - me, and Kate and Joe with their family -

Desmond and Judith McCaugherty and young Donald and Christine. Others came too on the bus who knew Sarah Jane well. It was such a beautiful place to be buried. There were many neighbours and friends come to bid her farewell.

After the service and burial, we all went to a hostelry in Comber for refreshments. Kate's husband, Joe McCaugherty, is a wonderful host and great entertainer and singer, and it didn't take him long to get on to his favourite "The Green Glens of Antrim" - what a beautiful song. He also treated us to Robert Service's "The Cremation of Sam McGee", which he could quote off by heart from beginning to end. I wasn't sure that it was quite the thing for the occasion, but no-one seemed too worried. It certainly was quite amusing.

I will miss our little trips. Kate and Sarah and I often took the bus down to visit Eva at Portavogie. It is a fishing village with a harbour, and we sisters love going to sit on the quay so we can chat and watch all the activity. Sometimes we buy fresh prawns or herrings from the fishermen. Of course, Kate and I will still be able to visit Eva, but it won't be the same without Sarah. We will miss her so - always full of such funny stories and witty observations.

So four of us are now gone, and the rest of us seem to be doing OK, especially you, now eighty if I'm right. It was good to hear about all your children and grandchildren. You have so many and I only ever had my Margaret. I have not been so well recently and she takes good care of me in my little flat here in Bangor. I shall never know the joy of such a family as you have, but there, that's life. There's no point in dwelling on what might or might not have been.

We got news from Boyle that our cousin Fred died recently. He was seventy and Grange now stands empty. How strange. I can only think of it full of our cousins, and playing in the hay loft, and always in trouble with Aunt Kathleen and Uncle John Duke. That leaves our cousin Abraham living nearby in Grange Farm, which he bought when he went to America to seek his fortune. He lives there with his wife Lily and their three children Elsie, Harold and Dorothy, all almost grown up by *now. I met them all once when I went down visiting. They have a little dog called Jack who loves to run after sticks - very entertaining.*

I hope when I write again it will be with some better news.

Your baby sister,

Queenie

PS Eva and Kate and everyone send their love and best wishes.

How far off were those times. How far away were my little sisters and the places of my childhood. How sad to hear news of those that I had not seen for so long, those I would never see again. How helpless I felt. More and more also Minnie's health became of great concern to me. Her circulation was getting bad, particularly in her legs, and it was causing her great pain and discomfort. She had always been so active. As well as the pain came a great frustration.

The following spring, news came from Hasluck in Devon that he, like me, was now widowed. As ever it was an interesting and newsy letter.

Ridgedale
Dawlish Road
Teignmouth
Devon

20th May 1966

Dear Cousin Lizzie

I hope that this letter finds you and the family well. My wife May passed away last summer and I have been meaning to write. It has taken me a while to get myself into a new routine. I have had to teach myself to cook. I was always banned from the kitchen, so this is all quite new to me. It's not been as hard as I expected, and I seem to have got it all organised and managing to keep myself going! I'm now a dab hand at stew, and poached egg on toast and I've discovered that the local bakery makes an excellent date and walnut cake, and they keep one for me each week. May never wanted any new equipment in the kitchen. She said it was an unnecessary expense. Now I have an electric kettle and a toaster and a new stove. I hope she will forgive me!

A few years ago, I retired from the London accountancy firm and now I have a good deal of leisure time. I enjoy regular games of bowls at the local club, and I meet up with my friend Peck for refreshments in Teignmouth at least once a week if I can. It's always a very jolly affair. When we've finished, it's an opportunity to get some shopping and, of course, collect the cake! I enjoy watching the football on the television. Now that I'm on my own, I can turn it up as loud as I wish - you see, I'm rather deaf. My wife, May, always complained that I had it on far too loud!

I keep my hand in with doing the accounts for a couple of large estates, including Ennis, down in Cornwall, which is a very nice place to visit. It's owned by a Reverend Ennis, a dour old chap. My main point of contact there is his older sister, Miss Ennis. She's a real character, and is quite convinced that the estate should be hers. It never will be as the inheritance is down the male line. When the old reverend dies, it will go to a cousin in Canada. He will be fortunate indeed!

Miss Ennis has shown me around the family mansion. It's a beautiful place, but all shut up. No-one lives there now. There is an impressive library and I have spent several hours looking at some quite spectacular books. In my opinion, the most handsome are the hand illustrated volumes of flowers and herbs. Miss Ennis doesn't know what will happen to everything. It will be a heritage lost, I think. The Ennis family goes back hundreds of years. The present house replaced an original Elizabethan mansion. There is an oil painting of it in the main hall of the 'new' house. The Ennis Estate covers many miles and takes in most of the area of Penryn, on the South Cornish coast. There are still rents collected from many properties in the town, though it is not as wealthy and influential as it once was.

I have just spent a couple of weeks at Ennis, doing the end of year accounts. I always stay at the cottage of a lovely lady, Mrs Nicholls, who was once the housekeeper at the big house. She is *a very good cook, and very good company and we have some entertaining conversations. After Ennis, I then went on to visit my colleague, Sir Harry Graham Vivian. He has a beautiful home and gardens on the Lizard Peninsula, not so far from Ennis. Cornwall has a Mediterranean climate, even milder than Devon, and his gardens are splendid, with all sorts of unusual and semi-tropical plants. My favourite time to visit is now as the rhododendrons at Trelissick are in glorious bloom.*

Over the years, I have met some very interesting people. I expect you will remember some of those visitors my parents received at Willesden. I went on to work with some of them during the War when I was appointed as a financial adviser in the Ministry of Agriculture. There was concern with problems of food production, and ships bringing imports of Australian wheat were being bombed by the Germans. I was part of a team looking at ways to cultivate vast acres of the country for cereal production during the shortage. Later in the war, we were looking to find areas where flax could be produced following a fall-off in imports from Russia. It was most interesting but challenging work, helping to ensure that the nation was fed during those harrowing times.

I look forward to further correspondence between us.

With fond thoughts from your cousin

Hasluck.

I was always fond of Hasluck, and delighted to hear so much about him and his life and experiences. Once more, I wondered whether we might have got together if things had been different.

An unusual event occurred at about that time. My brother Thomas and his wife Delia were living in Scotland, when his son, James, made the decision to come out to Canada. I got a letter out of the blue from him, and it took me quite by surprise.

2nd July 1967
Johnstone, Scotland

Dear Cousin Elizabeth

We've never set eyes on each other but I feel I know you, and I'm sure we will meet at some time in the not too distant future. My father, Thomas, has told me a lot about growing up with his big sister in Coolnagranchy before she (you) and Mary Ann went homesteading to Canada all those years ago.

Well, now it's my turn to come to Canada. I'll be moving to Medicine Hat in Alberta, a bit over 150 miles from Climax. Far enough, but I hear that the roads and transport are improving all the time. I've got a job at the Empress Gas Plant. There's a three-bedroomed house with the job, so I won't have the trouble of looking for somewhere to live. I'll be flying over later this month and getting everything sorted out, then my wife Patsy will follow early in September with our six children. We have four boys and two girls. The oldest is twelve and the youngest is three, so I'll be looking around for schools for the older ones before Patsy comes out.

I'll let you know my address, etc when I get out there.

With best wishes

James Monson

A couple of months later, I heard more from James, or Jim as he liked to be called, and in time I did get to meet him and his family, and to hear more about my little brother Thomas and his life in Glasgow.

That was 1970, and about the time of metrication here in Canada. Once before, I managed the change from Irish money and measurements to the Canadian system, but then I was young and it wasn't so hard. To thrust a new system on an old lady of eighty five, almost eighty six, is cruelty indeed. It was all started by the Liberal federal government of Pierre Trudeau and the Metric Commission. And many things have been changing gradually since then. All my life, both in Ireland and Canada, I was used to seeing the road signposts and signs showing distances to places in miles. Suddenly it seemed that the places I knew had got further away – no longer miles but

1970 Me, aged 85.

kilometres. Then, when the packets in the stores were printed with grams and kilograms, I was lost. The newspapers were filled with articles about folk who were resisting metrication, even some government employees were making a fuss – and losing their jobs because of it. One official with Revenue Canada who publicly opposed mandatory metric conversion was dismissed for "conduct unacceptable for a public servant." Not even the weather forecast remained unaffected, with Fahrenheit temperatures replaced by Celsius, and rainfall measured in millimetres and snow in centimetres. Although I tried, I had no idea what was going on.

But I had lived so many years on the prairies that I have a good idea of what to expect. There is snow in the winter and there are surprises in the summer, some better than others. The hours of darkness never change – from 5pm to 8:30am in the winter months, and the longest summer days in June and July stretch from 5am to 9pm.

More news came from over the water, this time from my nephew, John.

Hazlemere, Surrey
December 1970

Dear Auntie

I am sorry to tell you that your brother John Duke, my father, has died at the age of 86. He's been living here in England with me and my wife. He was taken to hospital on Wednesday last having trouble with his breathing and he passed away peacefully on Friday. I have made arrangements for his burial here in Hazlemere.

We will miss him and his tales of the war and his various adventures. He had many friends, and always kept everyone laughing.

I have let people know where I can, but really I've lost touch with most of the family since I remarried and came to England. It would be nice to know how everyone is doing. I don't even hear from my sons, Jackie and Ronnie, in Canada.

I am now 68, and retired from work. My wife and I enjoy greens bowling and that's what keeps us both busy these days.

I hope this letter finds you well. I got your address from my Uncle Thomas in Glasgow.

With best regards
John

So my brother John was gone. I thought back on our time growing up. He was the second child, and for a short time we were the only two from Coolnagranchy at school together, and me having to try and protect him from his difficulties and troubles. He always preferred to be out with Father on the land, and there he learnt so much more than he ever did in the classroom.

When Minnie and I left for Canada, Mother still kept us up with John's news. I looked back over those letters from home and marvelled at John's continual good fortune – being spared the courts and imprisonment when he had thrown a trouble-maker out of the bar and killed him – his exploits in the war, and surviving on rum when the army had forgotten him on Perim Island. How I laughed, as I had done before. And then I cried. I cried for John, and for my daughter Irene, and my daughter stillborn when we first came to the homestead, for Mother and Father, for my William and his brother John, for my sister Martha, and those back home in Ireland, Blanche and Lillie and Sarah Jane. I was overcome with loss and sadness. It took news of Minnie's troubles to bring me back from the desolation that had descended upon me.

I got news that Minnie's circulation had got so bad and, with hardening of the arteries, she was admitted to the Hospital and Geriatric Centre in Swift Current. There her leg was amputated. From there she was sent back to Shaunavon Hospital where she spent several months recuperating, and finally went back home and Florence went over to care for her. It wasn't so far to Canuck, so I was able to visit and give Florence a break from time to time. But Minnie never really got over the amputation and suffered greatly with it.

Her spirits were lifted for a while when I went over to see her with news from Lois, who had gone over to England to visit Hasluck. He and I still exchanged letters from time to time, and when Lois became fascinated by this, she too started to write to Hasluck. This resulted in her making a visit there for five days at the end of September, before going on to Boyle to see Coolnagranchy and the places of our youth.

Boyle, Ireland
Oct 5, 1974

Dear Mother

I am having such a happy time here. The journey was not so bad - we were able to get a flight direct from Regina to Heathrow Airport near London and arrived very early on Sept 26. We then took the tube train to Paddington Station and then the train took us all the way to Teignmouth in Devon. The views of the English countryside were lush and green with beautiful trees and rivers, and interesting towns and villages. It couldn't be more different than our prairies back home, and our homesteads. How strange Saskatchewan must have been for you when you and Pappa first came.

Uncle Hasluck collected us from the station and took us to his lovely home overlooking the sea. What a charming man! His wife, May, died in 1965, so he has been on his own for some time but seems to be getting on well. He enjoyed that I did some cooking for him, as he seems to live on a rather grey stew which he makes at the weekend and then reheats each day. It's got everything in it, and he seems hale and hearty on it. He gave us that when we first arrived, and it tasted well enough. It's just not a good colour, and I have introduced him to browning so its appearance is much improved! I think he has enjoyed the bit of variety that I have been able to bring him!

I was surprised that he called his wife, May. I thought you told me that her name was Clara, and he said it was actually Clara Selina May, but he always called her May. And May is also the middle name of his third daughter, Cicely.

The house is quite interesting, to me anyway. Its design is what they call a dormer bungalow, with most of the rooms downstairs and then a bedroom up in the roof area with a wonderful double window with views to the ocean. The house has a sun room on the front where Uncle Hasluck has his sleep each afternoon, and we've joined him there and the warmth is soporific so we doze too. Uncle has a lot of red geranium flowers in the sun room, and they give off a most pleasant perfume in the warmth. It is very relaxing and very enjoyable.

In front of the house is a lovely garden which Uncle keeps quite trim, despite his age, and with a pond with red goldfish swimming around where you can sit and dream. At the back of the house, Uncle still grows vegetables and they are a main ingredient with beef or mutton for his stews. For a man in his mid-eighties, he's very active. A bit like you, dear Mother.

After 5 days with Uncle Hasluck, he gave us a lift to the port and we took the ferry to Ireland. The train journey showed a green and luscious land. We had to change in Dublin, then finally arrived at Boyle and looked around for somewhere to stay. While walking, we happened by chance to meet George Monson. First he took us to the hotel and then, when we got talking more and explained who we were, it turned out that his grandfather and your grandfather were brothers! We asked if he knew of Coolnagranchy and - you'll never guess what happened next! He actually lives there! We arranged to visit the following day and met his wife, Irene. It was thrilling for us to visit the place where you grew up.

He told us the history of the farm. Apparently, it had been in the family for over 200 years - did you know that? After your father left, it went to your Uncle George and Aunt Mary Ann in 1921, then to a cousin, another George, in 1927. When he died in 1937, it went to strangers for a while, then George bought it back and he and Irene took up ownership in 1949. Apart from the addition of a kitchen, George told us that it was the original house.

The next morning, we visited Knockadoo Estate, where you were born. It's a big farm now - about 300 acres. We met the steward and told him the reason for our visit. He was interested to hear that your father was steward there and that you were born there in 1884 and now living in Canada.

While we were at Coolnagranchy, George arranged for us to visit Dorothy Monson, daughter of Abraham who I understand was one of your cousins who lived at Grange. We also met her brother Harold. We spent a lovely evening there. All these people we met are farming folk.

I don't know how long it will take for this letter to reach

you. Probably I will be back in Regina before it arrives. But since I don't know when I'll get down to Climax, I'm sure you'll have a chance to read it before I see you next.

Please give my love to Auntie Minnie. I am so sad that she is suffering so.

With my love to you across the miles.

See you soon.

Lois

Once again, I thought that I might have visited the home of my youth, and cousins and family. But I had decided against that long ago, and now it was far too late. I was grateful to be able to see some of them again through Lois' eyes, and delighted to get news of my cousin, Hasluck. And I mused once more upon the thought that perhaps Hasluck and I might have wed if things had been different, as his parents, first cousins, had wed before. I chuckled at my foolish meanderings.

Minnie certainly enjoyed the news from England, and she smiled contentedly when I read Lois' letter to her. It was good to see her uplifted a little from her constant pain. The months passed and her troubles went from bad to worse. It was so painful for me to see her discomfort and not be able to do anything to improve things.

Just a couple of days before Christmas 1972, she died. She was eighty five and had lived a life of hard farming on the prairie. We buried her in Climax Cemetery, along with other family members who had gone before. We left her there in the peaceful grounds with her first husband George and her two little sons, Herbie and baby John.

It was only six months later that we got news that Minnie's husband, Edner, was also dead, not from illness but by a sad accident. He was working on his farm in Bracken when he fell out of his truck and died as a result. I was reminded that he was the same age as me, but I always thought of him as being much older. He took his place in the Climax Cemetery next to Minnie.

Life continued, and birthdays passed. The family always made a special occasion of them, especially when I celebrated my birthdays leading up to my ninetieth. And that was the proudest one of all for

Minnie 1887-1972 and Edner Skalbeck 1884-1973, Climax Cemetery.

me as, on 12th November 1974, I received a plaque from the Canadian Prime Minister, Pierre Trudeau, marking my ninetieth birthday, with my name and signed by him in person. By the time the day was over I had posed for that many photos, including the photographer from the Shaunavon Standard. The reporter asked me about my life and how many children, and grandchildren, and great-grandchildren I had. I was even able to point out that I had a couple of great-great grandchildren! I slept very very soundly that night.

Such happiness only lasts until it is kicked out by other occurrences. And so it was that the joy of the occasion only lasted a few days. I got news that my beloved only son, Clarence, was in hospital with appendicitis. It went into peritonitis and they operated. As a result of the surgery, he died, aged fifty eight, on 18th November, less than a week after my special day. Clarence was buried with great honours in the Veteran's Plot in Shaunavon Cemetery. Then in the following spring, in March, Clarence's wife, Helen, died. She was buried next to Clarence.

1974 was the year that the Mounties took in their first female recruits. There was much fuss made of it by those women who felt that there should be equality for women in all things. I wasn't too sure as it seemed to me that there were jobs that men could do, and others more suited to women. On the other hand, Minnie and I and other prairie wives were often engaged in the same hard work as the men. I think it was more the burning of female underwear that made me unsure as to what they were fighting for.

It was good to get news in 1975 of the marriage of Lois' son, Lyle. I wasn't able to attend but I was treated to a piece of cake and a photo of Lyle with his new bride, Eileen Graham. What a handsome couple they made.

It was about this time that I moved to the duplex bungalow which much suited me. I was slowing up, and always grateful that Rochelle and her family lived nearby. She came to visit several times a week, and she and the girls helped me with little jobs around the place. I looked forward to her visits, and it became a highlight of my life to sit and chat over tea and biscuits. Rochelle kept my up to date with local news and gossip, and we often laughed at the antics and disgressions of this one and that. At Hallowe'en each year, it was the time to empty the biffys, and there was always a tale to tell around the traditions that went with that custom, some not too pleasant.

By 1976, If felt that I hadn't much time left. In the previous three years, so many seem to have gone. News of the death of Clarence's son, Wayne, was followed shortly after by the terrible news of the death in June of my sister, Tillie, over in Calgary. She was eighty seven. I got a telegram from her daughters, Gladys and Marion, the same week as I heard from my nephew Jim Monson in Medicine Hat. It was news of my brother Thomas in Glasgow.

My 'retirement' home, and the view out to the prairie.

Medicine Hat
June 1976

Dear Auntie

I'm afraid this news has taken some time to reach you. On January 14, my father (your brother) Thomas passed away peacefully in Canniesburn Hospital in Glasgow at the age of seventy five. As you may recall, he was diagnosed in 1972 with cancer on the tongue - and the tip had to be removed in hospital. This affected his speech but after therapy he was doing alright and otherwise fairly healthy and in good spirits although his working days were over. I pleaded with him to come back to Canada with us, but there was no way he was leaving Scotland. He reassured us that Patsy's sister, Sadie, was looking after him really good. But 2 years later the cancer reared its ugly head again and had spread to other parts of his body so he was in and out of hospital for treatments but he was obviously terminally ill.

When I wrote to my mother in New Zealand to let her know about his illness, she wrote him a beautiful letter. She said she took full responsibility for all that had gone wrong in their lives. Uncle John's son James and wife Margaret took over the responsibility of looking after him in his final days as I was back home in Canada with the family and my sister, Blanche had gone to New Zealand. I flew over to Scotland to attend the funeral and to settle his affairs. I met all Uncle John's family while I was there and was delighted to see Auntie Eva who flew in from Northern Ireland with her husband, George Mahood. She's in her 80's and still going strong. She took home his ashes to scatter over the Irish Sea as he requested.

I hope to get over to Climax to see you soon.

Your nephew, Jim

Later that year, Gladys and Marion sent me a photograph of Tillie's grave in Port Elgin, Ontario where she was buried beside her husband, Frank. I started to dread what the next batch of mail would bring – I seemed to have so many letters in these few years telling me of brothers and sisters lost. In 1977, it was the turn of my sister Kate.

Portavogie, Summer 1977

Dear Sister

More sad news I'm afraid. As you know, we lost Thomas at the start of last year, well now it's the turn of our dear Kate. She gave up to influenza days before her seventy eighth birthday. Joe and the family are devastated as you can imagine. She is to be buried tomorrow near Sarah Jane at Comber.

We have much to do today, so I will write again shortly.

Queenie and I send our love, Eva.

It was at this time that I wished I had been braver and visited my family back home when I had the chance. One by one, my siblings were dying and I was denied the chance of bidding them farewell. A sort of unhealable sadness descended upon me. I spent hours, sometimes days, reflecting upon those who had gone before me. I thought of my parents and those of my brothers and sisters now lost to me, especially Minnie and Tillie. I pined for my William; I had been a widow for almost twenty years and yet I still missed his gentle kindness and his sense of humour. And how I missed my children who had gone before. It's hard to comprehend – the passing of a child before its parent – it's not the way things should be. Irene and later Clarence were both taken too soon. More and more I wondered how my little stillborn daughter would have been. I never mentioned her to anyone, but in my heart she was as real as all my other children. I thought of her as Eliza, named for me, and that's what her name was to be. I've always thought of her as a young girl with her hair curled and a great light around her, as she appeared to me shortly after I lost her over sixty years before.

Portavogie, Spring 1978

Dearest Sister

Now we've lost our Queenie so there's only you and me left out of twelve. She's been frail for some time and now she's passed away. Seventy seven years is a good number. My George has been a great support to me, and Queenie's daughter Margaret has been doing her best to deal with everything. I

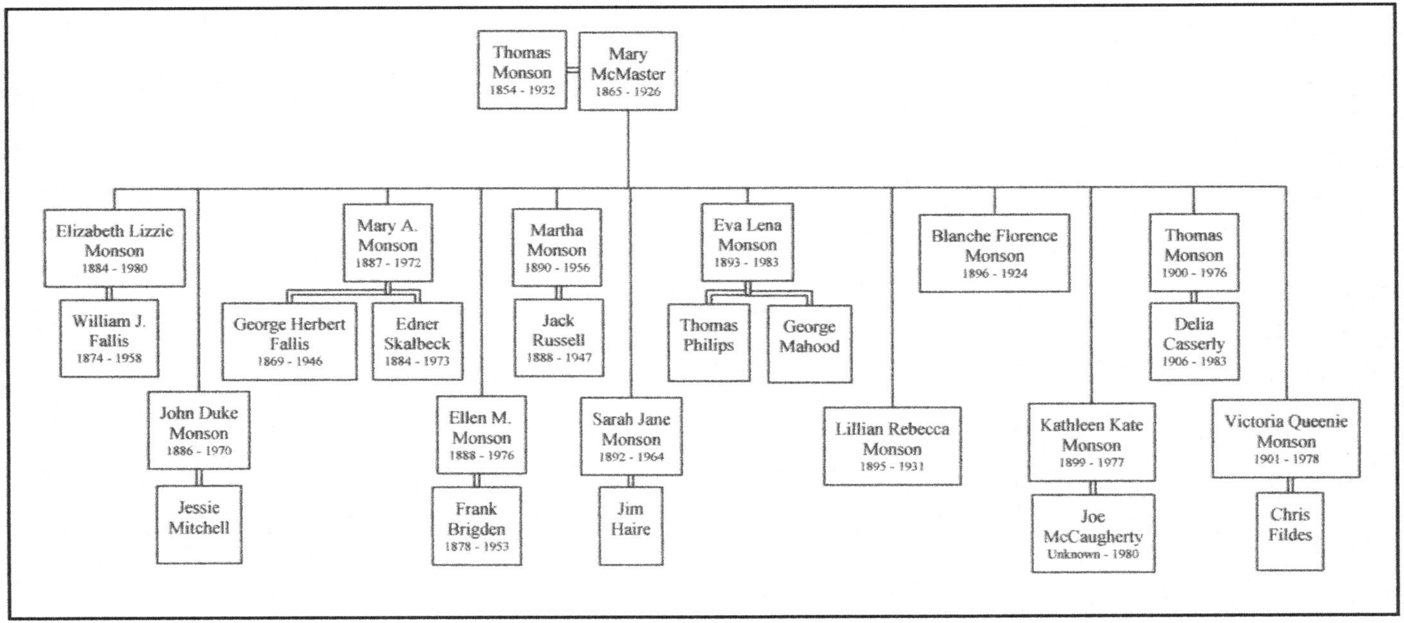

Family tree – siblings and husbands.

shall miss Queenie so. She, Kate and I have been so close since we moved to this area all those years ago, not to forget Sarah Jane - I can't believe that it's over 10 years since we lost her.

I send you my love from over the miles.

Your sister Eva.

Not Queenie too! I could hardly grasp the death of three dear siblings in the same number of years: Thomas two years ago, Kate last year and Queenie this year 1978. I was outliving all my brothers and sisters – only Eva was left now, and she was my junior by nine years.

How life threw such changes, never anticipated, ever surprising – and too often not in a good way. And in town and in the news, there was always talk of progress, but I was finding it hard to cope with change. All the new things were adding complication to life, and the simple life seemed far more attractive to me. I didn't want to cope with new ways of doing things.

Not so long ago, I watched a programme on my little television about other agricultural struggles such as ours – in Spain and Tenerife, I think it was. I think back on the hardships of our prairie life and realise that we were not alone. My short time spent with my Aunt and Uncle in London showed me a comparatively pampered life and was no preparation for Manitoba and Saskatchewan. Our homesteading existence was far more compatible with our roots in Ireland where we led a very basic farming life. I often wonder if Canada targeted us Monson girls for our survival skills. In our lives on the prairies, Minnie and I were lucky not only to know many of the skills required for survival but also what was possible.

And what of the changes I have seen over my years, the best part of a century. There are the obvious differences between growing up and adulthood, differences that everyone knows, though you could cut with a knife the separate parts of my life: my childhood in Coolnagranchy, the two years in England, the struggles on the prairie, and my settling in Climax and subsequent retirement here. The elements of living have changed very little; with hard work we always managed to put food on the table and clothes on our backs.

Clothes and materials have changed a great deal, now much more comfortable and well cut. But you'll never catch me in trousers! I never wore them and I never get used to seeing women and girls in them. Give me a smart dress and an apron any day!

I have known life and death as everyone has, some of it cruel but always borne with the support of family and friends.

I feel that it will soon be my time to go, and I am ready. I have lived an existence more varied and full than many, with a life that contrasts across two continents and has reached the deepest depths, while still surviving in triumph against the harshest odds. I have been blessed with a wonderful family. In my youth in Ireland, I was one of twelve children, in a poor but loving household. I have given birth to six babies, though only three remain, and I have been lucky to have my dear sister, Minnie, with me at my side for so much of my life. Of my thirteen grandchildren, there are still ten, and my line reaches further still with nineteen great-grandchildren and five great-great-grandchildren, and no doubt more to follow. They are spread far and wide, from nearby in Saskatchewan, across neighbouring Alberta, and further to Ontario, and beyond. I haven't met them all, but my birthdays and Christmases are always blessed with news and cards from so many of them. It's hard to keep in touch with such a wonderful dynasty. It seems strange that not one of them carries my maiden name of Monson.

My story would not be complete without mentioning them all by name, if I can. I hope that I am able to list them all and not upset one or other that I have missed. I have them all recorded in my address book and do my best to remember all birthdays and Christmases, especially as most of them are so good at remembering mine.

My first daughter, Irene, died eighteen years ago as the result of a car accident. Her first daughter, Hilda, has eight children, Gail, John, Debra, Susan, Wendy, Cindy, James and Belinda. My five great-great grandchildren, Lynne, Robert, Andrea, Shaun and Aaron, are the children of Gail, John and Debra. They all live in Chatham, Ontario, or thereabouts. No doubt there will be more to follow as all Hilda's children are now married. The family of Irene's second child, Ernest, have all set up home not so far from here, some in Shaunavon, some in Medicine Hat. Ernie's three children, Randolph, Brian and Tammy, are all grown up and no doubt shortly to have children of their own.

Irene's youngest child, Faye, has a son and a daughter, Shaun and Shalene, living in Swift Current, the town where William, George and John went, along with other homesteaders, to register their land and their betterment title back in the 1910's and 20's.

Clarence, my second child and only son, died five years ago. I often felt that his time fighting in Europe contributed to his early death. He had five children. Clarence's first son Gordon, has two sons, Gordon and Bradley, both living in Alberta, in Carseland and Stettler. Clarence's second son, Wayne, died three years ago aged thirty four, and neither he nor Clarence's next son, Leonard, had any children. Clarence's two daughters, Lenore and Marcia, each have a son and daughter. Lenore's two children are Natalie and Jamie, in Hinton and Stettler, both in Alberta. Marcia and her family are close by in Shaunavon.

Three of my daughters, Lorraine, Lois and Jean, are still with us and visit when they can, to my great delight.

Lorraine, has two daughters, Rochelle with one son Terry, and Shaaron's three children are Shelley, Donna and Darren. They all live here, in Climax, which is a great comfort to me.

Lois, my fourth child, has a teaching career that has scanned from McNutt and Whitewood to Regina. She has two children: Pam her eldest, and Lyle, married four years ago. They are all in Regina, to the north of Climax.

Jean is my youngest child and lives over at Eastend, not so far from here. The oldest of her four children was Terence, who we lost in '64 when he was just twelve. Then there is Margo, mother of Terence and Cherie, all in Calgary over in Alberta, and Dennis, now in Penticton, BC. He's written to tell me that it's a beautiful place, with lakes and mountains and rivers. Trudy is Jean's youngest – and the youngest of my thirteen living grandchildren.

That's my tale told, or at least as much as I can do. It's been with the help of Hasluck's grand-daughter, Rosey, who has crossed the t's and dotted the i's for me. And now all the papers and letters are tidied and filed, and my chest of memories and souvenirs is closed. Now I can go to my Maker knowing that my family around me, and those far away, as well as those who will follow after, can sift through my memories and experiences and know how I was and how I am. I'm sure they will want to know as there is ever one or other of them asking, "Gram Fallis, tell us about ...".

And so it is complete at last, and here for any who wish to know. I feel at peace with a certain relief that it is done. I hope it is a story of interest to my descendants, telling how I came to this land, and maybe others will get some pleasure from it too. I can sit and see it all again, and all those people and places that I love and have loved.

Update 2016

Lizzie Fallis, nee Monson, died in 1980, the year after her story was told. She was ninety six, the last but one of the twelve brothers and sisters. She is buried in Climax Cemetery in Saskatchewan, along with several of her Canadian family. Only Eva survived Lizzie; she died in 1983 at the age of ninety, at her home in Portavogie, County Down, three years after Lizzie.

All but two of Lizzie's siblings left their childhood home; Lillie and Blanche never married and are buried with their mother, Mary McMaster, in the graveyard at Croghan, in County Roscommon. Lizzie, Minnie, Tillie and Martha, finished their days in Saskatchewan or Manitoba. The other four sisters, Sarah Jane, Eva, Kate and Queenie all moved to County Down and are buried there. Lizzie's two brothers, John and Thomas, died in Surrey and Scotland. Their descendants are spread far and wide.

Lizzie and her siblings grew up in Coolnagranchy near Boyle in County Roscommon. Her extended family included grand-parents, aunts and uncles, cousins and second cousins living on nearby farms at Derrymaquirk, Grange and Carrick-on-Shannon, and in Dublin and Boyle. She heard stories of other close relatives who had gone further afield, some as far as Ohio and New Zealand. Before setting off on her homesteading voyage to Canada she spent two years in London living with her aunt and uncle and cousins, including my Grandfather, Hasluck Monson, two years her junior. They kept in touch over the years, and he died in 1981 in Devon, UK, also aged 95.

In fact, that aunt and uncle who Lizzie lived with in London returned to live in Coolnagranchy in the 1920's, but Lizzie never went back to the place of her birth so she never met them again.

All the family farms in County Roscommon are still there. Ernest Monson farms beef at Derrymaquirk, and uses Coolnagranchy as a cattle shed; Ernest is the son of Lizzie's second cousin, William Monson. The land at Grange is farmed by David White, the grandson of Lizzie's second cousin Abraham Monson; The Grange and Grange Farm houses stand empty. Lizzie's cousin, Molly, lived over at Killukin in Carrick-on-Shannon, and her grand-daughter, Rosie, now runs The Bush Hotel in the town.

In Saskatchewan and Alberta, there are several of Lizzie's and Minnie's descendants, including some of their grandchildren and great grandchildren who live in Climax and nearby Shaunavon, close to where Lizzie and Minnie and their husbands worked the land. They have abandoned the homesteads and the land lies untended, apart from a small area still farmed by another family. The Geodetic Survey marker remains, and the slough, and the railway track across the land. There is no evidence of the cabins that the Fallis families toiled so hard to build. The ground is still full of stones, despite their labours to remove them. It's as if there is an infinite supply, waiting deep in the ground, forever working its way up to the surface. The prairie grass has re-established itself, along with the wild sage. The wind blows across the land, the land which goes on as far as the eye can see. The sky and the prairie seem endless, as if they both go on forever.

The prairie wheat has given way to oil. Small rigs are dotted across the land, with the pumpjacks rocking slowly and rhythmically as they draw the oil from deep in the earth. The pumps send it on its way into the underground pipelines where it flows to mighty collection tanks. From there, the oil is distributed by train to the depots for processing. Saskatchewan produces almost 20% of Canada's oil, second only to neighbouring Alberta. They call it "liquid gold" and it lies deep beneath that same ground that Lizzie and her family strove to make productive. There seems no justice that the same land that broke the backs and spirits of so many is now the source of great riches.

Lizzie Fallis (nee Monson), Climax Cemetery.

IN LOVING MEMORY OF

MRS. ELIZABETH FALLIS

BORN
Boyle County Roscommon, Ireland
November 12, 1884

PASSED AWAY
Shaunavon, Sask.
May 30, 1980

FUNERAL SERVICE FROM
Climax United Church, Climax, Sask.
Monday, June 2, 1980, at 2.00 p.m.
Venerable Howard Shurvin officiating

INTERMENT
Climax Cemetery, Climax, Sask.

Binkley's Funeral Service, Shaunavon, Sask.

Lizzie's Funeral. Lizzie is buried in Climax Cemetery.

Lightning Source UK Ltd.
Milton Keynes UK
UKOW07n0809290517
302165UK00004BA/22/P

9 780956 298089